R_X

for

$UCCESS

OPTOMETRIC MANAGEMENT

Bob L. Baldwin, O.D., F.A.A.O.
Bobby Christensen, O.D., F.A.A.O.
Jack W. Melton, O.D., F.A.A.O.

Vision Publications

R_x

for

$UCCESS

OPTOMETRIC MANAGEMENT

Copyright© 1983 Bob Baldwin, O.D., F.A.A.O.
Bobby Christensen, O.D., F.A.A.O.
Jack Melton, O.D., F.A.A.O.

All rights reserved

No part of this book may be reproduced in any manner
without written permission of the publisher.

International Standard Book Number; 0-912063-00-9

Library of Congress Catalog Card Number;.83-80795

Printed in the United States of America

Preface

There is an old adage, "Success has many fathers, failure is an orphan."

Failures do not write books about success; successful practitioners who combine their knowledge and experience and are motivated to share their "secrets," do indeed father a significant contribution to the future of optometry.

The authors of this book are three successful urban doctors of optometry, two in a partnership practice housed in a superb modern facility with imaginative computer capability . . . the third in a specialty practice utilizing associates in a uniquely designed office to compete professionally in the highly competitive contact lens market. The common bond is a deep personal and professional relationship based upon respect and friendship linked together by a commitment to professional optometry and a mutual philosophy as to how it can be practiced successfully. Realizing that there are many ways to put a philosophy into practice, the authors have combined their experiences with those of other successful practitioners who share their basic concepts and offer a Rx for success.

The credibility of the authors was firmly established in my mind when they insisted that I visit and evaluate their practices before accepting the role as editor. Not only did I find impressive, well run offices, but three doctors who indeed "practice what they preach." Not only do they preach on the optometric "lecture circuit," but they travel over 350 miles a week for two semesters each year to present a well-rounded course in practice management to the students at Northeastern State University College of Optometry in Tahlequah, Oklahoma.

While targeted at graduates entering the practice of optometry and established successful practitioners who are reluctant to consider associate practice, this book is recommended to all doctors of optometry who are looking for ideas to enhance their practices and provide better patient care.

From a literary standpoint, this book is a maverick . . . an unconventional easy-to-read dissertation on successful practice from the early considerations of entering practice to the sophisticated techniques and advanced management skills of a growing established practice.

It is a "how to" book that offers alternatives and examples . . . a common sense book based on real life experience, not theory. It offers professional advice from professionals in related fields, brainstorming ideas, and a supplement that asks notables in the profession, "If you had to start in practice again in a new city with no equipment and very little money, how would you do it?"

It is a book to read, savor and then save for the time in one's career when a major decision has to be made. It then becomes a reference book offering advice and guidance.

Even though the book title implies that success begins with the dollar sign, it must be stated at the outset that true success in optometry is not always measured by the bottom line on a financial statement. Success is a happy, enthusiastic doctor caring for satisfied, enthusiastic patients in a professional practice situation that is rewarding to both parties.

To this noble purpose and no other, this book is dedicated.

Milton J. Eger, O.D.
Editor

About The Authors

BOB L. BALDWIN, O.D., F.A.A.O.

A graduate of the University of Houston, College of Optometry, Dr. Bob Baldwin is in general practice of optometry with Dr. Bobby Christensen. Active in the field of contact lenses, Dr. Baldwin has served as clinical investigator and in a leadership role in the Southwest Council of Optometry. A Fellow of the American Academy of Optometry, he serves as a practice management instructor at Northeastern State University College of Optometry. Dr. Baldwin is noted as a pioneer in the field of computers for Optometric use and his office is a prototype of advanced computerized capability. His innovative thinking has made him a leader in practice management.

Dr. Baldwin has served his profession in various capacities in the local and regional societies and is a past president (1974-1975) of the Oklahoma Optometric Association.

The Baldwins, Bob, his wife, Margie, and their three daughters, Cindy, Peggy, and Terri, make Midwest City, Oklahoma their home.

BOBBY J. CHRISTENSEN, O.D., F.A.A.O.

A graduate of the University of Houston, College of Optometry, Dr. Bobby Christensen joined the practice of Dr. Bob Baldwin in 1974. A Fellow of the American Academy of Optometry, Dr. Christensen's interest in education has stimulated his efforts as an adjunct professor at Northeastern State University where he organized the format for the practice management courses. He has shared in the responsibility and creativity, with Dr. Baldwin, of computerizing their joint practice.

His other professional activities include clinical investigation of contact lenses and lecturing to both doctors and optometric assistants. Active in professional affairs, Dr. Christensen was president (1983-1984) of the Oklahoma Optometric Association and has served his state association as chairman of its Practice Management Committee.

The Christensens, Bobby, his wife, Jayne, and their three sons, Jeremy, Jay, and Corey make Midwest City, Oklahoma their home.

JACK W. MELTON, O.D., F.A.A.O.

A graduate of Southern College of Optometry, Dr. Jack Melton limits his practice to the specialty of contact lenses. Dr. Melton has been active in the clinical investigation of several new soft contact lenses prior to marketing.

Active in professional affairs, he has gone through the chairs of the Oklahoma Optometric Association and has served as president (1983-1984) of the Heart of America Contact Lens Society. Dr. Melton lectures extensively both in the field of Contact Lenses and Contact Lens Practice Management. He serves as adjunct professor of optometry at both Southern College of Optometry and Northeastern State University. Dr. Melton also has the distinction of being a Fellow of the American Academy of Optometry.

The Meltons, Jack, his wife, Janet, daughter, Lori, and sons, Ryan and Rodd make Oklahoma City, Oklahoma their home.

Acknowledgements

Our deep appreciation needs to be expressed to many for their contributions in the writing of this book. Many of the ideas have come from other O.D.'s as we have visited their practices or from seminars and conventions. We have simply revised them to fit our situation and practice. To all optometrists who have shared their thoughts and philosophies with us over the years, we are grateful.

Without the patient understanding and the help of the authors' families, the conclusion of this task could not have been accomplished. Margie Baldwin and Jayne Christensen have spent untold hours helping to produce this book and to them we express our special thanks.

The counsel, direction, editing, typing, and encouragement of the following people is acknowledged.

Milton Eger, O.D.
LeRoy Oxford, Ph.D.
Jayne Christensen
Margie Baldwin
Janet Melton
Galen Taylor, C.P.A.
Harris Nussenblatt, O.D., M.P.H.
Wes Wyatt
Dennis Kuwabara, O.D.
Stanley Yamane, O.D.
Barry Farkas, O.D.
Wayne Cannon, O.D.
David Hansen, O.D.
Daniel Klaff, O.D.

Robert Koetting, O.D.
Donald Getz, O.D.
Kathy Miller
Carol Lancaster
Nancy Laverty
Russell Laverty, O.D.
Elizabeth Wilkerson, O.D.
Joel Naegele, O.D.
Gene Murphy
Jim Stark, O.D.
Sam Oliphant, O.D.
Loretta McFarland
Peggy Wike, O.D.
Joseph Phillips, O.D.

i

Table Of Contents

ii

Chapter 1 | Planning Your Own Success

Goals should be a priority for the professional, whether starting a new practice or becoming part of an established one. One year goals and projected goals of three to five years are approaches that can stimulate practice management and growth. Goals must be realistic to be of any value. Therefore, all available information and statistics should be studied and evaluated. One's philosophy of practice must be the guiding principle in setting goals. Location and practice philosophies will determine the type of patient to be seen. Sub-specialities of favor will likely lead to more expertise in those areas. Population, age, and economic standards are also determinants. The necessary income to reach personal goals will determine how many hours per week and the amount of effort that will be required to achieve this income.

Projected growth can be evaluated from population statistics available for most areas. An optimistic estimate can be made for practice growth but a pessimistic projection is a worthwhile safeguard. Probably the growth rate will be somewhere between these projections. Other professionals in the area can be helpful. Great insight can be gained from collaboration with those who have been "through it before." One should project an optimistic or maximum volume of patients as well as the least amount of patients needed to remain solvent.

After the information has been evaluated, short range goals are in order along with a plan. When a systematic approach is finalized on how to reach the short range goals, they are to be stepping stones toward future goals. A systematic approach will set goals to insure small successes, all moving toward the long range plan. An effective plan will move on to new and higher goals once each short range goal is obtained. Complacency will stagnate the practice and stunt future growth.

Establishment of practice philosophies and achievement of goals is "practice management." Achievement of professional goals will determine success of personal goals. Personal achievement and eagerness to meet personal goals usually determine management of a practice.

GOAL SETTING

Goal Setting Begins By Listing Long Range Goals And Determining What Short Range Goals Are Needed To Achieve Them. Listed Below Is A Simple Example Of This Process.

Goal #1: To increase patient examinations from five to eight per day. Contact lens fittings will account for 20% of the total patient volume.

   Time Period: 36 months.
   Short range goals to achieve goal #1.

 1. First six months.
    a. Design and incorporate a recall system.
    b. Develop a contact lens service agreement.
    c. Start staff meeting and training sessions for personnel.

 2. Second six months.
    a. Redecorate reception room (new carpet and furniture).
    b. Send a six week progress letter to patients wearing glasses or contact lenses.
    c. Evaluate and increase contact lens inventory.

 3. Second year.
    a. Evaluate recall system.
    b. Send follow-up letter to patients not keeping recall appointments.
    c. Redecorate styling and dispensing area. Increase and update frame inventory.
    d. Warranty frames and lenses for one year.

4. Third year.
   a. Hire an additional assistant for styling and contact lens care (can be done sooner if the practice builds faster).
   b. Redecorate the remainder of the office.
   c. Buy a photo slit lamp for contact lens care and documentation.

The rest of this chapter highlights some fundamentals which will be discussed in detail in other chapters. Employees, equipment, office decor, office location, communication systems, contact lens and frame inventories, recall systems, public relations, scheduling, etc. are all tools with which to achieve goals. Management of all these resources should be directed to that end.

COMMUNICATIONS

Communication both in the office and out becomes an immediate priority. Proper communication includes the use of the telephone system and a trained staff who can answer questions and give an understandable explanation of fees. This would include explaining the services that are rendered for these fees. The staff should be able to handle most problem patients by using tact, listening skills and keeping their composure when approaching the problem raised by the patient. Employees also need to understand the amount of time needed for specific appointments and all other questions that arise at the front desk or in a dispensing area. Appropriate literature will answer questions and explain office procedures so people will be aware of what skills and services are provided. These tools become useless if the doctor cannot communicate with the patients. It is imperative for him to explain the diagnosis, making them feel confident that the problem has been addressed and the doctor is moving toward helping them resolve it.

OFFICE APPEARANCE

The next step toward achieving goals is office appearance. The office must be attractive and appealing upon entering. It should be warm and comfortable. A professional office needs to be colorful and appealing to the eye with furnishings in good taste and condition. Patients and staff should both be comfortable in the surroundings. Staff and doctor appearances must also be included in this category. There should be some guidelines established for dress codes for assistants as well as for the doctors. The doctor should look like a winner and act like one. A genuine concern in appearance and attitude translates into superior performance and the patient feels that they are receiving the best.

SCOPE OF PRACTICE

Another step to achieving your goals and philosophies would be the determination of the scope of practice which will be provided. This would include the quality of service and materials that you are going to offer and the time required to perform these services. From these philosophies an appointment schedule can be established to provide the necessary time for each service that will be rendered.

PROFESSIONAL IMAGE

A professional image conjures varied thoughts in the patient's mind. It should be a positive one. It must not be an arrogant God-like image, but rather an image of gentle kindness of a person who can make intelligent professional judgments. Patients respond to the confident authority of someone who knows what they are talking about. Making a patient feel important establishes a strong image. Remembering people's names is most impressive. The staff can be helpful in this area as well as providing patients' interests and characteristics whether from mental notes or records. Recognition fosters mutual respect. Office and personnel images which develop will be difficult to change later.

Everyone has special life goals and these will remain unfulfilled by straying from the guidelines of your philosophies. An image is not only established in the office, but in community affairs, with neighbors and friends, and with professionals in other fields.

FEE STRUCTURE

Achieving goals involve developing a fee structure which is within range of others in the same field. A fee structure must be high enough for one's level of skill, and meet personal income needs. Projected volume statistics must also be considered when establishing the fee program.

SPECIALTY SKILLS

Developing specialty skills enhances goal achievement. These must be areas in which the doctor has a strong professional interest and skill level. There must be a patient population available that will capitalize on these talents. Specialty areas improve professional image and can increase referral sources. Fees should be set to commensurate with skills and specialty training.

SELF-EVALUATION

Goals cannot be reached without critical self-evaluation. The enterprising doctor will realistically evaluate and use his communication skills and ability to meet people. His personality should reflect an attitude of being friendly, warm and caring. This is sometimes the most difficult area for an individual to change. Even the best rounded persons have certain personality traits that annoy or turn off other people. Awareness of these traits leads to correcting them. This change will make a tremendous difference in personnel management, patient management, and ultimately the growth of a practice. Life can be more enjoyable when built on positive aspects and the avoidance of negative personality traits.

CONTINUING EDUCATION

Continuing education is a tool in achieving goals. Attendance at seminars, lectures, and reading professional literature keeps the doctor current on new products, new tests, techniques, and the latest advances in research on eye health and general health findings. Knowledge gained, however, must be incorporated into practice, resulting in better patient care by adding new services and improving practice management . . . otherwise continuing education becomes merely a mental exercise.

THE PROBLEM PATIENT

Goal oriented professionals are prepared to handle the problem patient by having some guidelines set up for dealing with specific situations. It is important to remember the patient is always right when a problem occurs, although it may not be resolved the way he thinks it should. If this approach is taken, most problems can be solved. Patients must be approached with gentleness so that they can voice their concerns. Good listening skills will determine the problem. Once pinpointed, a solution is usually possible to make that patient happy. Then he will not be lost from the practice and perhaps will become a good referral source for the future.

ADVERTISING

The authors have not approached the subject of advertising in the media. The intent of this book is to provide information which can be used to build a successful professional practice without resorting to commercial advertising. It is the authors' opinion that advertising is not conducive to the development of a professional image.

SUMMARY

The format for goal achievements can be condensed into the use of proper planning, the use of new resources that become available, and willingness to use the personal energy needed to achieve stated goals. Upon achievement one can feel proud of his accomplishments, having a practice that will undoubtedly have grown as personal goals are being fulfilled. The doctor can then set new goals, lay new plans, and work toward their achievement. Practice management is an area that continually needs to be evaluated and will always have room for improvement.

Chapter 2 | In The Beginning . . .

Starting an optometric practice can be one of the most important, yet difficult, decisions that will ever be made in the life of a doctor. There are several general approaches that can be taken when going into practice: (1) start a new practice, (2) buy an existing practice, (3) buy into an existing practice, (4) join an associate practice (as an employee non-owner), (5) enter a partnership practice (as an owner).

STARTING A NEW PRACTICE

When starting a new practice, there are some basic realities to remember; first, there will almost always be a slow beginning with few patients. Practical experience must be developed and is not achieved overnight. Often the new professional will be a stranger in town, with few contacts to help build the practice. Becoming known in a community takes time and personal involvement.

Of prime importance is the cost of establishing a new practice. This is an age in which sizable funds are required to open an office. High interest rates coupled with inflated costs, are making it harder to produce a profit in any profession or business. To establish a following, one must be competitive. There must be excellent facilities, trained personnel, and modern equipment, or patients are going to look elsewhere for someone who fills their professional service expectations. All this requires an investment of capital. Success can be directly related to doing a better job and providing more than expected.

Many facets are discussed in other chapters about starting a new practice. The location, office space, growth potential, population type, lab services, equipment selection, etc. must all be determined. These involve critical decisions which in turn can create expensive mistakes.

Offsetting these concerns is the pride and the sense of achievement that cannot be replaced by any of the other alternatives.

MULTI-DOCTOR PRACTICES

When buying or joining another practice, there are a number of questions to be answered before any agreements can be reached. Such questions are: Does this practice meet the goals and philosophies envisioned by you? What is the growth potential of the practice? Is the practice in a posture of growth, staying the same, or one of decline? What type of specialized care is provided, such as contact lenses or visual therapy, or is it primarily a geriatric practice that has aged with the doctor who started the practice? Are there ways to increase the type of services being provided in the practice? How often are patients programmed to return for professional care, and is there an effective recall being used? How old is the property and equipment presently being used in the practice? Will the patients likely return and be seen by the new doctor?

Another important question to consider is whether the previous professional or his office personnel are going to leave or stay, and if so for how long? This consideration can be an asset or liability, and must be evaluated on an individual basis.

Another weighty concern is the reason for the sale. Is it because the practice is not doing well? Is it because the professional wants to retire? If there has been a death in the practice, how long has the practice been idle?

Before looking into a situation requiring years of payout, the wise doctor must avoid the hindsight of regret. The guidance of an attorney, CPA, insurance agent, and a banker is strongly recommended because these professionals are trained to help far beyond the skill level of "do it yourselfers." These professionals have experience and wisdom with which to advise and guide you, saving both money and heartache.

VALUE OF A PRACTICE

a. Partnership Practice

After answering these questions and numerous others, comes the task of determining the value of the practice. Formulas abound and range from one dollar to fifteen dollars per record, and from the average yearly net to the average yearly gross. In reality, each practice is an individual business and must be evaluated on that basis.

Two primary areas constitute the value, the tangible assets and the intangible value called "goodwill". The tangible assets of the practice such as actual property, equipment, accounts receivable, cash in the bank, etc. are one area. In evaluating this part of the practice, some give and take is often necessary to arrive at a fair book value for the equipment. In most instances, both doctors should be able to decide together on the value of the equipment. A third, mutually respected professional can be called upon to help arbitrate any disagreements. If agreement is difficult, one should be alerted to the probability that a successful partnership is unlikely.

Assuming that both potential partners reach an agreed value for the tangible assets of the practice, then one half of that value would be paid over the period of "buy in" into the partnership. If the assets were determined to be $100,000 then $50,000 would be paid back with interest. It is often helpful for the senior partner to carry a note at a reasonable interest rate eliminating the stress of the junior partner having to qualify for a fairly substantial loan often before a line of credit has been established.

The intangible assets or "goodwill" of the practice are the second area of value. This is the part of the practice that reflects the growth potential and the renumeration for the years of labor the senior partner has put into the practice to make it successful. While this area is much harder to assign a value, statistics of practice growth can be used to determine some guidelines for reaching a value.

b. Professional Corporation

If you are buying into a professional corporation already existing, the value of the corporation is determined by the number of shares of stock that have been issued and the book value of each share. The book value changes as the practice grows and usually becomes more valuable as the years of successful practice continue.

Negotiations for shares of stock become less complex than trying to determine the value of the fixed assets each year. Shares of stock also represent ownership and usually voting strength, and can be bought individually or as a parcel depending upon the agreement between the doctors.

THE TRIAL PERIOD

When going into an associateship with the potential of partnership, there should be a trial period of at least six months with a maximum of eighteen months. An employment agreement between the doctors involved should be written so that each understands the conditions of the contract. This will greatly reduce future misunderstandings.

It is important that the basics of the partnership agreement be considered even at the beginning of the trial period. Too often one or two years go by just to discover that the conditions are completely unsatisfactory to one party, and disagreements begin. The original contract should provide a method for arbitrating disagreements. Often disagreements can be resolved by utilizing good communication skills and allowing a time lapse for each party to fully consider the other's view. The attitude should be one that strives for appropriate compromises rather than a "win". If the partnership contract is agreed upon before the expiration of the trial period, the employee contract should be considered void (samples of contracts, Appendix B).

A PRACTICAL PLAN THAT WORKS

Before establishing any partnership agreement, it should be determined whether there is enough potential in the practice to make a living for both partners. Again, there is no magic formula to determine this, but every statistic should be considered before the partnership is consummated. If the practice is not strong enough to support both practitioners, the partnership will eventually fail. Probably the most likely reason that most partnerships fall apart is due to division of the monies or that there is not enough money to divide.

There are two major considerations in bringing in a partner . . . (1) income for each doctor, and (2) ownership. Income is sometimes based on longevity and productivity — ownership on investment.

The most attractive situation for both the junior and senior partners, is a sliding scale of salaries. A proportionate higher salary pays for the goodwill that has been established by the senior partner. Yet, the new partner can be assured of a minimum income.

An example of this sliding scale might be that the first year in practice, the senior partner would receive 75% of the net and the junior partner 25%. The second year would be followed by the same 75–25 split as a cushion for the senior doctor who may have experienced a drop in income from his original 100% during this transition period; the third and fourth years 70–30, the fifth and sixth year 60–40; and beginning the seventh year a 50–50 split.

This method assumes that ownership increases by 1/12th each year up to 6/12ths or 50%. During the same time span the junior doctor is making payments to the senior doctor for the tangible assets.

In the examples an agreed upon value of the practice assets is $100,000, 50% of which is sold to the new doctor using a payment plan plus interest. Interest should be well below that charged by a bank and the term of the buy-in can vary depending upon the ability of the new doctor to pay it while still maintaining an appropriate lifestyle expected of a doctor.

Following are some examples that demonstrate how this approach works using different statistical values. Listed are a number of observations to keep in mind while reviewing the examples:

1. The usual estimated net of a solo practice is 33 1/3% of the gross. 36% is projected for the partnership practice, but may vary with circumstances.

2. A $250,000 maximum solo gross may be high or low for different practices and locations.

3. Two average figures are used for yearly increases but they would actually change each year.

4. Note how difficult it would be for the junior partner to live and make his tangible assets payment "if" his first year percentage draw was too low.

5. The percentage can increase at any rate, start at any point, or not change at all until the buy out period is completed, which is six years in these examples.

6. The estimated set of figures are arbitrary and your statistics need to be inserted into the formula.

7. An additional assistant's salary should be considered as the practice grows.

8. Notice that inflation is not considered in these figures, yet it can have a significant impact on the actual amount of in-pocket dollars.

9. Expenses for additional equipment has not been considered in the statistics.

EXAMPLE NUMBER ONE

Projected Gross Increase Per Year	Year	$250,000 Maximum Solo / 36% of Gross		Percent Draw Per Partner		Junior Partner Salary	Senior's Solo Net at 33% $82,500	Senior Partner's Net Loss or Gain
		Practice Gross	Net Income	Junior	Senior		Senior Partner Salary	
$45,000	One	$295,000	$106,200	25%	75%	$26,550	$ 79,650	−$ 2,850
$45,000	Two	$340,000	$122,400	25%	75%	$30,600	$ 91,800	+$ 9,300
$45,000	Three	$385,000	$138,600	30%	70%	$41,580	$ 97,020	+$14,520
$35,000	Four	$420,000	$151,200	30%	70%	$45,360	$105,840	+$23,340
$35,000	Five	$455,000	$163,800	40%	60%	$65,520	$ 98,280	+$15,780
$35,000	Six	$490,000	$176,400	40%	60%	$70,560	$105,840	+$23,340
	Seven			50%	50%		Total	$83,430

$ 83,430 Dr. Senior Gain from Salary Difference
$ 50,000 For Tangible Assets (Plus Interest)
$133,430 Total Received for half of the Practice

Taking in a partner with minimum investment capability resulting in equal equity and income in the seventh year.

EXAMPLE NUMBER TWO

Projected Gross Increase Per Year	Year	$250,000 Maximum Solo 36% of Gross		Percent Draw Per Partner		Junior Partner Salary	Senior's Solo Net at 33% $82,500 Senior Partner Salary	Senior Partner's Net Loss or Gain
		Practice Gross	Net Income	Junior	Senior			
*$35,000	One	$285,000	$102,600	25%	75%	$25,650	$ 76,950	—$ 5,550
$35,000	Two	$320,000	$115,200	25%	75%	$28,800	$ 86,400	$ 3,900
$35,000	Three	$355,000	$127,800	30%	70%	$38,340	$ 89,460	$ 6,960
$45,000	Four	$400,000	$144,000	30%	70%	$43,200	$100,800	$18,300
$45,000	Five	$445,000	$160,200	40%	60%	$64,080	$ 96,120	$13,620
$45,000	Six	$490,000	$176,400	40%	60%	$70,560	$105,840	$23,340
	Seven			50%	50%			

*Compare this example with example one and note the difference in the Senior's Net Gain if the Projected Gross increase per year is reversed.

Total $60,570

$ 60,570 Dr. Senior Gain from Salary Difference

$ 50,000 For Tangible Assets (Plus Interest)

$110,570 Total Received for half of the Practice

A variation of example number one showing a different growth pattern of the practice during the 1st seven years.

EXAMPLE NUMBER THREE

Projected Gross Increase Per Year	Year	$250,000 Maximum Solo 36% of Gross		Percent Draw Per Partner		Junior Partner Salary	Senior's Solo Net at 33% $82,500		Senior Partner's Net Loss or Gain
		Practice Gross	Net Income	Junior	Senior		Senior Partner Salary		
$45,000	One	$295,000	$106,200	25%	75%	$26,550	$ 79,650		− $ 2,850
$45,000	Two	$340,000	$122,400	30%	70%	$36,720	$ 85,680		+ $ 3,180
$45,000	Three	$385,000	$138,600	30%	70%	$41,580	$ 97,020		+ $ 14,520
$35,000	Four	$420,000	$151,200	30%	70%	$45,360	$105,840		+ $ 23,340
$35,000	Five	$455,000	$163,800	30%	70%	$49,140	$114,660		+ $ 32,160
$35,000	Six	$490,000	$176,400	30%	70%	$52,920	$123,480		+ $ 40,980
	Seven	Note the difference in the Senior's Net Gain when the percentage stays 30-70 for the last five years.		50%	50%		Total		$111,330

$111,330 Dr. Senior Gain from Salary Difference

$ 50,000 For Tangible Assets (Plus Interest)
_____
$161,330 Total Received for half of the Practice

A variation of examples one and two showing a different percentage of draw during the seven year period.

A SECOND PLAN TO CONSIDER

Ownership and income do not necessarily have to increase at the same rate. Consider the following conditions upon which the next example is based:

1. The maximum solo gross of the professional association was considered to be $250,000 with a net of $82,500.

2. It assumes an average yearly increase in gross of $40,000 for the first four years and $30,000 for the following seven years.

3. The formula utilized is that the junior doctor will buy 5% of the stock for 10% of his salary and will have equal ownership in ten years. Equal salaries will start after the sixth year.

4. It must be understood that there will be other expenses that will modify the net . . . such as new personnel and new equipment. This has not been considered in this table so as not to complicate it.

5. Allowances must be made for inflation which is not considered in this example. (see inflation table following)

A professional association (P.A.) or professional corporation (P.C.) is a different entity than a solo practice. The ownership of a corporation is determined by the issuing of shares of stock whose value changes each year as the profitability of the corporation changes. The purchasing of ownership is transacted by establishing a value for the shares of stock at the time of purchase. However, the same principles apply when purchasing stock or undivided assets.

EXAMPLE NUMBER FOUR

Projected Gross Increase Per Year	Year	250,000 Max Gross / Practice Gross	36% of Gross Net Income	JUNIOR					SENIOR				Solo Net 33% 82,500
				Percent Draw	Salary	Less 10% For Stock	Percent Owner-ship	Total Income	Percent Draw	Salary	Percent Owner-ship	Salary + Junior's 10%	Net Loss or Gain
40,000	1	290,000	104,400	30	31,320	3,132	5	28,188	70	73,080	95	76,212	— 9,420
40,000	2	330,000	118,800	30	35,640	3,564	10	32,076	70	83,160	90	86,724	660
40,000	3	370,000	133,200	35	46,620	4,662	15	41,958	65	86,580	85	91,242	4,080
40,000	4	410,000	147,600	35	51,660	5,166	20	46,494	65	95,940	80	101,106	13,440
30,000	5	440,000	158,400	40	63,360	6,336	25	57,024	60	95,040	75	101,376	12,540
30,000	6	470,000	169,200	40	67,680	6,768	30	60,912	60	101,520	70	108,288	19,020
30,000	7	500,000	180,000	50	90,000	9,000	35	81,000	50	90,000	65	99,000	
30,000	8	530,000	190,800	50	95,400	9,540	40	85,860	50	95,400	60	104,940	
30,000	9	560,000	201,600	50	100,800	10,080	45	90,720	50	100,800	55	110,880	
30,000	10	590,000	212,400	50	106,200	10,620	50	95,580	50	106,200	50	116,820	

Total 68,867 For Stock

Total 40,320 Salary Difference

$ 40,320 Dr. Senior Gain from Salary Difference
$ 68,867 Dr. Junior Payment for Stock
$109,187 Total Received for half of the Practice

A planned approach to equal income over 7 years and equal ownership over 10 years. Gross income, percentages of draw and percentages of the stock purchased per year are variables determined by negotiated agreement.

INFLATION TABLE

Percent	1st Year Salary	5th Year Salary	10th Year Salary	15th Year Salary	20th Year Salary	25th Year Salary
5%	$ 30,000	$ 36,464	$ 46,537	$ 59,392	$ 75,798	$ 96,737
8%	30,000	40,814	59,968	88,110	129,459	190,216
11%	30,000	45,541	76,737	129,305	217,884	367,145
5%	50,000	60,775	77,563	98,990	126,336	161,238
8%	50,000	68,023	99,946	146,851	215,585	316,761
11%	50,000	75,902	127,897	215,511	363,146	611,920
5%	75,000	91,162	116,347	148,489	189,511	241,867
8%	75,000	102,036	149,921	220,281	323,663	475,565
11%	75,000	113,853	191,845	323,358	544,874	918,143
5%	100,000	121,550	155,131	197,989	252,687	322,498
8%	100,000	136,048	199,896	293,710	431,553	634,091
11%	100,000	151,806	255,799	431,034	726,315	1,223,881

An example of what income is necessary over a period of years to stay even with different inflationary rates.

A THIRD PLAN TO CONSIDER

Many large corporations start executives at a base salary and give a bonus according to productivity. This concept can be applied to Optometry in the following example.

Ownership is obtained by paying for the tangible assets. This is accomplished by reaching an agreed value for the tangible assets and establishing a payment schedule to the senior partner.

Jr. Partner	Base Salary	Bonus
Year One	$30,000	% of
Year Two	35,000	productivity
Year Three	40,000	to be
Year Four	45,000	determined
Year Five	50,000	by original
Year Six	55,000	agreement
Year Seven	50-50 Salary Division	

Loan payment period should be determined by the ability of the junior partner to repay the loan.

VOTING RIGHTS

Let's carry it forward. Two partners have an equal number of shares of stock and a third partner who is brought into the practice and has been given one share of stock. The senior partner has the specter of losing complete control of the practice. . . for the two new partners can out vote him if they so desire. While this is a rarity, it can happen.

The solution to this dilemma is that while the senior partner, when selling or giving the stock to the new partners, does lose ownership, it is arranged that he retains the voting rights of that stock until he dies or leaves the practice. . .not all the stock, but enough to avoid being outvoted.

This factor is the greatest concern for the senior doctor who may be willing to share his income and establish a low selling price for his stock to bring in a junior partner, but to lose control of his practice is a stumbling block to negotiations.

A wise arrangement should insist that all major decisions that affect the future of the practice would require agreement by all partners and the voting right retainer would be a "security blanket" for dire emergencies only.

A graduation of salary as discussed allows the junior partner to come into the practice with very little cash outlay, paying for his part of the practice through hard work and building the practice. The senior partner will enjoy a gradual increasing salary level to pay for the goodwill.

When productivity is placed in the formula, it is not unusual for the junior partner to earn more money for working longer hours and more weeks than a senior partner who is seeking time off, even though the junior partner owns a minority portion of the stock.

MARRIAGE, ANNULMENT AND DIVORCE

Partnerships are often referred to as being similar to a marriage. It is that much and probably more. In fact, the doctors spend at least eight hours a day together making important decisions.

Like a marriage, even though the intention of both parties at that time is to "live happily ever after," there should be a plan to annul or divorce one another.

1. What happens if the senior doctor wants the junior partner out?

2. What happens if the junior partner wants to leave voluntarily?

3. What happens if one becomes disabled?

4. Will there be an insurance program in the event of the death of one of the partners?

5. How about retirement of the senior partner? Is there a buyout plan and a contract requiring purchase?

These are only some of the contingencies that must be planned for and put in writing by a mutually agreed upon attorney.

Then there are contingencies requiring the advice of a tax expert such as:

1. How does the senior partner handle the sale of stock? Is it subject to capital gains taxation?

2. Does a buyout over a long period of time (10 years) require an interest payment and, if so, at what rate?

3. How is the difference in book value of the stock and the sale price handled tax-wise?

4. How much is paid to the junior partner for his stock in the event of dissolution of the partnership? How is that handled from a tax standpoint?

Some of these questions can be answered by referring to Appendix B prepared by a C.P.A. and Corporate Tax Attorney.

So again, focus is returned to the concept that partners must have compatible philosophies and goals and be able to sit down with a plan to determine what direction the practice is to take. The magic is a commitment on the part of both doctors to make it work. If each treats the other as he wants to be treated, problems will be minimal and the working relationship will be a pleasant one.

This outline lists major areas and additional questions which should be asked when considering a partnership.

A. Personal Philosophies

   1. Are practice goals the same?
   2. Are personal life styles compatible.

B. Retirement Plans

   1. Retirement funds; is a trust fund available?
   2. When will the senior partner retire and how will his portion be sold?

C. Attitude Toward Patients — can the doctors' ego stand patients seeing the other doctor?

D. Spouses

1. Can the spouses get along?
2. Can the doctors get along with the spouses?
3. Can the doctors say only positive remarks about their partner when at home?
4. Will practice decisions be discussed with the spouses? (they should be)

E. Finances

1. Will income be based on productivity?
2. What is the philosophy of the practice towards buying equipment, etc.?
3. Does the practice have the potential to produce the income necessary?
4. Can the doctors refrain from judging the other's personal spending habits?
5. Can agreements be easily reached on fair value of practice equipment and goodwill?

F. Professional Skills and Reputation

1. Does the patient care of each doctor meet the expectations of the other doctor?
2. Do the doctors feel confident in each other's skills?
3. How much continuing education is expected?
4. Are the doctors willing to learn from each other?
5. What is the reputation of the senior partner in the community and health care society?
6. How has the junior partner performed in the classroom and clinic?

G. Partner Communication — these are items which must be established after the above questions have been answered.

1. Must be honest with each other.
2. Write and file all decisions made.
3. Use professional consultants.
4. Develop goals and establish practice concepts.
5. Moral standards must be high.

MAKING THE NEW DOCTOR PRODUCTIVE

When a new doctor comes into the practice, it is usually quite some time before he becomes as busy as the senior partner. There are the items of initial help, such as contact lens checks and modifications, adjustments, styling and seg height confirmation, progress checks, and examination of the senior doctor's overflow of patients. These services do little to increase the cash flow into the office. However, involving him in the administrative duties of the office, such as hiring and firing, training aides and establishing working schedules can be a decided benefit to the office.

Another idea is to share each patient between both doctors so that they are equally busy. This can be accomplished by the new doctor entering the examination room first. After the introduction, Dr. Junior announces that he will be doing some tests and then Dr. Senior will be along to complete the testing. Stating that the expected doctor is, in fact, coming and not replaced eases the patients' resistance to another doctor seeing them. It also seems very natural when multiple aids are utilized and when the patients are accustomed to more than one person performing tests.

The new doctor can proceed with the case history, slit lamp, keratometry, external and internal examinations. An explanation of the findings is given to the patient about this portion of the examination. He then excuses himself and the senior doctor enters and finishes the vision analysis and case presentation. During that same time Dr. Junior is starting the next patient, and the same routine is repeated.

After the new doctor has been in the practice for a while the roles can switch. If the doctors are truly compatible and approach visual care in the same manner, anticipating the actions and instructions of the other, they can even switch in the middle of the visual analysis if the need arises. Obviously, this approach requires a great deal of harmony and good records.

As the working relationship progresses and the patients become familiar with "both" doctors, then the patient sees the doctor who is available at that time. The exchange of roles continues to be practiced with new patients.

There are some considerations the senior doctor must make:

1. Some of the old faithful patients may actually prefer the new man and ask for him. It is crushing to the ego, and while an effort is made to honor the request for a specific doctor, it is never encouraged.

2. Along with sharing patients, goes a sharing of the glory. It is not just the senior doctor's practice anymore.

3. A junior partner may have brought a specialty skill such as low vision. The senior partner must be prepared to refer loyal patients to his pártner.

Advantages sharply outweigh any misgivings with this approach:

1. It immediately exposes the new doctor to each patient who comes in for care.

2. It eliminates the slow time for the new man during the first few years because he is working as hard as the established practitioner.

3. The patients enjoy the concept of two doctors for the price of one and it becomes a PR tool for the practice.

4. By exposing the patient to both doctors, it is possible for either doctor to see the patient the next time if the need should arise. (vacations, sick, day off, etc.)

5. Two optometric minds can make better judgments, and the counsel of the other can often provide better care for the patient.

6. The assistants have an equal loyalty to both doctors and can keep the traffic flow moving more smoothly than if they were working for two different practices in the same office.

7. It gives a feeling of harmony to the office atmosphere rather than a feeling of competing with each other.

This approach to a new partner entering into a practice can increase production and enhance practice growth.

Chapter 3 | Practice Location: A Philosophical Approach

Selecting a location is more than just a practice site. This is a major decision that applies to any type of practice you may be considering . . . solo practice, a new practice with a colleague, an associateship and even a partnership.

Location is a total way of life for the doctor and his family. You must determine whether it is an appropriate environment for the family, and a proper setting for your community involvement, your religious preferences, and your pursuits for leisure.

Therefore, it is necessary to decide in which part of the country and in which type of community you want to live. There are similar opportunities in almost any community, but it is wise to start surveying a community a few years prior to graduation. The most important objective, therefore, is to fulfill your own personal philosophies and goals. Consider the climate, the people, and the number of miles to the children's grandparents. Pick communities that meet your personal criteria, then examine each one to find which best meets the needs of your family and your anticipated practice.

Is it the kind of an area which accents the personality of the family? The atmosphere and informality of a rural area could be a real problem to the family who desires the hustle and bustle or the cultural and entertainment offerings of city life. This chapter will establish some guidelines to help examine a community as to whether it will fulfill the expectations of the doctor and his family.

SOLO PRACTICE

Solo practice is still today a viable alternative and should not be discarded because of financial restraints. An enterprising doctor with confidence in himself and a predetermined plan for success can usually find the financial backing necessary to purchase a practice from a retiring doctor or to go it alone. There is, at least, one major financial organization, Western Capital, with millions of dollars available (with government help) committed to finance and purchase new professional optometric practices. Selecting a community for the solo doctor adds, however, some new dimensions to his guidelines.

1. Determine the number of optometrists in the area. As a good rule of thumb, 10,000 people will support one optometrist. When considering this figure, the doctor should be aware there are many communities that attract people from outside the community for shopping, business and health care services. There are some areas that are "bedroom communities" with people actually seeking health services from nearby localities.

2. Consider too, the number of ophthalmologists and opticians in the community who are providing the same or related services.

3. Look to the number of other health professionals. A guiding ratio is three to four dentists for each optometrist. If there is a great number of other health professionals in the community, then chances are an optometrist will suceed in that community.

4. Plot the locations of practitioners on a city map. This may give indications as to what part of town could possibly support a new professional.

5. Determine the average age of the population in an area. A doctor who enjoys working with children and fitting contact lenses would be very unhappy in a community of older people.

6. Explore the economy! Is the area in a growth pattern or is there evidence of decline? What is the unemployment rate of the area? How do the people make a living? Are the people primarily white collar or blue collar? Is one individual industry furnishing most of the jobs? Some communities depend on one primary employer. If that business were to decline or close, could the practice still survive?

Carefully study the strengths of these businesses and whether the company will have a marketable product in the future.

7. Evaluate the growth of the retail community. Is there a steady pace of retail businesses, particularly chains, moving into the community? Fast food franchises and oil companies spend vast sums each year researching communities for the same information needed in establishing a practice. If some of these major companies are in a specific area, then that area has a good healthy population expectation and business activity.

8. Seek advice! Community leaders are generally a reliable source of information. They are usually involved in the Chamber of Commerce and the political happenings of the community.

Chambers of Commerce can provide much statistical information. They provide a good feel of whether or not the community welcomes new health care practitioners. Chambers of Commerce sometimes help the community seek new professionals. They can help find office space and in some communities help in financing the practice.

Bankers have a pulse on the community and are a necessary and recurring contact. They are usually involved in the community and in tune with its growth and potential.

Other optometrists in the area can make significant contributions. A new optometrist who moves into the community without contacting other doctors will isolate himself. Discussions with optometrists will tell what kind of services are being provided. This helps determine what services the community expects from its eye care professionals, as well as exposing those services not currently provided. Observations can be made as to whether they are making a good living and inquiries into the need for another optometrist in the area can sometimes evolve into associateships or partnerships. Be aware that some optometrists may be negative in their responses fearing competition; others may be negative for your best interests, being very honest. You must decide.

Other health professionals, including dentists, medical doctors, opthalmologists and osteopaths afford insight not gained elsewhere. Discuss health care delivery within the community.

Does the philosophy of health care being provided meet the standards of your philosophy? Especially in smaller communities, the optometrist must be able to work with the health care team if he is to become a viable part of the community.

9. Satisfy family needs. Other areas that any family looking to enter a new community should explore would be: the school system and facilities, community activities and facilities, churches, recreational activities and local governments. If this list of family needs is met, one of the largest obstacles has been hurdled.

If practice and location philosophies have been thoroughly evaluated, communities can be visited and rated. All the positive evaluations of the guidelines should be weighed against the negatives and compared with the ratings of other communities under consideration. Hopefully this procedure will enable you to reach a well thought out, unemotional right decision on the community in which to live and practice.

MULTI-DOCTOR PRACTICE

Today, the first choice among the student body of the schools and colleges of optometry as the most desirable practice situation after graduation is the associate practice.

As to the subject of location, only the community or area selection is the responsibility of the new practitioner for the site location has been made by the established practitioner years before.

This is not to infer that once a location is selected it is forever, for times change, socioeconomic factors fluctuate and practices outgrow current facilities.

Multi-doctor practices, in fact all types of practices must constantly reassess these factors. Has the neighborhood changed for your type of practice? Has there been a shift in the shopping — health care locations in your community? Has an important industry relocated elsewhere? Is your practice outgrowing its facilities? Are you ready to enlarge your scope of practice . . . vision therapy? . . . low vision care? . . . an in-office finishing laboratory? Are you able to add new technology equipment in your present office without sacrificing needed space? Have you reached the point in your practice where the office needs remodeling and refurbishing, but to do so might close down your operation and the alternative of relocating might well be an economic advantage?

All of these considerations and more should be evaluated periodically and the decision to move should not be viewed with trepidation, for the experience of most doctors who have relocated, is that a practice grows more rapidly with the image of success. A new, modern facility offering greater service to patients is indeed an image of success.

THE SPECIALTY PRACTICE

The location of a practice limited to a specialty is probably more critical than the location of a general practice. A vision therapy practice in a retirement area is as senseless as a low vision practice in a community of young couples. Specialty practices usually take a large population from which the number of patients necessary to support such a practice can be drawn. Specialty practices often require referral from colleagues and other professionals. This is usually a great practice builder so long as the specialty doctor does not compete in any manner with the referring doctor.

THE BRANCH OFFICE

If we make the assumption that a branch office is a means of increasing income until the primary office is affluent enough to support the financial needs of the doctor, the following location factors are among those to be considered.

a) Driving distance from home and primary office.

b) Weather factors during the winter.

c) Overhead versus income. Often rent for a branch office for part-time occupancy is as great as the primary office rent.

d) Competition.

e) Parking.

f) Economy and mix of the community

BASICS ABOUT OFFICE SITE LOCATION

Most offices will be acquired through lease agreements. Real estate experts, CPA's, attorneys, and bankers should be used to aid in the execution of the lease. Most offices are leased by dollars per square foot per year. As an example, a 1,000 square foot space at $12.00 a square foot per year, would be $12,000.00 for a one year period of time, or $1,000.00 per month. The same 1,000 square feet at $15.00 per square foot would be $15,000.00 per year or $1,250 per month. Square footage is customarily calculated from the outside walls to the middle of the perimeter interior walls and includes all of the interior office walls.

Measurement
of Square Feet

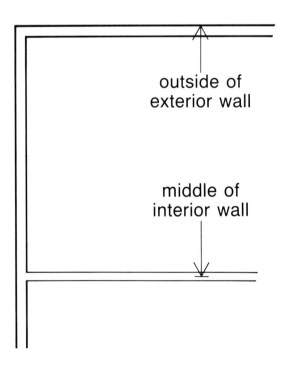

Be aware that there are some leases that are based on the gross of the practice. This is prevalent in high traffic locations such as a mall and the rent might have an escalating clause based on inflation factors (increased taxes, insurance etc.).

When leasing one might weigh the merits of long term leases. The advantage of the long term lease is locking the rent payments at a fixed rate while everything else inflates. Space is being bought for the same price per square foot that held true at the beginning of the lease. The disadvantage of the long term lease is that often there exists a situation of being locked into the space without the option to expand or change to another location.

The most ideal lease situation in a beginning practice is a one or two year lease with options to renew at the same or only slightly inflated lease payments with the right to sublet; in an established practice, a longer lease is more appropriate. Again, this must be negotiated on an individual basis with professional help to guide negotiations. A lease is an important and binding document that can greatly affect the overall success of the practice. (Sample lease agreement Appendix B).

When entering into a lease situation, maintenance of the property is a special item to consider. Who will pay for the maintenance and what type of upkeep can be expected? Is the space older and one that is highly susceptible to problems, or is it new space that should incur very little maintenance? In a lease agreement, the cost of utilities and who pays them must be determined. Figures can be acquired from most utility companies that will give the average utility bills over a specific period of time.

A close look at the other tenants in the building and the adjacent businesses may be rewarding. They are not only neighbors, but they form the image by which patients will judge your office. Other businesses in the location should complement the philosophies and goals of the doctor. Your lease should restrict another eye care practitioner from practicing within the same business complex for a specific number of years.

An alternative to leasing is to buy existing space. The same factors important in leasing are doubly important in buying because of the permanence of the situation. The amount of available cash flow and borrowing capability will often determine the method of acquiring space at any given level of practice development.

People are drawn to ample as well as convenient parking. A good rule of thumb for number of parking spaces is one parking space for each 200 square feet of office space. If there is a parking problem, then there will always be a problem for patients. Traffic of the area should also be noted, including the traffic flow and how easy it is to gain access to the office parking. If there is a fee for parking, who pays? Who pays for maintaining parking lots? Are they lit at night? Who pays for snow removal? . . . restriping?

Traffic is important in regard to the number of people who pass the location daily. Often the city traffic department can supply exact numbers at given locations. If there is an isolated single building, people have a tendency to make a mental note of the building being there, much more readily than in a complex. At the same time, a complex setting offers exposure to people who visit the other businesses or professions within the complex. Each is important and can greatly influence the growth of the practice.

Selecting the proper location needs to be more than satisfying someone's personal whim or arbitrary guess. Much is at stake, from family fulfillment to professional success, so take a planned approach using the suggestions and ideas that are applicable to your situation.

Chapter 4 | Office Design And Decor

Design of an office is a reflection of personality and a personal expression of goals and philosophies. In turn, this expression of personality will attract a certain type of patient to the office. It is, therefore, important to express through office design and furnishings a feeling of success and confidence while achieving a mood of relaxation.

Probably the most violated rule of practice management is: "Your office should be nicer than your home." Too many practitioners live in a nice home while totally neglecting their office. It is fine to have a nice home, but priority should be given to obtaining and sustaining a nice office. That commitment will provide the income for a nice home as well as other personal pleasures.

When constructing a new building or remodeling an existing structure, the doctor should work very closely with an architect. An architect, however, is not an optometrist and needs to be given guidance and understanding toward general operations of the office. Your architect should be willing to visit your office and/or other offices to learn responsibilities and duties of assistants and doctors.

Before attempting to start any design of an office, one should visit as many optometric offices as possible. Note carefully general design, attractiveness, and traffic flow. The state optometric association can often indicate those offices that are likely to have special design or decor ideas.

The American Optometric Association has a collection of floor plans and designs for offices. The AOA library can even supply slide presentations of attractive offices from around the country. This service is provided to you as a member of the AOA. In addition, laboratories can often supply design and office plans. This includes both local laboratories and national manufacturing companies.

Designs should have an eye to the future, and the design plan should project a minimum of five years. An objective projection should be made to the future physical demands of the practice. Space for multiple examination rooms needs to be planned for the future. Practice growth will be limited if exam rooms cannot be added. Provisions for expansion should include adequate electrical outlets, plumbing and telephone jacks to provide for future needs. Filing and storage areas need to have capacity for expansion. Plan ahead in office design rather than planning for today.

ROOM DESIGN

The reception room should be an invitation to the office. This is the room where patients gain their first and lasting impression of the doctor and his office. It, therefore, should be an expression of the doctor's personality more than any other room. The reception room should be well lighted with a relaxed and cheerful atmosphere. The decor should be appealing to typical life styles of patients one expects to serve. Even ethnic or cultural decor may be appropriate in some areas.

Durability of the reception room furniture should be of prime importance since the furniture of this room will receive the most wear. Regular household furnishings are usually the most attractive for the reception room, but are not ordinarily designed for extensive wear. Often, however, it is best to buy these, planning to replace them every few years. Commercial lines of furniture are quite attractive and durable, but may not be as personal and expressive.

Furnishings needed include chairs which are high enough for older or disabled patients to get in and out of. Couches and loveseats tend to intimidate the strangers who are forced to sit together. Thus, individual seating or a combination of individual and group seating is the best choice. A game table located in the central area of the reception room adds extra seating and a surface to fill out paperwork. Lamps on small lamp tables add a personal touch and may enhance the room by direct or indirect incandescent lighting.

Space is needed for a coat and hat rack. The coat rack should be located within view of the receptionist to insure confidence to the patient that his coat is attended.

Have a specific display area for magazines. Magazines should always be current and may be best presented in binders. Bound books with pictures or photography add a touch of class to the reception area.

Live plants provide the reception room with a homey, friendly touch. These may be purchased and maintained by the staff or may be leased through professional plant services. Dying plants are not attractive and should be replaced or removed.

The walls should reflect personality and taste in art, keeping in mind the dual function of appealing to patients, as well as catering to the doctor's taste. Displayed art may be purchased, leased, or even checked out at the public library. Many doctors make photography a hobby, using photographs to add a personal touch to the office decor. It goes without saying, however, that the finished product must be of the highest quality and professionally displayed to achieve a desirable effect.

Colors, wallpaper, window dressings and paint should add an element of cheer. The reception room in general should reflect and convey an air of confidence and success.

An effective way for an office to attract children as patients is to have a children's area within or adjacent to the reception room. This tells the parents that you invite children to the practice. The area should provide activities for small children while anticipating an examination or waiting for mother. Children's toys should be of the highest quality and be very durable. If practice goals do not include expanding in children's vision care, it may be preferable not to have this special area. Thus, parents will not be encouraged to bring children with them to the office.

BUSINESS AREA

The receptionist's desk should be easily visible from the reception room while at the same time providing enough isolation for the receptionist to have privacy in conducting business arrangements and carry on telephone conversations.

The reception desk should be 42 inches high for patient check in. The receptionist work desk is 30-32 inches high with a typing area included which is 28 inches high. Filing compartments built under the patient check-in area gives the receptionist storage for stationery, appointment cards, etc. The width of the business area is most efficient when it is four to six feet wide from the receptionist desk to the files or back wall. Three inch deep drawers can be built under the 30-32 inch desk top. A three foot cabinet is excellent storage space which can be at one end of the reception desk. The length of the desk should be a minimum of six feet. It may be divided into a check-in area and a check-out area.

The filing system influences the floor and wall space necessary for the business office. A built-in filing system requires a depth of 18 to 24 inches. File cabinets and many commercial filing systems require additional space that will allow for opening and closing drawers with enough space for personnel to pass by when it is open.

The business office is best located adjacent to the reception area. It is important to make some physical separation to provide privacy. Such an arrangement makes it possible to work without disturbing the reception area function. The business office should have a place for private telephone conversations that can be made to the patients for collection and recalls. There should be adequate space for filing and, most importantly, for file growth.

EXAMINATION ROOM

The examination room should be attractive and warm, not cold and sterile. It should provide a relaxing atmosphere to help relieve patient apprehensions. Such an environment will aid in establishing doctor-patient rapport, resulting in better patient care.

Equipment, whether new or old, should look new to the patient. The equipment must always be clean. As a provider of health services, cleanliness is an obligation.

It is advantageous to have lighting on rheostat controls with easy access to the doctor. Rheostats do not work well with fluorescent lights since they are expensive to install, and often have maintenance problems. The preferred situation is to arrange adequate incandescent lighting or a combination of fluorescent and incandescent lighting for examination purposes.

A visual examination is usually performed with the projection screen area dimly lit while the examination chair area is brightly lit. The ideal length of the examination room is approximately 23 feet with the patients' eyes being 20 feet from the screen. More practically, however, anything beyond 14 feet can be used as a direct projection length without appreciable testing differences. Ten to twelve foot rooms can be adapted to mirrored projection. There are several combinations of mirrored refraction rooms. It is also wise to look at twelve foot rooms as being more flexible for adapting to a different purpose in the future. The conventional long narrow rooms have more limited adaptability.

Windows in any room, including the examination room, provide openness, but are generally covered by drapes to control light during the visual examination . . . negating the openness effect. Wall and ceiling insulation will help to provide proper sound absorption. Carpeted walls and some wall coverings also help reduce noise levels and give more privacy. These wall coverings can be used to color coordinate with examination equipment.

The minimum width of the examination room is seven feet with the ideal being eight to ten feet. The eight to ten foot width allows cabinet space parallel to the exam chair with light switches, writing area, equipment, supplies and sink easily accessible.

Switches for lights, projector and other frequently used equipment should be within easy reach of the doctor. It may be possible to locate a panel of all switches on the cabinet front. A writing surface, 30 to 32 inches high while sitting or 36 inches standing could be provided by the cabinet top or, perhaps more conveniently, by a pull-out board.

The examination room should have two additional chairs for family members who often accompany the patient. Some doctors discourage visitors in the examination room but most recognize that family members and friends can be a source for new patients.

If the office includes multiple exam rooms, the decor should vary, but the outlay and position of the equipment should be standard. This is another opportunity to appeal to children by the type of art and crafts used in decorating. Bold colors attract children. Puppets are particularly popular for decor and may also be of value in communication. Other examination rooms can be decorated to be appealing to target groups of patients. Examples include a sports oriented decor, a decor featuring a cultural or ethnic theme, murals on the walls of mountains or other nature scenes. Decorating ideas are only limited by one's imagination.

THE STYLING AREA

The frame or styling area should reflect an attractive boutique atmosphere. The presentation and marketing of any product, eyeglasses included, can be presented more successfully if there is appeal to the consumer. Before setting up a styling area, one might profit from a visit to some of the large successful optical chains and department stores to observe marketing techniques. These businesses are competitors and will probably be presenting products in an updated and appealing manner. Individual practitioners have a tendency to present their products in an unplanned, helter–skelter fashion. Merchandising and retailing have for a long time been ugly words in optometry, but today's consumers expect a professional presentation when they buy. Frames are, and should be emphasized as an important part of fashion. Anything less than the best is shortchanging the patient and, in the long term, the doctor.

Lighting in the styling area should accent and highlight the frame while making the patient look attractive. Conventional fluorescent lighting makes the patients' skin look harsh. There are special types of fluorescent bulbs that will highlight the skin and make it look more natural. The electric utility company employs lighting consultants who can give specific recommendations for lighting needs. Incandescent bulbs add appeal to the patients' skin tone. Spot and track lights are good to highlight the frames and add an attractive appearance to the styling area. Mirrored walls and frame displays add size to the room and give the illusion of more frames.

Frame displays may be designed as open or closed displays. Open displays allow patients freedom in seeing all the possibilities, but may be overwhelming to many. A good stylist may prefer a closed system with perhaps a few key styles displayed. The stylist's expertise in frame selection can then be a great advantage to the patient and to the organization of the frame selection process.

Men's, women's and children's frames should be displayed separately. As a baseline in a general optometric practice, frame inventory can be best divided: women 45%, men 35%, and children 20%. There is no magic number for frame inventory. The critical issue is providing current fashions with a variety that will satisfy people of different lifestyles and income levels. Excessive inventory creates disarray and extends selection time.

Wall space available in the styling area determines the number and size of frame displays. If the area has several entrances the wall space is reduced. Center islands can be used to help separate the styling areas and add additional display space. Seating can be available in each styling division of the center island. Such an arrangement will assist the stylist in controlling the frame selection process while making it possible to work with more than one patient at a time.

Dispensing and frame adjustment, if at all possible, should be isolated from the frame selection area. Patients coming to the office to pick up glasses or to have frames adjusted should be served without interrupting someone in the process of making a frame selection.

A bar height of 42 inches for the patient with a working height of 36 inches for the dispenser works well for frame dispensing in the adjustment area. Bar stools should have a height of 27 inches to 31 inches from the floor to the seat. The bar allows the technician to stand while the patient is seated allowing both to be comfortable. The bar overhang provides a place to conceal optical tools. Some dispensing tables are designed for both the technician and patient to be seated. Consider the additional time involved if the technician must be up and down to retrieve tools. Storage for frame cases and supplies such as lens cleaner should also be included. A small display area can exhibit repair kits, goggles, eyeglass chains, cleaners, etc.

CONTACT LENS AREA

The contact lens areas should be bright and cheery, ideally with a window view. A new patient getting contact lenses is not only experiencing a different way of seeing, but often transforming his personality and appearance. The area should project the excitement of this new experience. Learning to wear contact lenses can be frustrating, or it can be a time of joy and excitement at the new sense of perception. Experience shows that the patient who is happy and excited about his contact lenses will be the one who refers others. People who have a bad experience will react to the contrary.

A cabinet or desk for the contact lens dispensing should be arranged both to accommodate the patients and the assistant giving instructions. Thirty inches is a comfortable height. An arrangement that allows multiple dispensing is advantageous. Mirrors and sinks should be set with convenient accessibility to both patient and assistant.

Storage for consignments of contact lenses should be planned. Whether the lenses are stored in racks, small trays or in other arrangements, they need to be stored at a height that is easily accessible with labeling visible. The storage area needs to be expandable for future increases in inventory. Precautions to prevent theft should also be considered when designing the storage area.

The lab should be an area for contact lens modification, frame repairs and storage of work in progress. It should have adequate space, lighting, counter tops, electrical outlets and sinks to accommodate these needs. Special emphasis should be given to sufficient electrical outlets and sinks. There seems to always be inadequacies in this area. The lab should be easily accessible from all parts of the office, but not easily visible to the patient.

SCREENING ROOMS

Screening rooms are indeed desirable, but not necessarily required. When a screening room is not available preliminary skills can be taken in the examination room. However, trying to do too many things in one room may adversely effect productivity. This may be an area to plan for future expansion if it is not possible to incorporate a screening area initially.

A screening area should have space for future additional equipment. Electrical outlets must be accessible and possibly put on separate breakers. Some instruments such as fields instrumentation, automated refractors, and photodocumentation instruments require controlled illumination. If the room has windows, blackout curtains are needed, especially if fundus photography and indirect ophthalmoscopy are performed. The room size can be planned after drawing a schematic of instrument size and placement within a space. Instrument tables require an area with acceptable width and depth. There are rotary optical tables that can make efficient use of numerous instruments with one sitting. Space must be ample for the doctor, assistant, and patient without danger of bumping the instruments.

ADDITIONAL ROOMS

The doctor's private office is an area where personal preference dictates size and how elaborate the furnishings will be. The office provides a place for private conversations and completion of many business details that are a part of private practice. The office may also be used for patient consultation and for meeting with company representatives. Its value as an "escape" area from a busy office should not be overlooked. A multiple doctor practice may choose to have only one private office or one for each doctor. Since duplications represent space that is not always in productive use, the cost must be weighed against expected benefits.

Depending upon what facilities are available within the immediate building, it may be useful to provide a lounge area for employees where they can take a short break or perhaps have lunch in the office. Such an area represents an effort to provide employees with a benefit conducive to a favorable work atmosphere, but again is a non-productive space and must be evaluated.

Preferably there should be separate restrooms for patients and staff. When this is not possible, the restrooms should be located in an area that has easy access to all parts of the office, yet isolated as much as possible from the traffic flow. An office building may provide common facilities. Depending upon accessibility, this may eliminate the need for restrooms within the office, at least for public use. Most communities require wheelchair capabilities to restrooms which means the door must be a minimum of two feet six inches wide with a turning diameter of 48 inches. Restrooms should include an exhaust fan system. The restroom should experience a home-like decor to enhance the warmth of the office.

DETAILS

There are countless details that must be a part of the initial planning as they have to be included in the original construction. The remainder of this chapter will review some of these details.

Background music is highly desirable as it establishes mood. Music can be provided by either a commercial system or a simple amplifier with speakers throughout the office. A commercial system can allow the speakers to also be used as a part of the intercom system. The choice of music should attempt to appeal to the majority of patients, but most importantly not be offensive to them. Music not only helps set a relaxed atmosphere, but also cuts the noise and conversation from other areas of the office. Speakers in the exam rooms should be located in a position that will not detract from the examination. This goal is assisted by individual volume control. Some doctors may prefer no music within the exam room, but may include a speaker to accommodate an intercom system.

Office design should incorporate a telephone system. It is necessary to include space for convenient telephone location and adequate telephone jacks with the possibility of expansion. Telephone facilities should include the ability to communicate and page between rooms. Such communication capabilities can greatly enhance the efficiency of the office. Telephone systems can be purchased from a variety of companies. The purchase should be adequately researched and compared, since quality and capacity of systems will vary significantly. Two points of consideration include the possibility of expansion and the availability and cost of maintenance.

When designing an office, make sure the telephone company runs adequate commercial lines to and into the building during construction. There should be designed a telephone closet of minimal size of two feet by four feet to house commercial telephone equipment.

Door location into the examining room and size of the door must be strategically planned. Anything less than a two foot six inch door will not accommodate optometric chairs and stands. A two foot eight inch door is desirable yet more awkward in opening and closing. Sliding doors can be a real space saver, as well as a traffic safety feature in a busy office.

Vent locations, as well as thermostat locations must be planned to keep each of the rooms at relatively even temperatures. As examination rooms are often closed and do not allow appropriate air circulation, both output and return air vents should be provided in each of these rooms to insure comfort. Uncomfortable room temperature or stuffiness can deteriorate a patient's impression of the very best office. Office staff performance will certainly be enhanced when in a pleasant temperature environment.

Good sound insulation between rooms and particularly around bathrooms should be included in building plans.

Providing adequate sinks requires careful review as plumbing is difficult to add at a later date.

Lighting should be adequate in all areas for efficient performance.

Decisions must be made regarding the type of filing system to be used in order to include space for the required furniture. It is critical to be able to expand in this area.

Security of the office should be included in the planning. Adequate lock systems can be recommended by a qualified locksmith. An alarm system may be desirable. This can range from a simple inexpensive battery operated door alarm to an elaborate system that dials the police. Upon request the local police department and insurance companies willingly make suggestions as to the method and need for protection.

Local fire codes must be incorporated in any office design. Often there are regulations regarding the type of carpet, type of exterior walls, the width and number of exits, the width of hallways and stairwells, and the type and number of fire extinguishers.

Local building codes usually require office entrances, parking facilities and restrooms to meet handicap specifications.

The choice of building materials, accessibility to the building as well as other factors will influence insurance rates. This may be worth checking into before making commitments to specific plans.

Good office design is the art of making the principles of practice management functional in an efficient environment. All of the design details that may seem as though they come after choosing or building the office must be well thought out in advance to provide for effective office management.

101 FACTS THAT EVERY DOCTOR
SHOULD KNOW

1. Parking — 1 parking space for each 200 square feet of office space.

2. Stripes on parking.
   Most Ideal — 10' Wide
   Most Common — 9' Wide   18' Length
   Minimum — 8' Wide
   Handicap — 12' Wide

3. Straight-In Parking and Turn-In space 40' width minimum.

Parking Designs

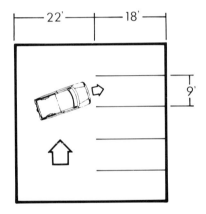

4. Angle parking and Turn space — 35' width minimum.

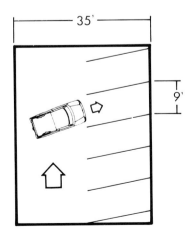

5. Double Straight-In and turn space — 60' width.

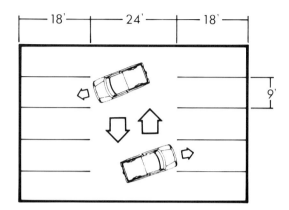

6. If there are steps outside, there should be a handicap ramp.

7. Professional Sign Outside — Maximum 4" letters to look professional.

8. Lights on exterior of building should be controlled by photoelectric switch or timer.

9. Incandescent lighting — short life, can freeze in cold weather. Fluorescent — good, but diffuse; inexpensive maintenance.

   Mercury — best and brightest lighting; can be diffuse or spot; inexpensive maintenance.

10. There should be outside electrical plugs and water faucets (silcocks).

11. Any sprinkler systems or electricity to signs should be planned before construction of sidewalks, drives, lawn, etc.

12. Automatic sprinkler systems are the best way to water plants and grass, but are expensive.

13. Northern exposure of doors will allow cold air in the winter.

14. Eastern and western windows will bring direct sunlight in during morning and evening hours.

15. Southern and northern exposures are good for indirect lighting. (More sun from the south).

16. Exterior doors should open outward in an office. In some cities this is required in accordance with fire regulations.

17. Standard wooden doors are 6'8" in height while standard glass doors are 7'0" in height.

18. Doors   Most Common
    Exterior 2'8" to 3'6"   3'0"
    Interior 2'0" to 3'0"   2'6"
    Private Bathroom Doors 2'0" or 2'6"
    Handicap Bathroom Doors 2'8" or 3'0"

19. Handicap regulations call for a 4'0" turning diameter within the restroom.

20. Restrooms need exhaust fans, preferably wired directly to the light switch.

21. Normal residential outside entry door will not hold up in an office setting.

22. Minimum seating in the reception room should be for six patients even in the smallest office.

23. People do not like to sit directly next to strangers in a reception room — do not overcrowd with couches and loveseats.

24. Children can often be occupied with books and toys in the reception room. Have something for them to do.

25. Humidifiers will reduce the amount of "static shocks" experienced in office during cold weather. There is also "anti–static" carpet available. Nylon carpet has more static than wool blends.

26. Air does not circulate in closed exam rooms unless equipped with some type of return air vent.

27. Thermostats should be set continually on fan setting rather than

automatic to keep air circulating within the office and to reduce utilities and equipment repairs.

28. Plan rooms, halls, openings with sound and sight of the patients in mind.

29. Stereo, telephone and intercom wiring can best be done before sheetrock and ceilings are in place.

30. Carpet and acoustic tiles absorb sound.

31. Background music is a sound insulator.

32. Plants and fresh flowers are pleasant additions to any office.

33. Moods can be established with colors;
    Red — Excitement
    Blue — Peaceful
    Earth Colors — Relaxing
    Bright Colors — Cheerful
    Dark Colors — Classy

34. Pictures should express art and should be framed in good taste appropriate for the picture.

35. Photography can add interest to an office, especially if the work is of the doctor or an assistant.

36. Every exam room should have a sink (preferably with a single lever faucet and/or a foot-peddle faucet).

37. There should be paper towel holders at every sink.

38. Placement of examination chair and stand should have a planned location with plenty of working room.

39. Size of Examination Room

Size of Examination Room	Length	Width
Minimum	10'	8'
Adequate	16'	9'
Ideal	22'	10'

40. Mirrored refraction is best in a room of less than 12' in length.

41. Mirrors for refraction should be front surface mirrors to eliminate a double or shadow image. THEY MUST BE ADJUSTABLE.

42. Advantages of Mirrored Refraction.

    (1) Better use of space.

    (2) Room can be closer to square in shape and allow the room to be converted to other uses.

    (3) Mirrored refraction intrigues patients.

43. Disadvantages of Mirrored Refraction

    (1) Mirrored image is not as "real" as direct projection.

    (2) Phorias and ductions are complicated with extra target.

    (3) The patient can often see the doctor and the instruments in the background of the room during the examination.

44. The diagram shows arrangement of the typical mirrored refracting room.

$$a + b = \text{projection distance}$$
$$c + d = \text{patient/screen distance}$$

Refraction Room Designs

Mirror Refraction

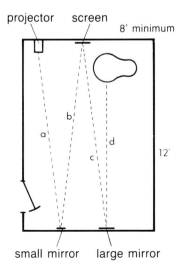

45. Two full length refracting rooms can often be offset with each other to most efficiently use space.

Refraction Room Designs

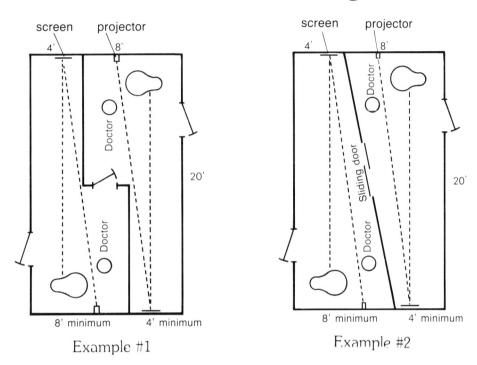

Example #1

Example #2

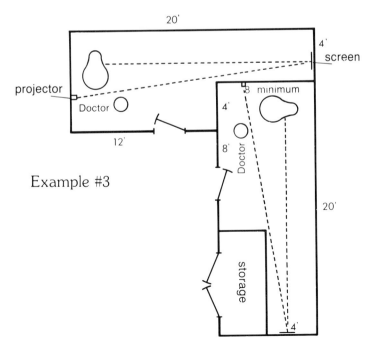

Example #3

46. Fixation lights or targets can be placed in the upper corners, at the end of the room, for patients to fixate upon during ophthalmoscopy.

47. Light switches should be placed where they may be controlled from the doctor's working position. A second set of switches at the room entrance is desirable.

48. Rheostats work best when used on incandescent lighting rather than fluorescent lighting.

49. The average life of a fluorescent bulb is two years and is dependent upon the number of times it is turned off and on. A fluorescent bulb uses very little electricity.

50. Utility companies have lighting consultants to help with office and exterior lighting.

51. Incandescent lighting has an average life of 1000 hours and is dependent upon the number of hours used. Incandescent light uses more electricity and gives off less useable light.

52. There should be more light directly over the examination chair (often fluorescent).

53. There should be dim light at the projection screen to enhance contrast.

54. Electrical cords look best "hidden". Hide them!

55. Floor plugs are good for chair and stand, however, they are expensive and somewhat limits the room ever being used for other purposes.

56. There should be a **minimum** of one electrical outlet on each interior wall.

57. The business office and the laboratory often need numerous electrical outlets. Strip plugs can be useful.

58. There should be separate electrical fuses or circuits for heavy equipment, coffee pots, refrigerators, computers, etc.

59. Frame display and both frame and contact lens dispensing areas should have incandescent or special fluorescent bulbs to accent the patient's complexion. Normal daylight fluorescent bulbs make the facial tones look unnatural.

60. Cabinet and Storage Rule: No matter how many cabinets and closets there are, they are full; and there is never enough!

61. Cabinets in the examination room should be located in reach of the doctor.

62. Cabinets

Standing Writing Surface of Reception Window	42" high
Normal Cabinet e.g. Cabinet with Sinks	36" high
Sitting Cabinet	30" high best
e.g. Reception Desk	29"-32" range
Normal Cabinet Width	20"-24"

63. DESIGN FOR CONTACT LENS TABLE

Contact Lens Table Design

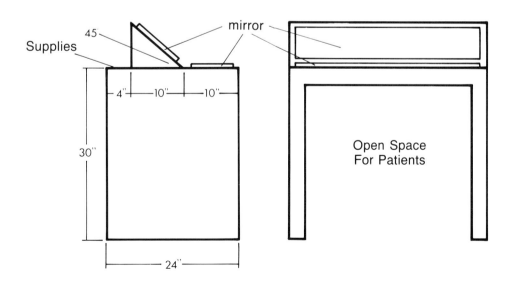

64. CONTACT LENS STORAGE CABINET DESIGNS

Contact Lens Storage Cabinet Designs

Pantry Style

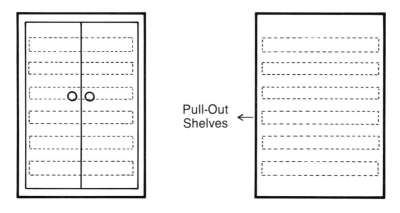

Pull-Out
Shelves ←

Slant Style

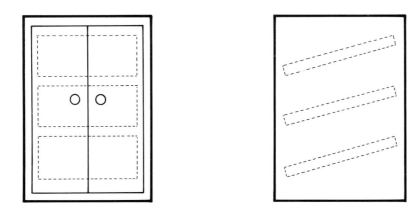

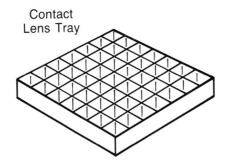

Contact
Lens Tray

65. Plan storage of contact lenses. Design cabinet so that contact lenses can be easily counted for inventory.

66. IDEA FOR GROUP SEATING. e.g. Reception, children's area, or audio–visual area.

Idea For Group Bench Seating

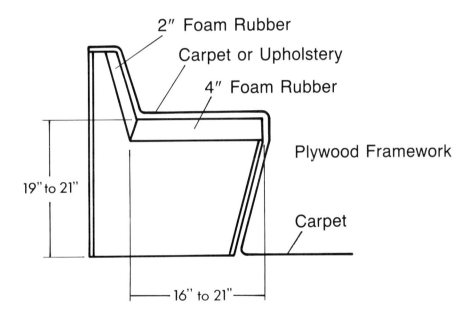

2″ Foam Rubber

Carpet or Upholstery

4″ Foam Rubber

Plywood Framework

Carpet

19″ to 21″

16″ to 21″

67. There should be dim lighting in the audio–visual area.

68. It is best to have a separate area for pre-testing. The area should be moderately lit.

69. A table may be built for pre-testing instruments.

Pre-Testing Station Designs

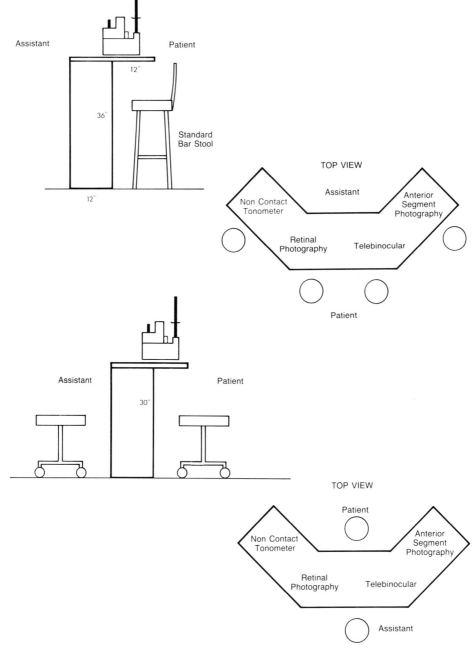

70. If building cabinets for instruments, don't forget the electricity.

71. DESIGN FOR FRAME ADJUSTMENT BAR.

Frame Adjustment Bar Design

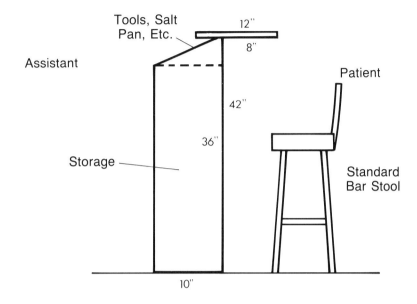

72. Check city codes and ordinances regarding fire, handicap, and general structure **before** building or designing.

73. Exam rooms, screening rooms and fields testing areas need blackout curtains if windows are present.

74. A polaroid screen can be built by covering a 1/4" pressed wood sheet with polarized screen cloth. The screen would be used in a long exam room and can be made in any size. The ribs on the material must run vertically to give stereo effect on vectograph testing.

75. Sliding doors save space within the office. They can be used as entrances to and between exam rooms. Rollers on the doors can be noisy depending on the material of the roller and track. Select the quietest combination.

76. Bracing in the wall behind and to the side of the exam chair will make it safe to mount equipment on the wall. (Projector or wall mounted stand).

77. Floor coverings around the exam chair, reception desk and lab area need to be firm so that stools with rollers can move easily.

78. When selecting carpet consider appearance, durability, safety, cost and fire codes. Rich carpet throughout the office adds class. Deep shags make it difficult for elderly and disabled to move.

79. When selecting the color of a carpet, be conscious of how easily it will soil or discolor.

80. Before buying carpet, drop a contact lens on it.

81. Tinted, thermal pane windows save energy.

82. Mini blinds and curtains add a finishing touch by adding color and contrast. Drapes add a formal, tailored touch to the area. Mini blinds are a more casual approach to the window dressing.

83. Formica cabinet tops should color coordinate with the rest of the room. Bright colors (yellow, orange, green) brighten and cheer the room. Gold, brown or light shades are soothing. White is sterile. Dark cabinet tops and woodwork tend to make the area gloomy.

84. Office decor should follow a theme (antiques, ultra modern, etc). Many furniture stores will provide professional decorating service with purchase.

85. Woodwork stain should be compatible with woodwork on furniture and accessories (e.g. magazine holder, coat rack and picture frames).

86. Vinyl wall coverings can be washed. They should be considered in high traffic areas. (e.g. halls, reception area, lab).

87. Hanging plants are attractive but heavy. Plan proper ceiling support where plants will be used.

88. Countertop corners can be rounded as a safety feature.

89. Plants can be used as room dividers.

90. Pictures should be hung at eye level or lower — never higher.

91. Clocks should be placed where doctors and assistants can see them, but not where the patients can see them.

92. A telephone in the reception area for patients use keeps the receptionist's phone free.

93. There is a need for a small refrigerator to store pharmaceutical agents.

94. If there is more than one examination room, there should be easy access between them for **doctors and assistants**.

95. Music systems should have individual controls for each room.

96. Design a space for a coat rack.

97. Chairs should be provided for additional people to sit in the examination room.

98. PLAN FOR GROWTH!

99. Whenever possible, arrange for a master switch near the main entrance that turns off all the electricity in the office except that which is necessary to control temperature and to light exits. This will save money on the utility bill and the life of bulbs in instruments that are inadvertently left on overnight time after time.

100. Three important rules in real estate. 1. LOCATION. 2. LOCATION. 3. LOCATION.

101. Golden Rules of Building:

    a. It will take almost twice as long as projected to complete any job!

    b. During construction; time is money!

    c. No matter how careful the planning, **you will** make mistakes!

    d. Whatever the estimated cost — it will always be more!

Chapter 5 | Buying Office Equipment

Cost, service involved, and terms of purchase are issues facing the optometrist when equipment is needed. Must it be new? If so, certainly it will be around for awhile and will show a pleasant tax depreciation.

Evaluations should be made comparing the cost of new and used equipment. New equipment will have a longer life expectancy and will show full tax depreciation much more quickly than it will wear out. It can also be considered a sound investment, since new equipment prices continue to inflate.

Often good used equipment may be worth more than the original prices. When looking at used equipment, one can figure the cost will be between fifty to eighty-five percent of what new equipment will cost. It will lose some of the tax advantages such as investment credit and some depreciation, but the initial reduced cost can sometimes outweigh the tax losses. The factors that determine the feasibility of buying new or used equipment should be determined on an individual basis. These decisions can best be handled through consultation with a CPA or tax counselor.

When buying new equipment it is wise to shop among suppliers to see if they have discounts for new practitioners and possible discounts in buying sets of equipment. The matter of financing and the possibility of delayed financing for new practitioners should be compared. The differences in the way a loan is set up can amount to thousands of dollars in final costs and can greatly affect monthly cash flow.

Compare different manufacturers, evaluating quality versus price. Sometimes the best is not that much more expensive. Equally important is the promotional value of the equipment. The visual impression the particular equipment gives the patient can be an asset. While new colors blending with the office decor can be beautiful, older equipment can be painted in other colors to look pleasant also. Either way attractive equipment can be a factor in practice growth.

Equipment maintenance should be evaluated. How much future maintenance can be expected on this item, and what will it cost? The true test of reliability is to seek advice from other doctors about their experience with the equipment. Discussion with others will give insight to the durability, general maintenance, and accessibility to parts.

Availability of service is a pertinent question. The service reputation of the supplier can again be best determined by asking other doctors. There should be a written agreement on the service policies, including the length of the warranties and the time it will take to respond to a service call.

Additional questions you should seek answers for are:

(1) Is there available equipment to be loaned while repairs are made?

(2) Are there enough technically trained service people available?

(3) Are there service agreements, and are these service agreements worthwhile when compared to the individual maintenance cost?

(4) Are the stock parts available at the local outlet or must they be ordered from elsewhere?

Leasing versus buying depends greatly upon individual cash flow and the initial available capital. Many types of leasing programs and lease-purchase plans are available. Each must be carefully evaluated to completely understand its complexity. Individual financial status can be reviewed by a CPA to help determine which approach is best (See Chapter 20).

Many things must be considered and what is right for one person might not be right for another. Only after all aspects are studied can a decision be made that will be the appropriate one for your situation.

OFFICE EQUIPMENT CHECK LIST

A. Business Office Equipment

    1. Essential Equipment

        a. quality typewriter

        b. calculator

        c. telephone (push button dialing)

        d. filing system

        e. swivel chair with rollers

    2. Additional Equipment

        a. word processor

        b. specialized filing systems

        c. postage meter

        d. electric pencil sharpener

        e. computer terminal with printer

        f. safe

        g. automatic telephone answering system

        h. light system for inter office communication

        i. hands-off speaker with the telephone

B. Laboratory and Dispensing Area Equipment

    1. Essential Equipment

        a. lensometer

        b. hand tools

        c. frame warmer (warm air or beads)

        d. lens box for sizing

        e. lens base curve gauge

        f. lab trays

        g. swivel chair with rollers

    2. Additional Equipment

        a. contact lens modification equipment

        b. radiuscope

        c. center thickness gauge

    d. autoclave

    e. contact lens observation and magnification instrumentation

    f. automatic lensometer

    g. small drill

    h. hinge repair kits

    i. grinder and buffer

    j. soldering equipment

    k. ultra sonic cleaner

    l. refrigerator

    m. lens cutting and edging equipment

    n. lens tinting unit

    o. lens and frame engraver

    p. microscope

    q. computer terminal

C. Examination Room Equipment

  1. Essential Equipment

    a. phoropter

    b. patient exam chair and equipment stand

    c. retinoscope

    d. ophthalmoscope (direct and indirect) (binocular–monocular)

    e. keratometer or ophthalmometer

    f. Snellen projector and screen

    g. trial lenses

    h. tonometer

    i. screening instrument

    j. occluder, PD ruler, nearpoint cards

    k. slit lamp

    l. color testing plates

    m. hand magnifier (reticule)

    n. Burton lamp

    o. fields testing equipment

    p. battery charger, if retinoscope and ophthalmoscope are battery powered.

2. Additional Equipment
    a. specialized screening equipment
    b. photo slit lamp
    c. fundus camera
    d. instrumentation to photograph and map corneal topography
    e. PD scope
    f. stethoscope and sphygmomanometer
    g. binocular testing equipment (vectograph, etc.)
    h. automatic perimeters and fields testing equipment
    i. objective automatic refractor
    j. subjective computer refractor
    k. computer terminal
    l. automatic Snellen projector
    m. slide projector
    n. cartoon movie projector
    o. gonioscope
    p. foreign body spud and agar brush
    q. Worth 4 Dot
    r. stereo tests
    s. children's acuity charts
    t. blood sugar quick tests
    u. quick cell staining solutions for slide preparation
    v. automatic keratometer
    w. pachometer
    x. electro diagnostic computerization

Chapter **⑥** | # Community Involvement

One of the quickest ways to become known in an area is to become active in the civic affairs of the people. Making yourself available for community service will not only be personally rewarding, but will get you acquainted with the leaders of the area, and establish a broader base of people to help announce your presence.

Such organizations as Jaycees, Chamber of Commerce, Lions, Kiwanis, Rotary, etc. are service oriented groups or have business and professional thrusts that would be worthy of membership.

It is important to become active in local government, primarily in political campaigns. Support of the candidate of your choice expresses your opinions on vital issues pertaining to you, your community and to your profession. It is imperative to become totally involved in professional organizations on the local, state and national level.

Camaraderie experienced with peers not only enhances knowledge in your profession but also provides a nucleus of friends who you can depend on for advice, consultation, and true friendship. Some of the deepest friendships that you can form are within your profession, due to mutual experiences with many of the same trials, tribulations and joys.

Offer yourself as a speaker, an expert on subjects relating to optometry, vision or visual problems. This could include speaking for PTA groups, senior citizen groups, business groups, other health professionals (nurses, dietitians, dentists, etc.) or teach eye safety to industrial employees. Organizing school screenings, glaucoma screenings and health fairs are important community involvements.

Whatever your personal religious belief might be, there is a church organization in which you can express a true and genuine involvement. Lasting friendships frequently develop since it is a meeting place for people who share similar ideas and concepts. Although being active in church is a way to become known and a source of patients for the office, real success only comes when God is allowed His proper place, making joy and contentment attributes that overflow into the office atmosphere.

Success in optometry is directly related to enthusiasm and involvement. Those involved are those who are successful. Anyone making a total commitment and concerted effort in their professional organizations, in their community, and in service organizations will develop friendships and business contacts leading to success and happiness.

Chapter 7 | **Personnel**

Personnel management is the most difficult area for any business. It represents a mixture of talent, skills and personalities. Personnel management involves an awareness of people's feelings and an awareness of reciprocal needs. Some points to consider when hiring, both from the vantage point of employer and employee, are forthcoming.

When is help needed? It is the authors' personal philosophy that a new doctor should have a receptionist, even if traffic does not appear to merit it. The awkward image presented by the doctor answering the telephone and greeting the patient will not be positive. Even though skills should be the true measure of the doctor's ability, patients have only the criteria of an image to choose their doctor. When choosing a doctor, patients want the best and the best does not answer his own phone.

When is additional help needed? If the doctor is having to spend time finishing work after hours, doing tasks that someone else could have done during the day, or if it becomes necesssary to schedule fewer patients so that other tasks will be finished, more help is needed.

New tests or new equipment may require additional assistants as it will lengthen the examination and consume more time. Specializing in one area, such as contact lenses, visual training or low vision will require more assistants if the patient load is sufficient.

Certainly the re-evaluation of job descriptions for existing employees would be the first step in providing new services. If you find after examining job assignments and observing personnel performing functions, that they are doing what is expected of them but not finishing their work, then more help is needed.

Additional assistants who can add to productivity are the frame stylist, contact lens assistant, lab assistant, business manager, receptionist, screening test assistant, dispensing assistant, computer visual screening assistant (someone who operates an automated refraction system), visual fields assistant, insurance assistant and executive secretary (someone who takes care of all secretarial duties, mail, and abstracts the articles and important information which the busy doctor does not have time to read). When the patients are available, the doctor should be using his time to see patients and delegating other functions. A list of some duties possible to delegate for each type of assistant is compiled at the end of this chapter.

A logical approach is to add an assistant when there is a need for someone in that area about half of the time. This will allow an opportunity to train and educate the assistant before the need becomes so critical that training time is not available.

One must meet or exceed the going pay scale in the area to employ and keep a good staff. Find out what the pay scale in your area is by checking with other doctors and businesses nearby. An employee should be considered as an investment in the practice, and must be reimbursed accordingly. If an employee is exceeding the assigned tasks and is truly an asset to practice growth, then her initiative should be rewarded. In the same light, if an employee is not achieving or is not an extension of the practice philosophies, the employee should be dismissed.

"Other benefits" can stabilize employment. To get good assistants the doctor must offer a future, and benefits can help insure that future. Common benefits are uniform allowance, medical insurance or some form of medical allowance, free vision care for the immediate family, pension fund, profit sharing plans, bi-annual salary review, vacations, sick leave and paid training seminars which offer the benefit of being at a resort area or close to shopping areas and entertainment.

Seminars can be a benefit to the assistant who in turn benefits the practice. They generate new ideas, create enthusiasm, provide training, and lend a social setting to meet other assistants and doctors.

Office decor can be beneficial. A colorful office, having new equipment to work with, and a friendly atmosphere are all meaningful benefits to personnel. The job of the assistant should be viewed in the community as a prestigious one. Fun and challenge bring forth greater effort. If employees can assume responsibility, perform new tests, work with new equipment, they respond with team work and enthusiasm.

Staff meetings give everyone a time to air opinions, griefs and complaints, as well as things they feel are going well. It also gives the doctors time to give constructive criticism, to give praise, and to do training. There should be an established time each month for a staff meeting. Adequate time should be devoted, whether it is one hour or one day, to training and meeting with the staff, going over changes that need to be made, and catching up on items that are backlogged.

Delegation of duties remains the critical aspect of personnel management. A staff member must have responsibility for certain tasks and be trained to accomplish them. Each member must be told specifically what is expected and which tasks are given priority.

Priorities must be explained and listed. Each doctor must decide and tell the assistants what he wants delegated. He then must let the assistant do the job and not keep back tracking to do it himself. Specific responsibilities should be in writing for each staff member. These tasks are her responsibility. If something goes wrong in her area, she is responsible. Assistants and doctors should be expected to help each other if their task happens to be a low priority at that time and someone else needs help. The most efficient and happiest office operates on teamwork.

Only the doctor can have the foresight to anticipate what type of employee he will need when hiring time nears. Before hiring an assistant, the doctor should decide on the skills that will be needed. Does he need someone skilled in math, a typist, someone with telephone experience, someone who has worked in an eye care office, or someone to do the preliminary testing? A predetermined job description will help expedite the hiring of a new assistant.

When interviewing, an applicant should have a resume or should be provided with a form asking pertinent questions. An applicant that has not had enough incentive to fill out a resume, or to have thought out the job application process, should probably be disqualified on that basis alone.

The information on the resume should include: age, telephone number, address, references, the last several places of employment (if applicable), high school education and college or other training. It is also important to know what salary is expected, the salary at previous places of employment, the reason for leaving the previous employment and if personal transportation is available. A very important part of the interview is finding out an applicant's job related goals and how she visualizes this job. If expectations of the job are totally different from the job description, she probably is not the person for the job. There is also the need to know what benefits are desired by the applicant as well as what benefits were received at previous places of employment, in order to compare what can be offered for the position in question.

The position and job description dictate how the interview procedures need to be carried out. A typing test may be needed when hiring someone for a receptionist or insurance assistant. Some doctors like to give tests for math and psychological skill profiles to learn more about the person's mental abilities and also some personality traits. Asking general questions gives the doctor an idea of the applicant's ability to communicate. When gathering general information about the applicant, ask about general health and visual problems. In an eye care office good vision and physical health are mandatory.

Information about the family of the applicants needs to include the age and health of the children. If the children have health problems the applicant may have to miss work often. The children may be involved in activities which require the parents to be present or provide transportation. The family plans of the applicant may determine how long she will work and also whether maternity leave might be needed. If married, the type of employment of the spouse will influence whether they are likely to move from the community.

It is the employer's obligation to be very specific to the applicant about job expectations and requirements. For the most part, this can be achieved through an office policy manual. Working hours, employee benefits, future opportunities and special office policies should be explained. If a decision is made to hire an applicant, the office policy manual should be reviewed for thorough understanding. The manual should cover the job descriptions, paid benefits, vacations, special days off, etc. The perspective employee should read it. The office policy manual can be used as a reference if any misunderstandings arise over benefits or job descriptions. A sample office policy manual is available. Reference is Appendix A.

The first ninety days of employment should be considered a trial period by both the doctor and the new employee. It must be clearly understood by the new assistant that she will be evaluated during this period and will be dismissed if progress is not satisfactory. With this understanding, a training and testing program is started. The training program should be set up listing the skills needed. The job description for the assistant will determine which skills take priority in immediate training.

The following is an example for initiating a training and testing program for a receptionist.

1st Day — Read office policy manual, start filing, practice writing receipts for glasses and contact lenses, listen to others make telephone appointments, practice making appointments.

2nd Day — Start making appointments, start writing receipts for simple charges, greet patients and ask them to fill out information forms.

3rd Day — Sort mail, post checks received, monitor reception area and start memorizing fees. Test at end of day:

1. Write a simple receipt.

2. Make an appointment.

3. Post a check.

4. Greet a patient.

5. Explain fees for an examination.

4th Day — Become familiar with confirming appointments, read list of basic optometric terminology, learn types of recall and the recall time, answer all second telephone line calls.

Each day additional duties can be added. If other assistants are employed in the office, they will be able to do most of the training. The doctor should take time each morning to review that day's assignments and training. Simple tests every week help the doctor check the progress of the assistant. An assistant learning rapidly and taking responsibility as planned, will likely be able to fulfill the job description. Using a specific training and testing program makes it possible to discover early those incapable of meeting job demands. Time and money will be saved by early dismissal.

The trial period can also be important from the employee's perspective. If the job is not meeting her expectations in any way, she has the freedom to make a graceful exit. The employee who has this option is spared embarrassment and will usually maintain a friendly attitude toward the office.

LIST OF RESPONSIBILITIES GIVEN EACH ASSISTANT

The following is a list of duties and responsibilities which is separated into specific areas for personnel in the office.

RECEPTIONIST

1. Greeting and receiving patients (Smile)
2. Scheduling (Smile)
3. Telephone calls (Smile)
4. Sort mail
5. Post checks received in the mail
6. Handle returned mail — change of address, etc.
7. Call patient and bank on returned checks
8. Print and send statements (25th of month)
9. Work collections when back-up help is available
10. Monitor paper supplies and other business office supplies and order when needed
11. Keep reception area in order — throw away old magazines
12. Confirm patient information and health history from the information sheet completed by the patient
13. Notify preliminary testing assistant when the patient is ready
14. Record time of next recall in the patient's master information file
15. Notify the dispensing assistant when a patient calls about glasses or when the patient arrives for dispensing and adjustment

16. Filing and pulling of records

17. Prepare deposit and balance cash at the end of the day

18. Statistical report daily, weekly, monthly

19. Confirm appointments two days prior to appointment

20. Type letters and general correspondence

21. Explain fees — CL's, glasses, service agreements, examinations, office visits, visual training, etc.

22. Weekly, send progress follow-up letters for glasses and contact lens patients.

23. Weekly, send thank you letters to referring patients and doctors

24. Monthly, send recall letters (20th of the month)

25. Monthly, send service agreement expiration letters (20th of the month)

26. At closing time, turn on the telephone message recorder. The next morning she should listen to any messages received after hours and respond.

27. Constantly monitor the reception area, chatting with patients if only to assure them they have not been forgotten and advising them if the doctors are running late.

CONTACT LENS ASSISTANT

1. Pull contact lenses for fitting

2. Patient instruction for contact lens care and insertion and removal

3. Explain CL fees and service agreement

4. Help choose sun wear

5. Monitor contact lens and solution inventory, order when needed

6. Make money arrangements on contact lenses

7. Enzyme, clean, sterilize and recap stock lenses

8. CL modification

9. Inspection and verification of contact lenses

10. Take acuities, time worn, history, K's and lens inspection on contact lens annual exams

11. Order contact lenses for patients, post charges, call patient and schedule after lens verification

12. Keep contact lens instruction area clean and orderly

13. Make sure all credits and returned lenses are accounted for by checking invoices

14. Help with closing office at night, turn off instruments, empty trash, clean sinks, check supplies, set thermostats, lights off, doors locked.

PRELIMINARY TESTING ASSISTANT

1. Take patient to skills area or examination room

2. Take case history and check name, dates on record

3. Skills area — under age 15 — near acuities, color test, skills test, neutralize old Rx, K's, PD; age 15-30 — same except delete skills; over age 30 — near acuities, color test, PD, neutralize old Rx, fundus photos, K's, fields, blood pressure

4. Exam room — distance acuities, put prescription in phoropter, set proper overhead lighting and chair height, signal with light system that the patient is ready and leave the door open

5. Children's acuity test for those not knowing alphabet

6. Clean phoropter filters and lenses, clean sinks, keep skills room and exam rooms in order

7. Periodically check supplies in exam rooms and replace as needed — vision reports, other paper handouts, sample drops, alcohol swabs, Q-tips, paper chin strips on slit lamp, paper records, tonometer paper, pen lites

8. Contact lens fittings — take to exam room, put K's and refractive findings on CL sheet. The doctor can figure lens parameters and then the lenses can be pulled for insertion; signal the doctor when the patient is ready

9. Contact lens progress checks — take to exam room, get a brief history, take distance and near acuities, record the time lenses were worn today and yesterday

10. Help with confirmation and collections

11. Help check jobs and dispense glasses

12. Help with filing and pulling records

13. Perceptual forms on children as needed

14. Tensions when signaled after examination.

STYLIST

1. Guide patient in frame selection

2. Order glasses

3. Order inventory frames

4. Check-in frames when received, price and frame information

5. Clean and arrange styling area

6. Make money arrangements in styling area before ordering and note this arrangement on the receipt

7. Make warranty arrangements with labs and frame suppliers

8. Send warranty frames broken to the companies once per week

9. Substitute duties during free time

10. Make sure insurance and welfare claims have been approved before ordering

INSURANCE ASSISTANT (Part-Time)

1. Fill out insurance forms and follow-up on payments

2. Keep back business office in order

3. Help as backup in all other areas

4. Stay current on changes in types of coverages and the companies involved

DISPENSING ASSISTANT

1. Dispense glasses

2. Adjust glasses

3. Order repairs and post charges

4. Check in jobs — thorough verification

5. Fill out service agreement cards and laminate cards

6. Print five day lab reports and follow-up on late jobs and frames

7. Answer the telephone when the receptionist is busy

8. Watch for lab charges not entered

9. Call patient when Rx is ready

10. Call patient when Rx is late (7–8 days old)

11. Clean the lab

12. Explain the service agreement on the glasses and give the patient the warranty card

13. Explain any adaptation the patient might experience with the new Rx and how to care for the glasses

14. Select a case and tissue lens cleaner (glass lenses only)

15. Mention the time set for patient's next examination

16. Monitor case inventory and lab supplies, order when needed

BOOKKEEPER

1. Make certain invoices are attached to statements

2. Make all disbursements in time to realize discounts

3. Make sure each amount is recorded in the general ledger

4. Balance checkbook each month and make sure general ledger entries equal disbursements

5. Responsible for payroll checks

6. Must keep track of all federal and state withholding and FICA

7. File quarterly reports to I.R.S.

8. File quarterly reports to State Unemployment Commission

9. Pay as required all federal withholding, federal unemployment, state unemployment, state withholding and company income taxes

10. Correspond with state and federal agencies

11. File annual report on federal unemployment

12. Make certain CPA has all information needed to figure annual income tax reports

13. Figure and type W2's and give to employees

14. Realize all information is confidential and must be treated as such

Chapter **8** | **Patient Scheduling**

The first consideration in establishing a patient schedule is time slots. It must be determined what amount of time is needed for each type of appointment (i.e. regular exam, progress check, contact lens exam, contact lens check, etc.) and the schedule set up accordingly. The schedule will be subject to alteration and change as new equipment and procedures become available. Most types of appointment books purchased commercially do not provide the flexibility of establishing a variety of time slots. Often the doctor can design a customized appointment book that would specify the type of exam for each time slot and have it printed, thereby, accommodating the circumstances and preference of the particular office. Individual schedule sheets can easily be used in a loose-leaf notebook.

When establishing a schedule, it is important to be considerate of the patients' time and convenience. People do not like to wait and should not have to. It is poor practice management and poor manners to schedule in such a way that patients have excessive "waiting" time. Ideally, the patient should receive service immediately upon arrival with a minimum of lag time between segments of the exam, dispensing, etc.

Employees' schedules will dictate exam schedules, or vice versa. For example, if the contact lens assistant is working in the afternoons only, then contact lens examinations and follow-up visits should be scheduled at that time. Scheduling should always be done to allow maximum efficiency of employees as well as the doctor.

It may be helpful to use the scheduling concept of "grouping", i.e., scheduling certain age groups or types of cases together. In this way it would be possible to allow longer time slots for examinations of geriatric patients on a particular day, or utilize a particular assistant in contact lens instruction, or even to have one room of the office set up for vision therapy that may have other functions on a different day.

Professional meetings, conferences with lab representatives etc. should always be charted on the schedule. It is very embarrassing and wasteful to have to reschedule patients due to a forgotten commitment. It may be helpful to select a certain time each month to meet with lab representatives and inform them of that consistent time slot. Also, training sessions for employees should be scheduled. As discussed in another chapter, well trained employees will be one of the greatest assets to an optometric office.

After establishing the format of the schedule, the next step is explaining and listing for the receptionist what information is necessary when scheduling a patient. The following information should be obtained when scheduling a patient: patient's full name, responsible party, address, home telephone, business telephone, new or regular patient, age, type of exam, any problems requiring immediate attention (note: any unusual, specific complaints causing patient to seek care). It should not be assumed that a minor's charges will be paid by the mother or person accompanying the child. It is not unusual for the responsible party to have a different last name and/or a different address.

Scheduling an appointment is the first contact a patient has with the office. It is imperative that this be a positive encounter. The receptionist must be knowledgeable in order to answer patients' questions with assurance. Questions patients might have include such items as what will be the cost of the exam? How is payment received (check, charge cards)? Is there a payment plan? How long will the exam take? Can the doctor take care of a red eye? The receptionist must have a knowledge of contact lenses in order to be able to answer a variety of questions about the various types of lenses, and to be able to help patients understand that there are a number of criteria that will dictate what lenses will be successful.

The personality expressed by the receptionist over the telephone is probably the most critical issue in a new patient's concept of the doctor and his office. Being considerate, patient and pleasant should always be a part of the receptionist's attitude. The receptionist's voice over the telephone should be pleasant and easily understood.

One of the greatest turnoffs to a patient is to call for an appointment and hear "Doctor's office . . . will you hold please?" The frustration of not being able to respond and holding a dead line immediately establishes a less than competent image of your office staff. Even more disconcerting is if the caller is a doctor or patient calling long distance. A harried receptionist with a patient waiting for a receipt, one reporting in for an appointment and another seeking a re-check appointment finds little alternatives but to resort to the "holding procedure" for the unseen caller. If this occurs with regularity, the receptionist must consult with her doctor to find ways to solve this dilemma.

Appointments made several weeks in advance should always be confirmed one or two days prior to the appointment. This helps remind patients and also provides an opportunity to use any time slots made available by patients cancelling due to a change of circumstances since making the appointment. Confirmation of recall appointments is always necessary, as discussed in Chapter 10 on Recall Systems.

Chapter 9 | Developing Fees And How To Collect Them

There are two basic philosophies in professional health care: fees for services and fees for materials. The philosophy of fees for services follows the assumption that patients should be charged for professional services and that materials should be supplied at cost. Fees for materials emphasize a nominal fee for services combined with a substantial mark-up of the materials provided.

The fees for services approach is one method that can be used in developing a fee scale. Services are charged on a per service basis, and a charge made for each of the services rendered. This would include the examination, tonometry, fields, other special tests, dispensing fees and possibly a consultation prescription fee. This system must be explained carefully to work well. It is difficult for some practitioners to use this system because they do not feel comfortable explaining fees. If done properly, this is an excellent way for combating commercial optical care. Patients should be made aware that doctors are charging them for specific services and that the cost of the frame and materials will be very reasonable.

The second approach is material mark-up. This includes a mark-up on materials to cover the professional services involved when verifying and dispensing. This does not include the exam procedures, tonometry, fields and the other professional services which go along with the examination.

The fees, and the philosophy of fees should be somewhat consistent with the other practitioners in the area. Talk to the other doctors about their philosophies and any changes that they have made in their fees. Often the approach towards philosophies of fees may need to be dictated by the community and the people who live there. With this information as a guide, development of fees should be according to goals and personal philosophies.

The doctor must keep in perspective the fees and how they relate to the overhead and income. Awareness of all the costs that are involved in producing the services rendered is explained elsewhere. This includes not only chair time but also assistant's time, the time for checking the specifications of lenses, and the time involved in follow–up care. Included in the expenses required to produce services are the fixed physical overhead of contact lens and frame inventory, rent on office space, equipment and laboratory and material costs.

As well as being a professional, the doctor is operating a business and to be successful must employ general philosophies of business. "To make money, you must spend money" is pertinent. This means that for a business to be successful and to compete, it must have the finest in facilities, equipment and personnel. Fees, in turn, must reflect these expenses. As a businessman, the calculation of these expenses determines fees.

Fees should be evaluated periodically and increased with inflation. Expenses increase with inflation, and if fees do not change accordingly the doctor will lose money. The only time fees should be decreased is to increase volume. (This could easily mean longer hours worked to earn the same profit.) Volume will, however, never increase unless the patients are told of the decreased fees. Along the same line, an increase in fees will not decrease volume, unless completely out of line or unless an announcement is made accordingly.

A definite office policy toward professional discounts on fees must be established. Determine what professional courtesies will be extended to other professionals, other doctors and their families. This includes office policy toward fees for the assistants and their families.

It is necessary to have printed material discussing fees that can be given to patients. The staff must be very comfortable with the fees since they are the ones who make the presentation to the patients. It may be necessary, especially for new assistants, to have written explanations. This may include a notebook at the front desk or in the styling area which has a fee breakdown and a presentation of these fees. After a period of time, the assistants should be able to present fees without looking or needing the notebook. It must, however, be available to them. There is always the unusual circumstances which do not occur often and the fee explanation notebook can be referred to for the proper charge.

Patients are to pay for services when they are performed. Business consultants, CPA's and psychologists all tell us that the easiest time to collect a fee is when that service and material are offered, or when the service is rendered. Each day an account is on the books, the harder that account is to collect. Patients will rationalize not paying by complaining of services and materials that satisfied them earlier. As time goes on, this rationalization process becomes easier, making accounts 60 days old very difficult to collect.

A necessary office procedure is to decide who will present the fees, who will send the statements and who will work on collections. Returned checks are frustrating and call for further collecting procedures. Following through on slow accounts and bad checks is a distasteful necessity. The procedure to follow depends on the area and local laws. There are a number of ways in which this can be accomplished. An assistant can make calls or a letter program can be set up and worked at different intervals.

After 60 days, an account is a problem and calls for some type of action. After 120 days, the account should go to a collection agency or attorney, depending on local laws.

Other businessmen can help with the securing of a reliable, ethical collection agency or collection attorney. These firms must be well established and have developed a collection system that is proficient and follows state laws. These firms can invite lawsuits if they approach collections with debatable methods. Collection agencies are going to collect some accounts over 120 days which the doctor's office could not have collected.

The success of a contact lens fitting increases considerably when contact lenses are paid for at the time of dispensing. This is a very critical factor because the motivation level is much higher if the lenses are already paid for. A thorough explanation of fees will cut down on the problems of fee collection. This should always be done by the assistant. The exception is when a patient addresses the doctor directly and wants an immediate answer. Fees are to be presented proudly. They are an extension of the doctor's personal service and skill.

Contact Lens Service Agreements form a classification all their own. This is a prepaid service agreement extended to contact lens patients. A yearly fee entitles the patient to services and materials at a reduced rate. The greater the yearly fee, the more services and materials that are included. There are three main options. The first only supplies contact lens replacements; however, the second also covers the yearly examination. The third variation encompasses all degrees of contact lens care, including office calls, and cleaning and polishing of lenses. The Service Agreement can be handled through an insurance company or the doctor can set up his own. It is necessary to consult the state insurance laws before making this decision. An added benefit of the Service Agreement is that patients with insurance are more likely to return to your office for their future contact lens needs than uninsured patients.

All fees should be given proper thought and research. The doctor and staff must feel confident in the fees established and develop office policies for collection and explanation of charges. Guidelines should determine courtesies extended to other professionals, staff and family. Fees should be evaluated bi-annually to see if inflation is reducing take home income. In conclusion, remember that a doctor's office is also a business, and all costs of running that business must be included when deciding on a fee structure.

The following are samples of collection letters, a monthly statement, service agreements and a list of procedures and materials.

BALANCE DUE _____ LAST PAYMENT _____

DEAR

OUR RECORDS INDICATE THAT WE HAVE NOT RECEIVED A PAYMENT ON YOUR ACCOUNT SINCE THE ABOVE DATE. WE WOULD APPRECIATE YOUR TAKING CARE OF THIS MATTER IN THE NEAR FUTURE.

WE ARE ENCLOSING A RETURN ENVELOPE FOR YOUR CONVENIENCE. BALANCE DUE IS AS INDICATED ABOVE.

SINCERELY,

DRS. BALDWIN & CHRISTENSEN

Chapter 9 — Sample A.

First Collection Letter

DATE _____
NAME _____
ADDRESS _____
CITY _____

DEAR

YOUR ATTENTION IS RESPECTFULLY CALLED TO YOUR ACCOUNT WHICH HAS BECOME OVERDUE. THE AMOUNT IS _____ AND YOU ARE REQUESTED TO SEND YOUR REMITTANCE TO COVER THIS AMOUNT AT THE EARLIEST POSSIBLE MOMENT.

YOUR PROMPTNESS WILL BE APPRECIATED.

Sincerely,

LINDA JONES,
BUSINESS MANAGER
STILLWATER VISION CLINIC, INC.

Chapter 9 — Sample B.

First Collection Letter

BALANCE DUE _____ LAST PAYMENT _____

DEAR

AFTER SEVERAL STATEMENTS AND A PERSONAL LETTER TO YOU, OUR RECORDS STILL INDICATE THAT WE HAVE NOT RECEIVED A PAYMENT ON YOUR ACCOUNT SINCE THE DATE INDICATED ABOVE.

WE ARE REQUESTING THAT YOU PLEASE MAKE A PAYMENT WITHIN THE NEXT TEN DAYS.

BALANCE DUE IS INDICATED ABOVE.

SINCERELY,

DRS. BALDWIN & CHRISTENSEN

Chapter 9 — Sample C.

Second Collection Letter

BALANCE DUE _____ LAST PAYMENT _____

DEAR

THIS MATTER HAS GOTTEN OUT OF HAND. YOUR ACCOUNT HAS BEEN ON THE BOOKS FOR OVER 90 DAYS WITHOUT A PAYMENT, AND WE HAVE MAILED SEVERAL STATEMENTS AND PERSONAL LETTERS.

THIS LETTER IS TO NOTIFY YOU THAT UNLESS WE RECEIVE PAYMENT WITHIN THE NEXT TEN (10) DAYS YOUR ACCOUNT WILL BE TURNED OVER TO OUR LEGAL DEPARTMENT FOR COLLECTION.

BALANCE DUE IS INDICATED ABOVE.

HOPEFULLY,

DRS. BALDWIN & CHRISTENSEN

Chapter 9 — Sample D.

Third Collection Letter

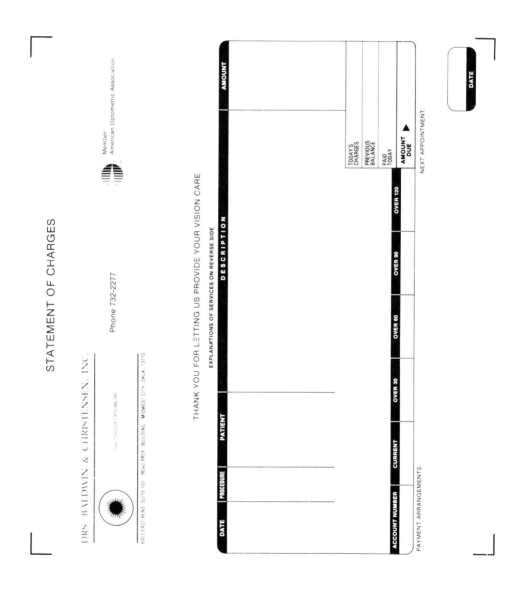

Chapter 9 — Sample E.

Statement of Charges (Front Side)

DEFINITIONS OF SERVICES

VISION ANALYSIS & DIAGNOSIS: Comprehensive evaluation of all components of the visual process in relation to the demands placed upon them by occupational, social and recreational use. This includes a thorough case history, examination of the eyes and related structures to determine the absence of disease, the objective and subjective measurement of the sight and the focus of the eyes, and their coordination and alignment both at far and near distances.

TONOMETRY: Recording and evaluation of the interior pressures of the eye. This is one of the tests utilized to detect the presence of Glaucoma.

VISUAL FIELDS: Specialized tests used to investigate the entire peripheral (side) area of sight. This is one of the tests utilized to detect the presence of Glaucoma.

CONSULTATION AND PRESCRIPTION(S): Planning and presentation of a treatment program to solve the visual needs.

PRESCRIPTION SERVICES: Determination of the optical characteristics of the lenses, design, selection and measurement of the frame, and ordering, verifying and fitting the finished prescription to the patient's face. Subsequent adjustments until the next assigned examination date.

MULTIFOCAL AND PRESBYOPIC SERVICES: Additional measurements and procedures utilized to determine the ideal form and position of bifocal or trifocal lenses required to satisfy all occupational, social, and recreational visual needs and problems.

PROGRESS EVALUATION: Subsequent consultation to determine the patient's response to the prescribed treatment.

OFFICE VISIT: Any office consultation with the doctor, concerning vision.

SUPPLEMENTAL CONTACT LENS EVALUATION: Additional specialized tests and procedures to evaluate the eyes for subsequent fitting of contact lenses.

FITTING CONTACT LENS: Lens/fit evaluation on the eye, patient instruction concerning contact lens insertion, removal, and care. Necessary contact lens modification and follow up visits for three months.

CONTACT LENS MODIFICATION: Changes in design and/or adaptation of the contact lens.

SUPPLEMENTAL V.T. EVALUATIONS: Additional specialized tests to determine the ability to maintain perfect alignment of the eyes, utilize and focus the two eyes together efficiently, coordinate eyes and hands and to judge size, shape and direction accurately.

DEVELOPMENTAL VISION: Analysis after specialized testing of a child's level of maturity in the development of all the learned skills of the visual process. These include the clarity of sight, ability to focus, move and aim the two eyes together accurately and with the rest of the body, judgment of size, shape and distance, etc. This type of testing is given children as young as six months.

VISION TRAINING, CONSULTATION, AND WORK-UP: Analysis, case planning and prescribing after additional specialized testing for vision problems requiring treatment through a series of re-training or re-educational procedures.

VISION SCREENING: Specific limited testing to determine the need of a complete vision analysis.

REPLACEMENT, REPAIRS: . . . to damaged or broken frames or lenses.

FRAME ADJUSTMENTS: Subsequent visits to maintain proper alignment of the frame on the face.

Rx VERIFICATION: Checking of a pair of glasses to determine if they were made according to the prescription, and within established quality standards.

SOFT CONTACT LENS FEE SCHEDULE

A. THE COMPLETE VISION EXAMINATION
    1. EYE AND HEALTH HISTORY
    2. BLOOD PRESSURE
    3. COLOR VISION
    4. DEPTH PERCEPTION
    5. EVALUATION OF PUPIL AND EYE MUSCLE REFLEXES
    6. MICROSCOPIC EXAMINATION
    7. INTERNAL EYE HEALTH EXAMINATION
    8. VISION EVALUATION AND DIAGNOSIS

AUXILIARY TESTS — TONOMETRY, VISUAL FIELDS, PHOTOGRAPHY

                                                TOTAL: $ _____

B. CONTACT LENS EVALUATION AND FITTING
    1. MICROSCOPIC EXAMINATION OF EYE SURFACE AND LIDS
    2. KERATOMETRY–CORNEAL CURVATURE MEASUREMENTS
    3. CONTACT LENS DESIGN AND SELECTION
    4. LENS FIT EVALUATED ON THE EYE
    5. INSTRUCTIONS TO PATIENT CONCERNING CONTACT LENS INSERTION, REMOVAL, AND CARE
    6. NECESSARY FOLLOW-UP VISITS UP TO THREE MONTHS
    7. MODIFICATIONS OF CONTACT LENSES UP TO THREE MONTHS
                                                TOTAL: $ _____

FEES FOR PATIENTS WHO ARE WEARING CONTACT LENSES AND NEED TO BE REFIT IN NEW LENSES MUST BE EVALUATED INDIVIDUALLY.

C. THE COST OF MATERIALS
    1. SOFT CONTACT LENSES .... _____
    2. NEW ULTRATHIN SOFT CONTACT LENSES .... _____
    3. SOFT LENS CARE KIT .... _____
    4. SPECIAL FEES APPLY FOR ASTIGMATIC LENSES AND OTHER SPECIALIZED LENS FITTINGS.

A CONTACT LENS AGREEMENT IS AVAILABLE AND ENCOURAGED, BUT IT MUST BE IN FORCE WITHIN 60 DAYS OF THE CONTACT EXAMINATION.
SERVICE AGREEMENT TOTAL: $ _____

FINANCIAL ARRANGEMENT MUST BE MADE WITH THE CONTACT LENS ASSISTANT ON THE INITIAL VISIT.
EXAMINATION FEES ARE NOT REFUNDABLE.
REGULAR FEES APPLY AFTER THE THREE MONTH FITTING PERIOD.

    B. L. BALDWIN, O.D., F.A.A.O.
    B. J. CHRISTENSEN, O.D., F.A.A.O.

Chapter 9 — Sample F.

Soft Contact Lens Fee Schedule

FIRM CONTACT LENS FEE SCHEDULE

A. THE COMPLETE VISION EXAMINATION
   1. EYE AND HEALTH HISTORY
   2. BLOOD PRESSURE
   3. COLOR VISION
   4. DEPTH PERCEPTION
   5. EVALUATION OF PUPIL AND EYE MUSCLE REFLEXES
   6. MICROSCOPIC EXAMINATION
   7. INTERNAL EYE HEALTH EXAMINATION
   8. VISION EVALUATION AND DIAGNOSIS

AUXILIARY TESTS—TONOMETRY, VISUAL FIELDS, PHOTOGRAPHY

TOTAL: $ _____

B. CONTACT LENS EVALUATION AND FITTINGS
   1. MICROSCOPIC EXAMINATION OF EYE SURFACES AND LIDS
   2. KERATOMETRY-CORNEAL CURVATURE MEASUREMENTS
   3. CONTACT LENS DESIGN AND SELECTION
   4. LENS FIT EVALUATED ON THE EYE
   5. INSTRUCTIONS TO THE PATIENT CONCERNING CONTACT LENS INSERTION, REMOVAL, AND CARE
   6. NECESSARY FOLLOW-UP VISITS UP TO THREE MONTHS
   7. MODIFICATIONS OF CONTACT LENSES UP TO THREE MONTHS

TOTAL: $ _____

FEES FOR PATIENTS WHO ARE WEARING CONTACT LENSES AND NEED TO BE REFIT IN NEW LENSES MUST BE EVALUATED INDIVIDUALLY.

C. THE COST OF MATERIALS
   1. CONVENTIONAL FIRM LENSES .... $ _____
   2. OXYGEN PERMEABLE LENSES .... $ _____
   3. FIRM LENS SOLUTIONS AND CASE .... $ _____
   4. SPECIAL FEES APPLY FOR ASTIGMATIC LENSES AND OTHER SPECIALIZED LENS FITTINGS.

A CONTACT LENS SERVICE AGREEMENT IS AVAILABLE AND ENCOURAGED. BUT IT MUST BE IN FORCE WITHIN 60 DAYS OF THE EXAMINATION.

SERVICE AGREEMENT TOTAL: $ _____

FINANCIAL ARRANGEMENTS MUST BE MADE WITH THE CONTACT LENS ASSISTANT ON THE INITIAL VISIT
EXAMINATION FEES ARE NOT REFUNDABLE.
REGULAR FEES APPLY AFTER THE THREE MONTH FITTING PERIOD.

   B. L. BALDWIN, O.D., F.A.A.O.
   B. J. CHRISTENSEN, O.D., F.A.A.O.

THE V.I.P. PROGRAM . . . A CONTACT LENS SERVICE AGREEMENT

THE "**VERY IMPORTANT PATIENT**" AGREEMENT IS NOT INSURANCE, BUT A PROGRAM PROVIDING A COMPREHENSIVE VISION CARE PLAN THAT INCLUDES "BOTH" THE YEARLY CONTACT LENS VISION EXAMINATION AND SPECIAL REPLACEMENT FEES FOR YOUR CONTACT LENSES.

CONTACT LENS SERVICE AGREEMENT

A. THE V.I.P. AGREEMENT INCLUDES THE FOLLOWING FOR ONE YEAR:
   1. OFFICE VISITS WHEN PICKING UP REPLACEMENT LENSES (USUAL COST $ _____)
   2. ONE CONTACT LENS VISION EXAMINATION (USUAL COST $ _____)
   3. SPECIAL LENS REPLACEMENT FEES

B. THE SPECIAL LENS REPLACEMENT FEES
   1. SOFT CONTACT LENSES
     A. THIN SOFT LENS REPLACEMENT PER LENS . . .
                         REGULAR COST . . . $ _____
                         VIP REPLACEMENT . . . $ _____
     B. ULTRATHIN SOFT LENS REPLACEMENT PER LENS . . .
                         REGULAR COST . . . $ _____
                         VIP REPLACEMENT . . . $ _____
   2. FIRM CONTACT LENSES
     A. CONVENTIONAL FIRM LENS REPLACEMENT PER LENS . .
                         REGULAR COST $ _____
                         VIP REPLACEMENT . . . $ _____
     B. OXYGEN PERMEABLE LENS REPLACEMENT PER LENS . . .
                         REGULAR COST . . . $ _____
                         VIP REPLACEMENT . . . $ _____

C. SPECIAL REPLACEMENT FEES APPLY FOR ASTIGMATIC LENSES AND OTHER SPECIALIZED LENSES.
D. SERVICE FEES NECESSARY FOR "REFITTING" LENSES ARE NOT INCLUDED IN THIS AGREEMENT AND SERVICE POLICIES ARE NOT TRANSFERABLE OR REFUNDABLE.
E. THE V.I.P. AGREEMENT MUST BE PURCHASED WITHIN 60 DAYS OF THE CONTACT LENS EXAMINATION.
F. SPARE CONTACT LENSES MAY BE PURCHASED THROUGH THE V.I.P.

   1. V.I.P. YEARLY TOTAL . . . . $ _____
   2. LENS AGREEMENT (NO SERVICE) . . . . $ _____

B. L. BALDWIN, O.D., F.A.A.O.
BOBBY CHRISTENSEN, O.D., F.A.A.O.

EXTENDED WEAR
CONTACT LENS SERVICE AGREEMENT

THE V.I.P. EXTENDED WEAR SERVICE AGREEMENT INCLUDES THE FOLLOWING FOR ONE YEAR:

1. OFFICE VISITS WHEN PICKING UP REPLACEMENT LENSES (USUAL COST $ _____)
2. A SIX MONTH AND YEARLY CONTACT LENS VISION EXAMINATION (USUAL COST $ _____ EACH)
3. SPECIAL LENS REPLACEMENT FEES
   A. LENS A

   REGULAR COST . . . $ _____
VIP COST . . . $ _____

   B. LENS B

   REGULAR COST . . . $ _____
VIP COST . . . $ _____

4. SERVICE FEES NECESSARY FOR "REFITTING" LENSES ARE NOT INCLUDED IN THIS AGREEMENT AND SERVICE POLICIES ARE NOT TRANSFERABLE OR REFUNDABLE.
5. THE V.I.P. AGREEMENT MUST BE PURCHASED WITHIN 60 DAYS OF THE CONTACT LENS EXAMINATION.
6. SPARE CONTACT LENSES MAY BE PURCHASED THROUGH THE V.I.P.

V.I.P. YEARLY TOTAL . . . $ _____

B.L. BALDWIN, O.D., F.A.A.O.
BOBBY CHRISTENSEN, O.D., F.A.A.O.

Chapter 9 — Sample I.

Extended Contact Lens Agreement

SYSTEM DATE:	FEE LIST	PAGE 1
PROC. NO.	STATEMENT DESCRIPTION	STANDARD CHARGE
1	VISION ANALYSIS AND DIAGNOSIS	
2	TONOMETRY	
3	VISUAL FIELDS	
4	CONSULTATION	
5	VISION ANALYSIS AND DIAGNOSIS/PHOTOS	
6	BIFOCAL AND PRESBYOBIC SERVICES	
7	TRIFOCAL AND PRESBYOBIC SERVICES	
8	SPECIAL PRESBYOBIC SERVICES	
9	PROGRESS EVALUATION	
10	OFFICE VISIT A	
11	OFFICE VISIT B	
12	OFFICE VISIT C	
13	OFFICE VISIT D	
14	SUPPLEMENTAL CL EVALUATION	
15	CL FITTING (SOFT)	
16	CL FIT. (SOFT TORIC & SOFT SPH.)	
17	CL FITTING (SOFT TORIC)	
18	CL FITTING (SOFT SPECIAL)	
19	CL FITTING (FIRM)	
20	CL FITTING (POLYCON)	

Chapter 9 — Sample J.

Fee List

Continued
next page

SYSTEM DATE:	FEE LIST	PAGE 1
PROC. NO.	STATEMENT DESCRIPTION	STANDARD CHARGE
21	CL (FIRM SPECIAL)	
22	CL MODIFICATION	
23	SUPPLEMENTAL VT EVALUATIONS	
24	DEVELOPMENTAL VISION	
25	VT CONSULTATION & WORK-UP	
26	VISION SCREENING	
27	REPLACEMENT REPAIRS	
28	FRAME ADJUSTMENTS	
29	RX VERIFICATION	
30	SV GLASS LENSES	
31	BIFOCAL GLASS LENSES	
32	TRIFOCAL GLASS LENSES	
33	SPECIAL GLASS LENSES	
34	SV PLASTIC LENSES	
35	BIFOCAL PLASTIC LENSES	
36	TRIFOCAL PLASTIC LENSES	
37	SPECIAL PLASTIC LENSES	
38	PHOTOCHROMIC	
39	TINT	
40	PRISM	
41	VARILUX LENSES	
42	GENTEX LENSES	
43	RIMLESS	
44	SPECIAL	
45	FRAME	

46 thru 49 open for future use.

50	SOFT CL'S	
51	SOFT CL SOLUTIONS & ACCESSORIES	
52	SPECIAL SOFT LENSES	
53	CSI LENSES	
54	LOANER CL	
55	FIRM CL'S	
56	FIRM CL SOLUTION & ACCESSORIES	
57	POLYCON CL'S	
58	SPECIAL FIRM CL'S	
59	VIP LOST SOFT REPLACEMENT	
60	VIP CSI REPLACEMENT	
61	VIP LOST FIRM REPLACEMENT	
62	VIP LOST POLYCON REPLACEMENT	
63	VIP SPECIAL CL REPLACEMENT	

64 thru 98 open for future use.

Chapter 9 — Sample J. (continued)
Fee List (continued)

Continued
next page

SYSTEM DATE:	FEE LIST	PAGE 2
PROC. NO.	STATEMENT DESCRIPTION	STANDARD CHARGE

99	SERVICE CHARGE	
100	CONVERSION BALANCE	
101	VIP AGREEMENT	
102	CONTACT LENS AGREEMENT (NO SERVICE)	
103	VIP AGREEMENT/EXTENDED WEAR LENSES	

104 thru 149 open for future use.

150	TERMS: PAID IN FULL AT ORDERING
151	TERMS: ONE HALF DOWN — BALANCE AT PICKUP
152	TERMS: ONE THIRD DOWN — BALANCE AT PICKUP
153	TERMS: ONE FOURTH DOWN — BALANCE AT PICKUP
154	TERMS: WILL PAY IN FULL AT PICKUP
155	TERMS: ONE HALF DOWN — BAL IN THIRTY DAYS
156	INSUR. DEDUCT. @ STYLING; BAL AT STATEMENT
157	INSURANCE DED. @ PICKUP; BAL BY STATEMENT

Chapter 9 — Sample J. (continued)

Fee List (continued)

Chapter 10 | Recalls: An Invitation To Success

The lifeblood of optometry is a neglected child. Samplings indicate a startling number of offices have no recall system. It is as though they either consider it unethical or an improper action to notify a patient of needed care. These colleagues fail to realize the enormous potential for practice growth that a recall system represents. No recall spells stunted growth for most practices.

Most of the really successful practices across the nation do utilize a recall program of some form to keep their practices growing and provide the necessary service that most patients expect when they seek care. Most providers of the health care field would conclude that the professional has a responsibility to notify and inform a patient when it is time for subsequent care. He has the responsibility to give a rationale of why the appointment is necessary and, thereby, create within the patient a desire to seek such care.

Most practitioners who maintain an active recall program would explain that on a few occasions people are disturbed when they are notified that it is time to return for visual care. However, many are disturbed when they are not notified. The majority of the people want to know that somebody cares for them and about them. A simple reminder from their doctor not only reminds them of the vision care needs, but also it speaks to the fact that someone cares about them.

An effective recall system does not just happen when one decides to instigate such a program. A certain type of preconditioning is necessary for a positive response to result. Next year's recall starts at the close of this year's vision examination. Following the case presentation, it is important that the doctor tell the patient when he should return for further care. At that time, it is important for the doctor to share reasons why regular care is important and why the particular period of time was chosen for them. Additional reinforcement can take place at the close of the styling and/or by the receptionist. She might say, "Did Doctor _____ tell you he wanted to see you in one year and we'll send you a card notifying you of the time?"

Additional reinforcement is given when the recall date, (at least the month suggested) is placed on a visit slip or a recall card, business card, etc. Some offices use some form of follow-up correspondence or a telephone call in ascertaining the progress of the patient. At that time, a reminder of when they are to be re-examined can be shared.

There are many techniques of recall that are used by different offices. One of the most commonly used forms is the sending of a card that notifies the patient that he is due to be re-examined. Some offices find that a telephone call is more effective and conveys the same message in a more personal way. However, this may be impractical in rural areas because of long distance telephone calls.

Another effective recall method is sending a card and following that card with a telephone call. The card alerts the patient that a telephone call will be coming shortly and the receptionist will then arrange a satisfactory time for him to have his visual care updated with re-examination.

Another method of recall is to send a card to the patient that already has a predetermined appointment time which you have saved for them. It carries the message that says, in effect, "Before filling appointment times with new patients, it is important to save time for regular patients first. We, therefore, are reserving you a time for your vision examination on _____ date. If this time is inconvenient for you, please feel free to contact our receptionist and she will be happy to change the date to a more suitable time."

Some practitioners might feel that this is going a bit too far to reserve that time without their knowledge. Experiences have shown that it produces the highest number of positive recall responses when the patient is properly preconditioned and a follow-up telephone confirmation is utilized. In this day, people are busy and even though their motives are good, they often do not take time to do what is needed without structured follow through.

A typical conversation that could take place as the doctor concludes his examination with a patient as it relates to recall might go like this: "Mrs. Jones, we have found today that Amy's eyes have become more nearsighted and we will need to change the power of her glasses. It is also important that we re-examine her in one year, or sooner if symptoms should appear. Amy is at a very vulnerable age when visual changes often take place."

When the stylist finishes selecting the eyewear for the patient and financial arrangements have been made, she might reinforce earlier comments in this manner: "Mrs. Jones, the doctor has set a one year period to be the time for Amy's next vision examination. We will drop you a card and save her an appointment time so we can follow the progress of her nearsightedness. I will just write the month and year on your visit slip and you will have a record of when she will receive an appointment card."

Four weeks from this date a progress call can be made with explanation as: "Mrs. Jones, the doctor likes us to contact all of our patients after they have received new eyewear to be sure they are adjusting properly. We will be looking forward to seeing Amy at her appointed time."

After the patient has left following the examination, it is important that there be some method of keeping track of the recall time. A postcard can be utilized for notifying of a recall date. It can be preprinted or written at the time of the examination and filed in a drawer that is organized by the months of the year. When the month arrives which that patient has a time reserved, the cards are pulled, the appointment time written in the appointment book and the card sent two weeks in advance of the assigned appointment time.

Whether an appointment has been made by either the office or the patient, the patient's intention to keep that visit must be confirmed one to two days before the scheduled time. It is noteworthy how often people forget, or problems come up that cause them to miss appointments. When a recall appointment is not kept, a follow-up telephone call should be made which explains to the patient that an appointment was missed and rescheduling to a convenient time would be welcome.

Overbooking of appointments is sometimes needed to fill in the gaps of "office made" recall "no shows". When the office preassigns the schedule hour, rescheduling is often necessary to arrive at a suitable time between both the patient and the doctor. Occasionally there will be a family that will respond negatively to the recall program. They may say, "I don't care to come in now for whatever reason" or "I am unable to come now because of financial obligations." It is then wise for the receptionist to tell the patient in an understanding manner that a reassignment is being made six months hence and gain permission to follow through.

Keeping track of the number of recall appointments that are made will show what percentage of success the recall program is producing. It will also give direction as to what type of system is most effective. Any system, it must be stressed, is more effective than no system at all. A trial effort, embracing aspects that may seem counterproductive to the conservative doctor, can produce a surprising response.

Computerized recall programs are now very sophisticated. The recall messages are individualized by diagnosis (i.e. myopia, astigmatism, hyperopia, cataract, glaucoma, visual training), by age (i.e. presbyopia, child, college student), and by the type of visual correction (i.e. soft contact lenses, O_2 permeable contact lenses, astigmatism contact lenses, monovision contact lenses, bifocal contact lenses, progressive addition glasses, safety glasses). Computers reduce personnel time required to manage the recall system and add a personalized touch not easily accomplished with other recall systems. Chapter 18 further explains the use of computer recall systems.

Sample recall letters follow which may be of help when formulating a recall message.

NAME _____
ADDRESS _____
CITY/STATE/ZIP _____   DATE OF LAST EXAM _____

AT THE TIME OF YOUR LAST VISUAL EXAMINATION, WE AGREED TO NOTIFY
YOU WHEN IT WAS TIME TO BE RE-EXAMINED FOR ANY CHANGES IN YOUR
EYE HEALTH OR FIT OF YOUR FIRM CONTACT LENSES.

WE TRY TO SAVE OUR PREVIOUSLY EXAMINED PATIENTS TIME IN OUR
SCHEDULE BEFORE ACCEPTING NEW PATIENTS AND WE HAVE RESERVED A
TIME FOR YOU ON DAY _____ TIME _____ DATE
_____ .

IF THIS TIME IS INCONVENIENT FOR YOU, PLEASE CALL OUR OFFICE. WE NOW
HAVE SOME NEW ASTIGMATISM SOFT LENSES AND STILL HAVE A ONE YEAR
WARRANTY ON GLASSES.

SINCERELY,

OPTOMETRIC ASSISTANT

Chapter 10 — Sample A.
Eye Examination Reminder Card

NAME _____
ADDRESS _____
CITY/STATE/ZIP _____   DATE OF LAST EXAM _____

AT THE TIME OF YOUR LAST VISUAL EXAMINATION, WE AGREED TO NOTIFY
YOU WHEN IT WAS TIME TO BE RE-EXAMINED.

WE TRY TO SAVE OUR PREVIOUSLY EXAMINED PATIENTS TIME IN OUR
SCHEDULE BEFORE ACCEPTING NEW PATIENTS AND WE HAVE RESERVED A
TIME FOR YOU ON DAY _____ TIME _____ DATE
_____ .

IF THIS TIME IS INCONVENIENT FOR YOU, PLEASE CALL OUR OFFICE. WE NOW
HAVE A ONE YEAR WARRANTY AGAINST BREAKAGE OF OUR FRAMES AND
LENSES.

SINCERELY,

OPTOMETRIC ASSISTANT

Chapter 10 — Sample B.
Eye Examination Reminder Card

NAME _____

ADDRESS _____

CITY/STATE/ZIP _____   DATE OF LAST EXAM _____

AT THE TIME OF YOUR LAST VISUAL EXAMINATION, WE AGREED TO NOTIFY YOU WHEN IT WAS TIME TO HAVE YOUR **EYE HEALTH** RE-EVALUATED.

WE TRY TO SAVE OUR PREVIOUSLY EXAMINED PATIENTS TIME IN OUR SCHEDULE BEFORE ACCEPTING NEW PATIENTS AND WE HAVE RESERVED A TIME FOR YOU ON DAY _____ TIME _____ DATE _____ .

IF THIS TIME IS INCONVENIENT FOR YOU, PLEASE CALL OUR OFFICE. WE NOW HAVE A CAMERA WHICH CAN PHOTOGRAPH THE BACK OF THE EYE TO HELP EVALUATE EYE HEALTH.

SINCERELY,

OPTOMETRIC ASSISTANT

Chapter 10 — Sample C.

Eye Examination Reminder Card

DEAR _____

YOUR EYES HAVE BEEN RECALLED.

IN ORDER TO ASSURE YOUR CONTINUED VISUAL COMFORT AND EFFICIENCY, IT IS NECESSARY THAT YOU HAVE A PERIODIC EXAMINATION. PLEASE CALL OUR OFFICE AT YOUR EARLIEST CONVENIENCE.

DR. MELTON AND STAFF

Chapter 10 — Sample D.

Eye Examination Reminder Card

Dear

After your last vision examination we recommended the next

appointment be in_____months. We have reserved your

appointment for _____ *Day.   Time.   Date.* _____

If this time is not suitable, please call_____ *Phone No.* _____ at your

earliest convenience.

Sincerely,

Optometric Assistant

Chapter 10 — Sample E.
Eye Examination Reminder Card (Front Side)

DRS. BALDWIN & CHRISTENSEN, INC.

 OPTOMETRISTS·

6912 E RENO, SUITE 101 · MIDWEST CITY, OKLA. 73110
ADDRESS CORRECTION
REQUESTED

NAME
ADDRESS
CITY/STATE/ZIP

Chapter 10 — Sample E.
Eye Examination Reminder Card (Back Side)

DATE _____

NAME _____

ADDRESS _____

CITY/STATE/ZIP _____

DEAR PARENT,

OUR RECORDS INDICATE THAT (CHILD'S NAME) LAST EXAMINATION WAS IN _____ OF _____ . THE NATURE OF (CHILD'S NAME) VISION PROBLEM WARRANTS MONITORING MORE FREQUENTLY THAN THE NORMAL ANNUAL VISUAL ANALYSIS.

SINCE CHILDREN'S AND YOUNG ADULTS' VISION CAN CHANGE FREQUENTLY, IT IS NOW TIME FOR A PROGRESS EVALUATION. GOOD VISION RELATES TO READING SPEED, COMPREHENSION, GENERAL SCHOOL ACHIEVEMENT, AND SPORTS ABILITIES. PLEASE CALL OUR OFFICE FOR A CONVENIENT APPOINTMENT.

WE HAVE APPRECIATED YOUR PATRONAGE AND CONFIDENCE AND HOPE WE MAY CONTINUE SERVING YOUR VISUAL NEEDS IN THE FUTURE.

SINCERELY,

DR. OLIPHANT
YOUR FAMILY OPTOMETRIST

SCO/ww

Chapter 10 — Sample F.

Eye Examination Reminder Card

DATE _____
NAME _____
ADDRESS _____
CITY _____

DEAR

OUR RECORDS INDICATE YOUR LAST CONTACT LENS EXAMINATION WAS ON DAY _____ MONTH _____ YEAR _____. WE ARE NOTIFYING YOU THAT IT IS NOW TIME FOR A COMPLETE VISUAL EXAMINATION AND ANALYSIS. PERIODIC VISUAL EVALUATIONS ENABLE YOU TO MAINTAIN GOOD VISION, INSURE COMFORT, AND MORE IMPORTANTLY, PRESERVE GOOD EYE HEALTH.

THE **EXTENDED WEAR CONTACT LENS** EVALUATION ENABLES US TO DETECT HOW CLEARLY AND EFFICIENTLY YOU ARE SEEING WITH YOUR LENSES AND TO MONITOR THE FIT, POSITIONING, AND CONDITION OF YOUR CONTACTS. CURRENT EXTENDED WEAR RESEARCH SUGGESTS FREQUENT INSPECTION OF THE LENSES AND FREQUENT MICROSCOPIC TISSUE EXAMINATION.

YOUR COOPERATION WILL HELP SAFEGUARD YOUR EYE'S HEALTH AND EFFICIENCY THROUGHOUT YOUR LIFETIME. PLEASE CALL OUR OFFICE FOR A CONVENIENT APPOINTMENT.

WE HAVE APPRECIATED YOUR PATRONAGE AND CONFIDENCE AND HOPE WE MAY CONTINUE SERVING YOUR VISUAL NEEDS IN THE FUTURE.

SINCERELY,

DRS. STATON AND STARK
YOUR FAMILY OPTOMETRISTS

BJS/JCS/TR

P.S. IN ADDITION TO HAVING THE LATEST IN VISUAL EXAMINATION EQUIPMENT, OUR OFFICE OFFERS THE FOLLOWING TO BETTER SERVE OUR PATIENTS:
 1. "NO LINE" bifocals in glass or plastic lenses.
 2. Extended wear soft contact lenses.
 3. Soft contact lenses for the correction of astigmatism.
 4. Bifocal semi-soft contact lenses.
 5. Oxygen permeable firm lenses (semi-soft contact lenses).

Chapter 10 — Sample G.

Eye Examination Reminder Card

CHAPTER

Communicating With The Patient In The Office

A cheery greeting by a personable receptionist paves the way to establishing rapport with an incoming patient. After providing the routine information, including the reason for the visit, the patient is directed to fill out a new, or regular patient information form, depending on the situation. Having verified all information, the screening assistant can be summoned and the patient moved to a preliminary testing area.

Different types of codes on the record jacket are helpful to let the doctor know later what has been done by the assistant. A notation should be made stating by whom the patient was referred. If the patient was a referral from another patient, or another doctor, a thank you card should be sent.

PRELIMINARY TESTING

At this time preliminary testing can be started. The tests should be explained by the assistant as she is performing them. A child can be given a Seymour Safely sticker or a button saying that he has had his eyes examined, making him more relaxed before he sees the doctor. The assistant can do other preliminary testing as needed and explain what tests are being done.

POST EXAMINATION

After the examination, the patient is presented with a fee slip by an assistant. It is necessary to present fees with a positive, firm, yet pleasant attitude. It is important to project to the patient the doctor's sense of worth for the fees charged. To avoid sensitive credit problems, the fee slip should provide alternative fee arrangements. Communication in regard to fees is a problem source, and this can be avoided with special arrangements for payment being made before incurring lab expenses. A fee slip is then filled out and a very thorough explanation of each entry is given with any questions being answered about the fees. On the reverse side of the fee slip there should be an explanation of each fee. A new concept being used in many offices is including on the fee slip all the information necessary to substitute as an insurance form. Thus, after the fee slip is filled out, one copy is stapled to a signed insurance form, requiring much less of the assistant's time. Also, this provides two copies of the fee slip.

Patients are told on the way to the front desk that they will be called when their glasses or contact lenses are ready, or when they need to set up an appointment for follow-up care.

DISPENSING CARE

When dispensing glasses, the assistant will adjust them and ask if they have any questions. Patients should be apprised of what to expect during the adaptation period. Top quality cases and specialty cases should be available to fill the needs of patients with special job requirements or who are very style conscious. Some examples would be hard cases for construction workers, cases with a flap on top for welders to keep hot slag out, cases with the local university mascot imprinted for student and alumni, high fashion designs and colors for the style conscious and children's cases with imprints of current cartoon characters.

Other special services and products that can be given are warranties on frames and lenses, lens tissues for glass lenses or a small bottle of cleaner for plastic lenses. The patient's name and phone number can be engraved in the temple for identification if lost. The assistant should explain that the fee for glasses includes the case, warranty, and frame adjustments for a specific length of time.

Four weeks after the patient has picked up glasses, an effective public relations tool is a follow-up letter. This letter will ask if they have any questions about their glasses or if they need further care. It will also state that a letter will be sent at a specific time in the future for their recall.

CONTACT LENSES

When the patient receives contact lenses, the fit will be evaluated and a thorough explanation of insertion and removal of lenses, proper hygiene, lens care, solutions, and wearing time is provided. If a service agreement program is available, patients should be made aware that the original fee "insures" the lenses for a limited period of time after which the total responsibility for replacement falls to the patient. Follow-up visits are mandatory and all instructions should be put into written materials. Since patients have certain expectations about contact lenses, they should understand the type prescribed and their benefits as well as limitations. A thorough explanation of lens durability, replacement cost, environmental factors, allergies, medications, etc. can help adjust that patient's expectations to the proper perspective and assure success.

With the contact lens patient, communication is probably more critical than with any other patient in the practice. A fee schedule should be presented to each contact lens patient with a detailed explanation given. This schedule can be broken down into parts: the visual examination, the fitting service, and the lenses. It explains the procedures in each part of the fitting and is vital in setting up the precedent of what professional contact lens care entails. In most cases, the fee should be paid when the contact lenses are dispensed to enhance motivation as well as assuring collection. The patient is much more motivated if they have already paid for the lenses and not as likely to fall into the trap of not trying if nothing has been invested.

A letter should be sent approximately six weeks after their dismissal. This letter stresses the importance of following all instructions given regarding wearing contact lenses and caring for them properly. It should also state the last date the Service Agreement on their contact lenses can be purchased and note that an appointment card for their next examination will be sent at a future date.

On the jacket of the contact lens patient record, a check list can be set up making sure information as to what type of contact lens the patient wears, their last exam, recall time, service agreements, etc. has been recorded. The check list can also be a reminder to send "thank you" letters and reports if needed.

CHILDREN

Children need something special. When examining children a favorable impression on the parent is part of the education process. After the examination, a child and parent should receive instructions on the care of their eye wear and possible future vision changes that could take place Then they get a prize from a "treasure chest" or other treat for being a good patient. (The author's "dietitian wife" objects to candy as a patient treat.)

MAKING NOTES

For any type of patient, it is necessary to make notes as to what was said in the explanation to that patient, including any telephone conversation. Was that patient told that this frame and lenses were going to be heavy; that this frame style touched their cheek; or that the tint selected was darker than recommended? Was it noted that the patient needed trifocals but rejected them at that time? Was it noted that the contact lens patient may have residual astigmatism or that he may not have a complete blink, or tear chemistry might not be what is needed for an ideal contact lens wearer? All of the explanations should be noted on the records so the doctor can later verify his previous communication with the patient.

NEEDED COMMUNICATION SKILLS

It is a long range benefit to review what is expected from the staff regarding communication with the patient in each of their specialized areas. The following are some of the communication skills needed by different assistants:

(1) The receptionist should be able to answer questions on scheduling, fees, general questions about eye care and contact lenses. She should be able to direct that patient into the proper type of appointment for the care needed. Another essential communication skill is being able to question patients in order to identify emergencies. The receptionist is also someone that must be able to communicate with the problem patient and stay calm and rational when dealing with them. The receptionist should have a superb personality and the ability to adjust to any situation.

(2) The assistant who performs auxiliary testing must be capable of explaining the tests being done and be able to converse with the patients making them feel at ease in the office setting. The screening

assistant should have the patient mentally prepared as to what to expect during the examination. The assistant must impress the patient with her skill and knowledge.

(3) After the examination, the styling assistant must be able to communicate with the patient about fees, current style and trends, lens types and tints, different reasons for special lenses, safety lenses and why different types of frames are better than others for that specific person. The styling assistant should represent "style" in her dress and mannerisms.

(4) The contact lens assistant must be able to explain the contact lens fees. She must know the specific type of care regimes for the different types of lenses. Communication skills of the contact lens assistant are critical for instruction on insertion and removal of contact lenses and explaining the different types of contact lenses. She must be familiar with the strong and weak points of the lenses used. A sense of what communication process will work best for that apprehensive patient getting his first pair of contact lenses will sometimes make the difference of whether the patient will successfully wear lenses. She must also excel over the telephone in explaining and understanding contact lens problems. She should not wear eyeglasses. The contact lens assistant must be patient and enjoy working with people.

(5) The lab assistant or dispensing assistant must be able to explain changes in the prescription, why an adjustment will make a certain difference in the way the patient sees or the way the frame feels on the face, be able to explain lens and frame types, and must be able to clarify and collect any balance of fees at the time of dispensing the eye wear. The lab assistant must have good hand dexterity and be somewhat technically oriented while expressing traits of organization and communication.

(6) The insurance assistant must be able to answer questions that are referred to her on insurance coverage and procedures for patient retrieval of proper forms from their specific insurance carrier. She must have knowledge on how to handle welfare and medicare forms which may differ from state to state and sometimes differ from patient to patient depending on the program for which they have been approved.

Often assistants must wear several hats and be able to perform a multitude of duties. But, even in a one assistant office, she should be expected to excel in all of these areas.

All office staff should be aware of programming patients with a positive attitude regarding vision care and use of contact lenses or glasses. Comments such as, "Call us when you have problems.", condition patients to anticipate problems. A more positive statement would be, "Feel free to contact us if you have questions or need further care." Contact lens assistants must be especially cautious not to predict problems when explaining the adaptation to contact lenses.

Inner office communications are probably the most important aspect of a practice and determine the kind of impression a patient has when leaving the office. If patients sense the staff being warm, friendly and competent with patient interests in mind, the practice can only benefit. A lack of caring and inadequate explanation of patient problems will usually result in their seeking future care elsewhere.

EDUCATING THE PATIENT

Overheard was this conversation from a wife to her husband as they were paying their fees at the business office:

"George, I've never had such a thorough examination in my life. You wouldn't believe the tests he put me through."
"What did he say was wrong with your eyes?"
"He didn't say! He just changed my glasses!"

This is a sad commentary about a lost opportunity that may never occur again. As you have read elsewhere in this book, one of the greatest practice builders is your involvement in community affairs . . . speaking before PTA's, service clubs and just about any group who will listen. And yet there are doctors who have a patient in the office ready and willing to pay for the advice and services he offers who for any number of reasons becomes mute and impersonal and expects his staff to explain his services to the patient.

Unfortunately this is the lament of many health care patients regardless of the discipline, "The doctor was too busy to talk to me!"

The subject being addressed is really not communication but patient care. The best doctor can delegate communications but must provide patient care himself. This is what he is trained for; this is what he is being paid for!

Patient care is the educational process by which a patient learns about his eyes, about what the doctor is doing during an examination and why, about the treatment plan being recommended and why, and about the necessary follow-up care and why.

There are many preliminaries that can set the stage for the doctor.

Educating the patient should begin in the reception area.

Doesn't it seem strange that most reception rooms of health professionals are alike. Often one is hard-pressed to remember which doctor's office he is in by looking around this room. All reception rooms seem to have chairs or benches around the perimeter with magazine racks containing new and old editions of popular consumer publications.

Here is a group of people in your office concerned about their eyes, being offered reading matter, performing a near point task which may be the reason they're in your office in the first place. In addition, if an office is well run, the waiting time for a patient should not exceed 15 minutes, hardly enough to get into a magazine of interest.

Why not use the time to begin the educational process of a patient by converting your reception area into a visual science information center?

Arrange your chairs in a back-to-back conformity in the center of the room and use the wall space to present simple visual displays that depict important information about eyes and vision. Too many waiting room walls contain hundreds of dollars worth of paintings selected by an interior decorator whose taste in art may or may not be better than the doctor's. But they serve no useful purpose except to give the waiting patient something to look at.

Why not use your imagination to attract, fascinate and educate the patient. A typical example is a visual display on the market that asks the question, "Do you know what the doctor sees when he looks into your eyes?" The display has a 3 dimension plastic mold of an eye which, upon the push of a button, lights up the pupil of the eye enabling the patient to look into the eye at a fundus photograph and see what you see in a normal healthy eye.

Too often we give our patients credit for knowledge they do not have. Ask your next patient a rhetorical question, "Do you know what the pupil of the eye is?" Most will tell you that it is a little black spot in the center of the eye. Few will tell you that it is a hole through which light passes to focus on the retina; few realize that an ophthalmoscope allows the doctor to see **through** the pupil to the back of the eye.

The visual display illustrates this quite vividly. In addition, in the corners of the unit are four fundus photographs that illustrate what the doctor sees if you had advanced conditions of glaucoma, hypertension, diabetes or brain tumor. Accompanying the display are complimentary color brochures that explain to the patients what they need to know about each of these diseases. An optional feature is an audio system that explains the display in about one minute.

This is only one of the many ideas suitable for displays in the reception area . . . others are:

1. What glasses do?
2. What is a cataract?
3. Color blind — NOT ME!
4. All about contact lenses.
5. Illusions.

Audio visual aids are available that explain many of these topics, and enterprising doctors can use their ingenuity to build visual displays to educate their patients.

THE EXAMINATION ROOM

It is at this point that the doctor must remember that the patient in the chair is not a pair of eyeballs but a whole person that he is examining through his eyes.

Every test performed by the doctor should be explained with the authority of a benevolent professional. It is not enough to tell the patient what you're doing, but why you're doing it and what you're looking for. Explain what retinoscopy is all about and what a tonometer determines. Explain why you must ask questions that require a choice by the patient during your subjective examination. Explain what a red-green check test is and why you are dilating the pupils.

Here you are sharing the data gathering process. When this is completed, it is now necessary to make a case presentation. It is here where the practitioner must be a **doctor** in the true sense of the word. This is the moment of truth that the patient has been waiting for. It is this point in time when you will keep the patient forever or lose him to a more caring doctor . . . or at least one that comes across as being more caring.

Regardless of how busy you are and how far behind in your schedule you are, you must take the necessary time to talk to your patient and to listen.

As this section began, it is not enough to say, "Linda, all the tests that were performed on your eyes today were normal and all you need is a prescription change."

Many doctors begin by reviewing with the patient exactly why she is in your office today . . .even if it is only because her frame broke and she is due for an examination.

Each test performed by the technician is reviewed, again briefly explained and the results interpreted.

There are three major concerns of most patients —

1. Are my eyes healthy? Am I going blind?

2. Why am I having difficulty (seeing, reading)?

3. Will my symptoms go away?

Are my eyes healthy?

It is necessary for you to explain that you carefully examined the external and internal parts of the eye and exactly what you saw. If you can use a visual aid to illustrate a normal fundus either by projecting a 35 mm slide or a light box system that ties into the visual display in the reception room, learning comes rapidly. An enlarged photograph transparency in a light box similar to how a physician views an X-Ray is an ideal way to explain a normal condition to your patient. Take 30 seconds to explain the optic nerve, the macula and the blood vessels using a magic marker that wipes off, to pinpoint your comments. There is a light box on the market that not only provides enlarged photographic transparencies of the normal fundus, but eleven other conditions that are relatively common.

It is sometimes invaluable to be able to place a photo transparency of a condition like diabetes next to a normal fundus and explain what is taking place and to emphasize the importance of the general treatment of diabetes to the preservation of sight and life. Admonishing a patient to adhere strictly to the insulin and diet therapy of her family doctor is much more meaningful when the advanced case of a disease can be displayed.

Explain what a cataract is and the several choices of therapy as well as any urgency for immediate surgery.

Explain a referral! Why, who, what and where and equally important, your role in their care.

Explain every test that you performed that ruled out or detected disease and the results.

Be warm, concerned, reassuring, but above all, be honest.

Why am I having problems seeing?

It is here where vision care takes center stage.

Explain your tests for vision care and the results.

Explain myopia . . . even if you did it two years ago during a previous examination.

Patients usually want to know if their eyes got worse? It is up to you to explain that a Rx change does not mean the loss or the diminishing of sight. Some doctors use examples to explain . . . examples that the patient can relate to in other parts of their bodies. Even if the example is not scientifically accurate, it may make common sense to a patient and relieve apprehension.

A typical example is the explanation to Mommy that Junior's eyes are now more nearsighted and that his glasses have to be changed and the lenses will be slightly thicker. Uppermost in their thoughts but not said out loud may be, "You examined Junior's eyes two years ago and told me that he was only mildly nearsighted — why did you let his eyes get worse?"

Some doctors anticipating this, use the parallel of Junior's feet. Explain that Junior's shoe size has changed frequently since birth and will continue to change until he reaches full growth. Ask the rhetorical question, "Did his feet get worse?" Explain that eyes grow too and will change every year until sometime in his late teens when this growth will slow down or stop altogether. Explain that changes following full growth are related to visual task requirements, reading habits and aging.

This type of presentation must spill over in all phases of vision care . . . why you are prescribing bifocals . . . why prism is necessary . . . even if you recommend that no changes be made in the Rx.

Will my symptoms go away?

It is here you might explain the enigma of headaches and the difficulty of an exact specific diagnosis as to cause. Some doctors use the reverse approach by assuring the patient that if headaches persist after new glasses have been worn for a short period of time, the patient should rule out eyes as a cause and seek other tyes of professional care to locate the source of the headaches.

Books have been written on the many different types of presentations made to explain eye care. Of prime importance is that a case presentation is a personal matter between doctor and patient. All the many answers should be carefully thought out and then orchestrated into a meaningful, personal, concerned presentation to your friend, the patient.

Search the field for visual aids, displays and audio visuals designed to educate the patient. Every optometrist is well acquainted with the multitude of brochures available from the American Optometric Association, BVI and many other resources. It is absolutely necessary for the doctor to have them available.

Supplement your case presentation with meaningful brochures that explain diseases that you have uncovered, visual conditions that you are correcting, types of materials that you feel to be necessary, and the importance of routine re-examinations. Make these brochures reinforcements of what you told them — that can be carried home. Memories are fleeting!

Conclude your presentation with the scheduling of time for the next examination and ask the patients if they have any questions. Allow them to vent their concerns and address their questions with authority and understanding.

In the long run, a 30 minute examination followed by a 15 minute case presentation is more valuable than an hour examination with a superficial, quickie case presentation.

You can never be allowed to forget that the patient came to see you . . . the doctor, not because of your eyeglasses, your beautiful office or the thorough examination you provided, but because of your reputation and image as a doctor who is knowledgeable, understanding and cares about his patients.

Educating the patient is the key to building a following of loyal, enthusiastic, satisfied patients.

PERPLEXING PATIENTS

Despite yeoman efforts to be good doctors, every practice has its share of "impossible" patients whose very nature is to be uncooperative, suspicious and unreasonable. They are the nomads . . . patients without a home . . . constantly moving from doctor to doctor, continually trying to find a new method of care, a new doctor or a magic pair of glasses that will solve their unsolvable problem. In fact, the new doctor in town will discover that many of his early patients are nomads for they have tried everyone else.

Satisfactorily dealing with these patients can be a significant source of practice growth. Making unhappy patients happy can be personally rewarding and beneficial to the total profession of optometry, as well as your own personal practice. Therefore, do whatever is required to solve a problem.

When dealing with a dissatisfied patient, either yours or someone else's, be sure that early in the conversation the patient is made aware of the fact that you are there to do whatever is required to make him happy. Sometimes it really comes to the fact that some people merely want to have someone to talk to and to know there is someone who cares. Even though often limited in the amount of time available to sit and visit with a patient, a certain amount is necessary. Listen carefully to what the patient is saying and try to note any underlying concerns the patient may exhibit.

One of the doctors' most difficult decisions is whether a change of this patient's lenses will help. The amount of difference in refractive findings may be very small, yet the cost to make such a change is significant. When you consider the cost of remaking a pair of glasses, especially with the fact that many laboratories will give a courtesy discount on a "do-over" prescription, the cost to turn a dissatisfied patient into a happy one is a small expenditure when considered over the years. This can be a valuable public relations tool that helps build a good reputation in the community. What is it worth to have a positive word spoken about your practice in your community? Obviously, it is worth quite a lot. There are people in every practice that do try to take advantage, and there is a time when no more "do-overs" are in order. However, that should be the exception rather than the rule that governs your practice.

The communication should be positive rather than negative when talking about adapting to glasses and contact lenses. It should be made known to the patients that you want to know if they have any questions or difficulties. It is much better for the patient to return to your office to air their complaints rather than to another office, their friend, or neighbor. Any office can make a mistake and the embarrassment of that mistake ending in another office can be avoided. Sometimes further explanation of adjustment to the glasses or contact lenses is all that is needed.

Many problem patients have legitimate complaints and sometimes a correct Rx placed on an improper base curve can create symptoms in a visually sensitive patient that would never bother other patients. Often unwanted prism caused by improper decentration but well within your tolerance for acceptance will exceed the patient's comfort range and result in asthenopia.

Sometimes you will find that the difficult patient masks his complaint and blames the new glasses for every symptom known to man. He gives you the clue to the real problem after you decided that perhaps you should change his glasses and prescribe the questionable +0.25 spheres over his recent Rx, when he casually remarks, "If you are going to change the lenses, would you change the frame too? — My wife thinks they're ugly." This was the problem in the first place but the patient knew that you probably would charge for a new pair of glasses without a legitimate complaint.

A new frame for the original Rx will often result in a happy, satisified patient. You must decide whether it is worth it to you — for, if you say "No", the new Rx in the same "ugly" frame may solve nothing.

Probably the most important rule to remember is to properly communicate on the initial visit. When proper explanations are given involving care and adaptation, few problems arise. A follow-up communication four to six weeks after the final visit can help find problems that would not have surfaced. With this approach, fewer patients will be lost to "problems."

CHAPTER 12 | **Telephone Systems**

For the patient calling an optometric office to make an appointment, the telephone is the first source of contact. For that reason, the telephone must be considered one of the most important systems in the office. The present concern is with installation concepts, rather than usage.

When looking for telephone systems, more than one choice is now available. Private companies have available sophisticated communication systems which can be individually engineered for a practice. These companies will sell or lease the telephones, install and service them, and engineer designs which would benefit your office and make an efficient communication system. A representative from the telephone company will come to the office and explain the different features, services and cost factors. The cost conscious doctor looks at both the private company and subsidiaries of Bell Telephone, then compares the total cost for each line coming into the office. Subtract that from the total cost and find out which system is going to be the more cost efficient. The investment credit and the tax advantages that are involved with depreciating the system should be considered. However, tax advantages and total cost savings by the use of either company can only be realized if the service is good.

It has been the experience of the authors that owning your own telephone system is more cost efficient. It will usually pay for itself in four to six years, depending on the amount of initial equipment installed. Because of the process of deregulating American Telephone and Telegraph Company, which includes splitting off the local Bell System phone companies into independent firms, telephones and communication systems that were set up by Bell can now be purchased. This will make it possible to directly compare costs of systems from Bell Telephone subsidiaries with private companies.

When moving into a new office space, telephone location is a factor in office design. When constructing the walls, the telephone company should be consulted as to where the cords and jacks will need to be installed. The height and location of the telephone and jacks must fit the needs of the functions in that area. It should be determined if the telephone will be used while standing or sitting. The telephone should be within easy reach from the primary work area. It must also be easily visible so that the lights for each line can be efficiently monitored. The telephone should serve the practice by saving time and steps; therefore, it is important to equip the office with telephones in every major work area. Refer to Chapter 13 for details as to how the telephones and a light system can be engineered together. Telephone location seems almost too elementary to mention, but many offices seem to overlook the importance of this practice management tool.

The telephone system should be developed for office flow. It is very important to have the proper number of telephone lines. A minimum of two lines is essential even for a new or starting practitioner. As the flow of the calls into the office increases, more lines may be necessary. When additional lines are installed, it may be necessary to assign a second assistant the responsibility of answering the second or third lines when they ring simultaneously.

Sometimes it is important to have an outgoing, unlisted line which can be used for ordering, personal calls for assistants, and for personal family calls. Some offices have a telephone which is used exclusively for the patients' outgoing local calls from the reception area. If this service is provided, it is important that there are enough lines in the office as not to inconvenience normal operations if patients use the telephone. If one number is unlisted for staff use, this same line could be used for the reception area, or a separate unlisted line exclusively for the reception area may be required.

When comparing telephone systems, there are some musts that need to be included. It should be a touch tone telephone rather than a dial. A touch tone telephone is similar to running a ten key. The number can be dialed very quickly, saving the receptionist's time as well as other members of the staff. A hold button and an intercom system built in is also essential.

After selecting the type of telephone system and the colors and capacities are decided on for the system, specific decisions about telephone locations are to be made. Locations must be readily visible to the personnel within the office. The receiver cords must be long enough to allow a certain amount of mobility in an area. If the telephone is a desk top model, it must have a long enough cord to be moved, making the telephone useful in different locations. Careful consideration should be given to the type of phone in order to maximize efficiency. In some areas, a wall telephone will fit the space much better than a desk top telephone. In the styling area, there may be inadequate room for a desk top telephone, making a wall telephone a more convenient choice. The same may be true in an examination room where all space needs to be used efficiently and effectively. The style is also important. A smaller size telephone might fit the space in a certain area, and a regular size or style telephone in another area would be more practical and cost efficient.

When selecting the telephone system, there is a wide variety of features available. Some options include music on hold, hands off speaker systems (communication without having the receiver off the hook) and different buzzer tones which can be changed relative to the level of sound in work areas.

The built-in intercom, which is adaptable in most telephone systems, can be as sophisticated as needed. Zones can be set up for a certain intercom number to call a specific area within the office such as the styling area, business office and the lab. Any number of different zones can be created. Only examination rooms might be included on one zone. After dialing a given number the intercom is activated and the message will be transmitted only to the particular zone for that number. The intercom system may also reach an individual room or the entire office by simply dialing the number established for that area. The intercom system should be tailored for each office and should allow for growth, as a more detailed system will be needed when the practice size and number of employees increase. The telephone system can be designed to have the capacity for additional communication functions as discussed in Chapter 13 on inter-office communications. These possibilities should be considered in planning and selecting a system.

Another item to remember is to communicate with the telephone company as early as possible about your listing in both the white and yellow pages. Telephone companies have cut off dates several months before the book delivery time; failure to sign their contract agreement could mean going over a year with no listing.

The office communications system should be planned for maximum efficiency and usefulness. A practitioner should anticipate an increase in telephone usage as the practice grows and be prepared to expand the system.

CHAPTER 13 | # Inter-Office Communications Systems

LIGHT SYSTEMS AND INTERCOMS

When developing a communication system within an office, one may want to incorporate the inter-office communication system with the telephone system. A principal requirement of the system would be to let the doctor and assistants know which exam rooms are occupied. The system should also let the assistants know the location of the doctor and where he is needed. If the practice is multiple doctor; a quick way is needed to communicate among themselves.

One exemplary communication system incorporates the phone with visual and audio signaling capacity. Consider an office with four exam rooms and four phone lines. With a ten button phone, four buttons are used for telephone lines and four of the buttons are color coded or numbered according to the color scheme or number of the examination rooms. On the row of buttons across the top of the telephone, four are the ordinary flashing lights when the telephone line is on hold, and the solid white light when the telephone line is being used. Four buttons are buttons that flash or stay constantly lit to let the doctor know which exam room is occupied. The remaining two buttons are for hold and intercom. The system also has a black button on the face plate of the telephone which is a buzzer used for audio communication among office personnel.

Two methods are used to activate a light indicating an examination room is occupied. The first method is for the light to come on when the patient sits down in the examination room chair. This activates a pressure sensor in the seat of the chair and the light stays on while the patient is seated. The second method is a manual switch that can be turned on when the patient is out of the chair, but still occupying the room. This same light can be switched to a flashing mode if the doctor wishes to signal an assistant. These lights allow the doctors and assistants to know which examination rooms are in use.

With inter-office communications, unnecessary traffic is reduced by utilizing audio and visual communication systems that instruct office staff "who" is wanted "where" and "why". Buzzer codes can be incorporated to let doctors signal one another without having to move back and forth between exam rooms or use the overhead intercom.

An added feature of the visual communication system is a separate panel of colored lights apart from that used in conjunction with the phone lights. For example, four additional colors can be assigned to specific individuals or referred to an area of expertise needed, whether it be contact lens assistant, stylist, etc. The additional panel of lights is located near the phones in all work areas. This informs, with the flip of a switch, which assistant or what type of assistant is needed and in which exam room. The capability of such an audio-visual in-office communication system is limited only to one's imagination. Light systems are available commercially, or, if one is so inclined, a system can be developed and fabricated with an electrician.

Following are some suggestions and specific ways in which the system can be used. Each assistant is assigned a specific color light on the auxiliary light panel. When the assistant is needed, her light is turned on and a buzz is given to get her attention. The switch in the exam room where she is needed is flipped to the flashing mode. At that point, she knows which exam room to enter. If a green light is flashing it indicates a contact lens assistant is needed. If the doctor were in the number one exam room, he would activate the switch of the exam room light. When it started flashing the contact lens assistant would know to come to that room. When the doctors want to communicate between themselves, they can give a long and a short buzz. This would tell doctor one that doctor two wants to consult with him.

When the circumstances indicate that verbal communication is required, the overhead intercom is used. It is set up in "zones" where a dialed number will activate the zone in which the assistant or the other doctor is working. The zone might be the styling area, business office, or laboratory area. A second zone could be the examination rooms. The assistant would dial zone #2 and ask over the overhead speaker for doctor one or doctor two. If the doctor wants to contact the receptionist, he simply dials her station where a hands-off speaker is located. She can respond immediately by speaking from anywhere in the room, or if she is taking an appointment, a message can be given over this speaker without interrupting her conversation with the patient. She can make a note and upon completion of her call, she can respond to the message.

Each room also has a number on the intercom system and can be dialed direct like any other intercom. To contact a certain room, dial that number and the buzzer signals the doctor or assistant to answer the call.

One other simple code that is useful: if the exam door is closed that means the patient is with a doctor. An open exam door with the patient information slip clipped by it, indicates that the preliminary tests are completed and the patient is ready to be seen by the doctor. In such a manner, the doctor observes the light system and notes which doors are open to guide him to the next patient in a multi-doctor practice.

Another technique is to seat the patient in an exam room, flip a switch for an identifying light above the door outside the exam room and place the patients' screening and history records in a plastic holder beside the entrance to the examination room. This enables the doctor to identify and greet the patient by name on entering rather than walking into the room empty handed and then picking up the records. This is particularly helpful to the doctor who has difficulty remembering names and has just seen this same patient a day or so previously yet fails to recall the circumstances.

As previously noted, many light systems are commercially available. The light system can be incorporated within the telephone system or on a separate panel by itself. They are usually installed on low voltage systems. A light system enhances any practice that is starting to produce a larger volume or flow of patients. It can increase the efficiency of the office through better communication resulting in quicker response from the staff.

Patients will sense an efficient office with everyone moving with purpose. The light and the intercom communication system approach lets the doctor know where the patient is within the office as well as the assistant and other doctors. The system reduces time spent on communication and this keeps the appointment schedule running smoothly. If assistants are signaling that a number of patients are waiting, the doctor can adjust his time to meet the patient load.

Communication within the office is essential and the forementioned examples are only a small sample of what can be accomplished with the technology available. Communication is one of the keys to practice management success and every professional should capitalize on its potential.

Chapter 14 | Practice Statistics

One important tool an optometrist can have at his disposal is the accumulation of statistical information about his practice. Statistical data can help determine goals and aid in locating the strengths and the weaknesses of the practice. Sometimes practitioners notice their gross or net income from the practice is not what they expected it to be. When they begin to analyze the conditions, however, there is not enough available information from which to make judgments. Commonly a practice can get very busy, even to the point of needing to take in an associate, but when arrangement times are at hand, there may be no information that quantifies the amount of business the practice is producing.

The Internal Revenue Service has a way of asking penetrating and personal questions when you least expect it. Because of poor record keeping, doctors sometimes have a difficult time explaining all the ramifications of their business. These reasons, and many more, speak to the fact that good practice statistics are a necessity.

What are some of the advantageous practice statistics that should be accumulated in any optometric office? The most obvious statistic is the **practice gross.** This data is usually the most readily available piece of information because of Federal Income Tax regulations. How much of that gross income really represents dollars in the pocket? **Net income** is what is of real interest; spendable dollars before taxes, and the amount of time required to accumulate those dollars. To determine the office net income, all of the office expenditures, with the exception of personal payroll and personal benefits, are subtracted from the gross income before taxes. In determining office net, good categorical statistical information on the expenses of the office is a necessity. One effective method of bookkeeping in accumulating these figures is a peg board system similar to the receipts system, but which is done for disbursements only. They are available through Reynolds and Reynolds, Control-O-Fax Company and others. These peg board systems are personalized checks that overlay a general ledger, which carbons the information from the check on to the ledger. This requires only one more entry of that expenditure into the proper category of expenses. Such categories of columns might be: laboratory expenses, office expenses, payroll, utilities, equipment, rent or office payment, taxes, miscellaneous expenses, etc. The total month's accounting is made for disbursements and can be accumulated on a quarterly as well as yearly basis. By knowing the total year's expenditures of different categories, the doctor can compare expenses against other practices or against national averages to give insight as to which categories may be out of balance in the practice. This information can also be passed on to an accountant for further financial guidance and income tax preparation.

The next statistic that needs to be kept is how many **total visual analyses** are done in the practice each day. These statistics can be further divided by listing whether the patients are new to the practice or former patients. These values obviously can show the optometrist if he is reaching out to new people in a community and whether the type of care he is providing is influential in bringing other members of the same family into the office.

Statistics about other types of visual care rendered in the office are also enlightening. For example, how many contact lens examinations and fittings are performed each day? How many visual therapy visits, developmental vision exams, and training sessions are done each day? How many progress or office calls are done daily and how much of the day's time is taken up in routine weekly contact lens follow-up checks? All of these visits do not necessarily represent income to the office, but they occupy time necessary to render care. When time studies of a practice are accomplished, a practice can be evaluated from a productive standpoint so that time allotted or fees for service can be adjusted.

When these statistics and other figures, which may be uniquely important to individual practices, are kept on a daily basis, they can be accumulated into weekly, monthly, quarterly and yearly values. They become informative to the doctor as to when the practice is the busiest or slowest, the areas of care where he is spending the greatest amount of time, and whether he is being adequately paid for his time.

One effective tool in helping a doctor establish a proper fee for his time is to determine the chair cost or overhead per examined patient. This can be determined by dividing the practice overhead by the total number of examinations performed during the year. This obviously will be an approximate figure since no consideration is made for the office calls, contact lens checks, etc. that are also a part of the office practice. It is nonetheless a helpful tool since visual examinations represent a majority of the time spent with patients.

One very effective and helpful tool in seeing the progression of a practice is making graphs of the practice growth. One graph could include the total number of examinations, another the year's total gross, and another a practice's growth over a period of years. These should be accumulated over a period of years in order to see what is happening in the practice. Following are some illustrations:

Sample Examination Trends

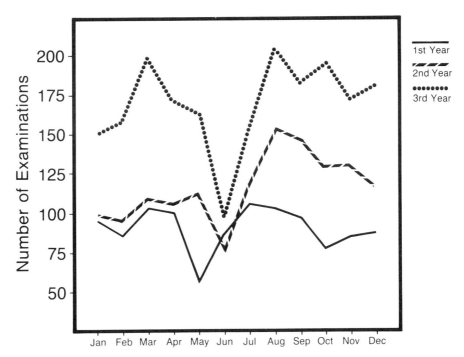

Sample Practice Income Trends

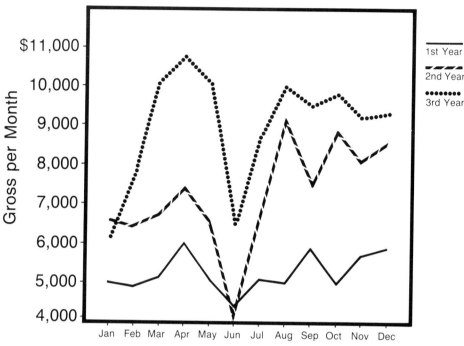

Sample Projected Growth Chart

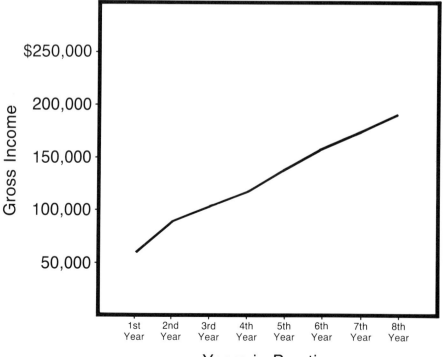

Statistics are only as valuable as the accumulations are accurate. When possible and appropriate, statistical values should be gathered on a daily basis while the business matters and patients seen are still easily remembered. Statistical information can also easily reflect when changes in the schedule have been made such as cancellations and no-shows. Obviously, the choosing of dependable people who have a knack for numerical accuracy is an important consideration when assigning the task of gathering statistical information to an employee.

Does the practice need a new associate? Is the practice growing at the rate necessary to reach planned goals? Are additional assistants needed? Keep good practice statistics and you will have a good basis from which to make judgments.

SAMPLE BUDGET

A planned budget makes good business sense. Listed below is a simple budget planning format.

MONTHLY FINANCIAL REVIEW

Month_____, 19_____

Income this month   _____
Income-Spent this mo.   _____
Income to Date   _____
Income-Spent this yr.   _____
Bank balance   (checking)_____
                 (savings)_____
                    Total_____

BUDGET

Column	Yearly Budget	Spent to Date	Remainder or Deficit for Year	Monthly Budget	Spent this Month	Remainder or Deficit for Month
Rent						
Utilities						
Automobile						
Office Exp.						
Salaries						

TOTAL

NOTES

PEG BOARD ACCOUNTING

Previous mention was made of the peg board accounting system as it relates to disbursement and basic collection of expenditure data. Far more widely used is a peg board system of receipts.

This program consists of a series of numbered receipts that are put on a notched peg board in numerical sequence. When money is received and the receipt is written, it carbons onto a family ledger card which is placed underneath the receipt ledger. It also carbons onto a daily ledger sheet that keeps track of the business done that day.

This daily ledger is a valuable source of information. At a glance, the doctor can tell how much money has been collected, not only daily, but on a monthly and yearly basis as well. A running figure of accounts receivable is available at any given time. Columns for cash, checks and charge cards make it easier in assembling bank deposits. The system includes balancing receipts against charges, making errors immediately obvious. This sheet will also show the money on hand, and since every penny as well as every receipt must be accounted for, theft by employees is difficult. Doctors should be alert to the fact that a dishonest employee can devise methods to beat the best system . . . peg board or other types. Spot checks and inventory controls eliminate temptation. This daily ledger is a great asset in reconstructing what has happened in case of a discrepancy with your patient, bank, or Internal Revenue Service.

Many health professionals use this method of receipts accounting because of its simplicity, accuracy, and ability to tell a story of the total value of services rendered. It will also provide a record of the date services were provided to a particular patient.

By having a family summary of every transaction made, it is easy to see at a glance the amount of business done, the type of services rendered, and is an easy method to provide income tax records for patients. Two of the numerous companies across the nation who provide this type of system are Reynolds and Reynolds Company and Control-O-Fax Company.

Following are some examples of receipts, day sheets and checks used with a peg board accounting system.

Chapter 14 — Diagram No. 1.

Pegboard with all three forms in place: The Visit Slip-Receipt, Family Ledger Card and Day Sheet.

DATE | FAMILY MEMBER | DESCRIPTION | CHARGES | PMTS. CREDITS | ADJ. | CURRENT BALANCE | PREVIOUS BALANCE | NAME

THIS IS YOUR RECEIPT FOR THIS AMOUNT
THIS IS A STATEMENT OF YOUR ACCOUNT TO DATE

Code	VISUAL EXAMINATION	Code	CONTACT LENSES & SUPPLIES	Code	SERVICE POLICIES
101	Eye Health Examination	301	Soft Contact Lenses	401	1 Year Service Policy
102	Tonometry	302	Firm Contact Lenses	402	VIP Service Policy
103	Perimetry	303	Continuous Wear Soft C.L.	403	1 Year Assurance
104	Blood Pressure	304	Flexible (Gas-Permable) C.L.	404	Replace C.L. ( ) ( )
105	Depth Perception	305	Toric (High Astigmatism) Soft		
106	Refraction	306	Toric (High Astigmatism) Firm	Code	PROFESSIONAL SERVICES
107	Prescription	307	Bifocal Contact Lenses	501	Contact Lens Evaluation
		308	Color Vision C.L.	502	Office Visit
	(A) TOTAL			503	Contact Lens Polishing ( )
Code	CONTACT LENS FITTING SERV.	310	Initial Contact Lens Supplies	504	Contact Lens Modification ( )
201	Biomicroscopy	311	C.L. Solutions	505	C.L. Power Change ( )
202	Keratometry		Salt Tablets-Bottle	506	C.L. Cleaning
203	P.E.K.	314	C.L. Case		
204	Contact Lens Design	315	Aseptor		(D) TOTAL
205	Contact Lens Evaluation		Enzymatic Cleaner		A, B, C, D TOTAL
206	Patient Instructions		(C) TOTAL		
207	90 Day Service Policy		RE EXAMINE		
	(B) TOTAL		NEXT APPOINTMENT		

NEXT APPOINTMENT JAN 1 AT 1:00 A.M. P.M.

jack w. melton, o.d., f.a.a.o.
practice limited to contact lenses

the omni offices
5000 northwest expressway
oklahoma city, oklahoma 73132
405-721-0877

FORM NO. 26-60112-R
Mifax-Oklahoma City
Oklahoma City, OK

Control-o-fax ®

Chapter 14 — Diagram No. 2.
Visit Slip and Receipt for a Practice Specializing in Contact Lenses.

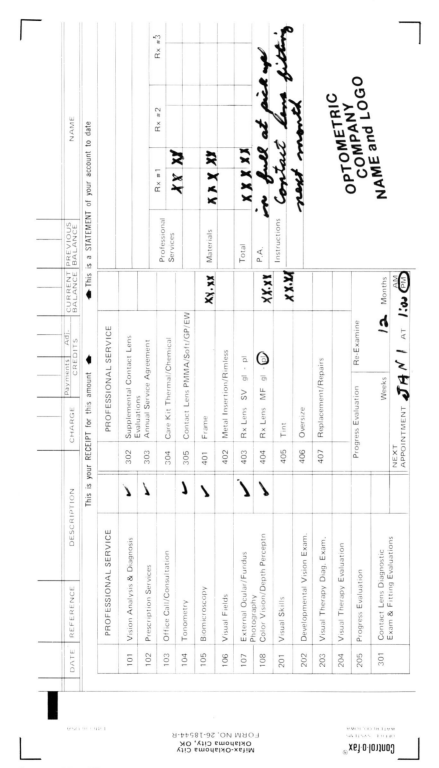

Chapter 14 — Diagram No. 3

Visit Slip and Receipt for Visual Care and Glasses in General Optometric Practice.

PLEASE RETURN THIS FORM TO THE RECEPTIONIST

ATTENDING DOCTOR'S STATEMENT

DIAGNOSIS (ICD9-CM)
PROCEDURE CODES: Current Optometric Procedural Terminology - 2nd Edition

EXAMINATION SERVICES

	CODE:	New	Estab.	FEE
☐ Minimal		90000	90030	
☐ Brief		90010	90040	
☐ Limited			90050	
☐ Intermediate		92002	92012	
☐ Comprehensive		92004	92014	

SPECIAL DIAGNOSTIC SERVICES

☐ Gonioscopy 92020
☐ Visual Field Examination 92081
☐ Perimetry - Kinetic 92083
☐ Tonometry V0010
☐ Provocative Test - Glaucoma 92140
☐ Ext. Color Vision Exam 92283
☐ External Ocular Photog. 92285
☐ Pachometry V0504
☐ Extended Ophthalmoscopy 92225
☐ Ophthal. - Fundus Photog./50 922
☐ Ophthalmodynamometry/60

VISION THERAPY SERVICES

☐ Vision Ther. Diag. Exam. 92060
☐ Strabismus/Amblyopia Therapy 92065
☐ Binocular V.T. Non-Strabis. V0150
☐ Vision Devel. Therapy V0152
☐ Visual Evoked Response 92280

LOW VISION THERAPY SERVICES

☐ Low Vision Diag. Service V0200

Progress Evaluation Re-Examination
Weeks │ Months

OPHTHALMIC LENS TREATMENT SERVICES

☐ Lenses Unifocal/0 Bifocal/1 V070
Invis. B.F./2 Prog. Add./3 Doub. B.F./4
Trifocal/5 Quadrifocal/6
☐ Aphakia Unifocal/1 V072
Bifocal/3 Trifocal/5
☐ Modifier
Mono./52 Replace/62

CONTACT LENS TREATMENT SERVICES

☐ C.L. Diag. Service Only V0500
☐ PMMA Spher./10 Toric/11 V05
Bifocal/12 Keratoconus/30
☐ Gas Perm. Spher./20 Toric/21 V05
Bifocal/22 Ext. Wear/23 Kera/34
☐ Hydro., Spher./16 Toric/17 V05
Prism/17 Bifocal/18 Extended Wear/24
☐ Orthokeratology V0540
☐ Therapeutic Contact 92070
☐ Aphakia V05
PMMF./51 Gas Perm/82
Hydro./61 Ext. Wear/91
☐ C.L. Modifier
Mono./52 Replace/62
☐ C.L. Service Agreement

OTHER SERVICES

☐ Prosthetic Eye Services 92330

PATIENT: Please keep this for Income Tax or Medicare & Insurance purposes - - See Back of Pink Copy for Insurance Instructions.

PREVIOUS BALANCE
N A M E

Date of Service

PATIENT:

		RX #1	RX #2	RX #3
FRAME SERVICES	V0800			
New Frame	V0801			
Previous Frame	V0802			
Frame Adjustment	V0803			
Frame Repair				
TREATMENT MATERIALS				
Frame	V1000			
Contact Lenses	V1000			
Lenses	V1000			

	RX #1	RX #2	RX #3
SUBTOTALS			
Professional Services			
Materials			
TOTAL FEE	$		
Payment Arrangements			

IRS # 99-2220115

SMITH and JONES
Professional Corporation
3070 W. Airline Highway ANYTOWN, U.S.A. 50704
Telephone 234-4651

☐ Wilbur C. Smith   ☐ Raymond J. Jones
SS # 265-50-1023   SS # 234-14-7728

89-12-2519

Chapter 14 — Diagram No. 4.
Latest AOA approved Visit and Receipt Slip.

STATEMENT

SMITH and JONES
Professional Corporation

3070 W. Airline Highway

Anytown, U.S.A. 50704

Telephone 234-4651

DATE	REFERENCE	DESCRIPTION	CHARGE	CREDITS		CURRENT BALANCE
				PAYMENTS	ADJ.	
		BALANCE FORWARD ⟶				

PLEASE PAY LAST AMOUNT IN THIS COLUMN ◀

CONTROL-O-FAX
FORM NO. 50 7LLR

THIS AREA FOR SERVICE CODES

OV—Office Visit	X—X-Ray	ROA—Received on Account
C—Consultation	NC—No Charge	TC—Telephone Consultation
EX—Examination	INS—Insurance	FA—Failed Appointment

89-15-0014

THIS IS A COPY OF YOUR ACCOUNT AS IT APPEARS ON YOUR LEDGER CARD

Chapter 14 — Diagram No. 5.

Family Ledger Card (Where all charges and payments accumulate).

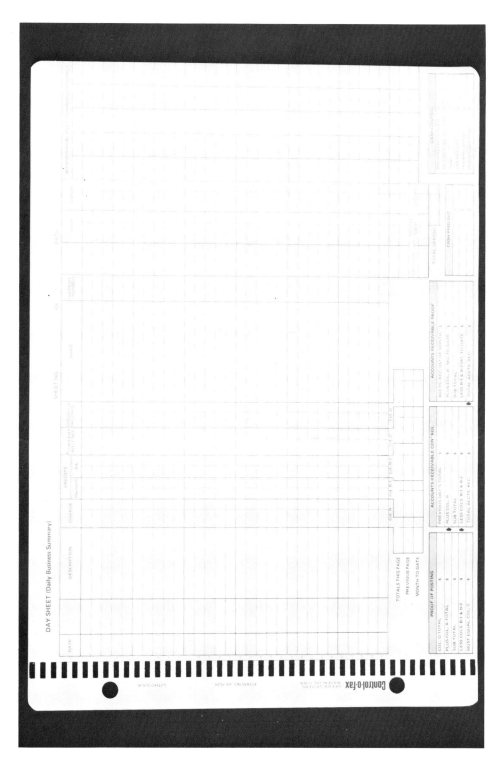

Chapter 14 — Diagram No. 6.

Day Sheet (Where all financial transactions for the day accumulate).

Chapter 14 — Diagram No. 7.

Check writing system with Payroll information.

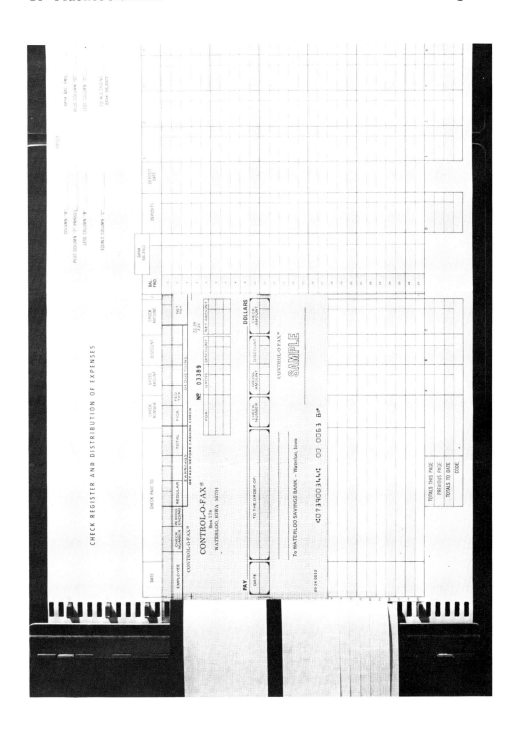

Chapter 14 — Diagram No. 8.
Check writing system with columns for different expenses.

Chapter 15 | Educational Meetings

As a professional, the doctor should continue to pursue his education after graduation. Many state licensing boards require additional education yearly. Even if not required, it is important to pursue postgraduate educational courses.

The American Optometric Association offers a continuing education award to those practitioners who wish to pursue extensive postgraduate education. Learning at one of these educational seminars not only comes from the courses, but also from interaction and conversation with other doctors, particularly those from other parts of the country. Participants will find their goals, philosophies and achievements similar to others. It is possible to learn from both accomplishments and mistakes of other practitioners.

The American Academy of Optometry offers some of the finest quality educational programs available to optometry. To become a Fellow of the American Academy of Optometry, one must file an application, complete case reports on individual patients, and pass the qualifying oral examination. Beyond the fellowship in the Academy of Optometry, one may wish to pursue the diplomate program in contact lenses, low vision, or children's vision.

The American Optometric Association and its affiliated state associations sponsor educational programs periodically on a national and regional basis respectively. Many other seminars are sponsored by manufacturers and private regional groups. It has been said that a continuing education program for optometrists can be found every week somewhere in the United States. It is important to seek out as many of these meetings as possible. Each one makes for a better optometrist and evolves into a springboard for professional achievements.

VISIT AND LEARN

Valuable practice management ideas can be learned by visiting other practices. Every doctor should make practice visitations before starting a practice and should continue making them while he is in practice. Very few ideas are original, but have been borrowed from others. When making a visitation, keep in tune to everything that is happening. Observe and evaluate ideas that might be used in your own individual practice.

One should visit as many rural and urban optometric offices as possible. Visit solo practices, multiple doctor practices, offices utilizing assistants, commerical practices, professional practices, offices that specialize in contact lenses and practices that specialize in children's vision. After leaving each office, list categories of practice management observations and rate each area . . . such as the attractiveness of the office, the personnel, doctor communication, fee presentation, etc. From this evaluation, the visiting doctor can glean solid ideas to improve management in his own office. Through this, organization of thoughts, philosophies and goals can be developed to establish a professional practice.

Visitations should also include ophthalmology offices, optical shops, and manufacturers of contact lenses and eyeglasses. If possible, one might also visit military optometric facilities.

When visiting these offices, it is best to call and make an appointment. No one will refuse a visit and most will be complimented that another doctor would like to see their office or laboratory facilities. Visits should be kept as brief as possible. Observe the practice while not disturbing the normal patient flow or the personnel.

Many large practices have tailored their management strategies from other successful practices. New equipment, communication techniques, office decor, personnel management, etc. observed in other offices can also be used by you in building a successful practice.

Chapter 16 Ophthalmic Mechanics: Attention To Detail

It is the intent of this chapter to emphasize to the doctor the importance of dealing with practice management aspects of providing glasses and contact lenses. Optometrists do all that is within their power to provide complete services to patients, emphasizing fees for those services. Usually the end result is the patient remembering "x" number of dollars that they spent for glasses. Considering then the importance of ophthalmic materials in the total framework of optometric care, attention to promoting them adequately is a valuable asset in optometric care.

COSMESIS

One of the most important aspects the patient considers about glasses is how they will appear cosmetically. Attention to making the lenses as attractive as possible will be appreciated by patients. Lenses that are of a high minus or high plus power can often be dramatically improved in appearance by making the lenses in minimal thickness glass (less than the standard 2.2) or in plastic. When using plastic lenses sometimes a considerable improvement in edge thickness can be made by using higher index of refraction plastics that are also harder and more scratch resistant. Edge coatings on the lens can also help disguise edge thickness, and lens surface coatings will help minimize reflections on glass lenses. Often the masking effect of a light tint in a lens can be helpful when a plastic material is involved and gives the illusion of drawing one's attention away from thickness to the color. It is usually advisable, all other things being equal, to consider zyl mountings versus rimless or wire frames in high minus lenses, so that more of the edge thickness can be disguised by an overlap of the plastic eyewire. When strong prescriptions are written and no warning is given to the patient, it is understandable how many can be disappointed and even hostile when they receive the new glasses you have just prepared. It is advantageous to have a number of lens demonstrators or glasses already made up in specific frames in order to demonstrate the good or bad effects that lenses can create.

Lens flippers are useful for displaying lenses that demonstrate different types of lens designs. Some of those examples are the following: a comparison of different basic bifocal or trifocal design, such as flat top 25's, 28's, 35's, and executives. Samples of lenses mounted into regular prescription frames can be helpful in demonstrating the expected appearance of high minus lenses in plastic versus glass when contemplating a large eye size. Many laboratories provide tint kits that give a patient an opportunity to view the way their tint will appear in his own prescription whether in plastic or glass lenses.

Another worthwhile demonstrational device is two lenses of high minus correction; one made in standard plastic materials and the other in a higher index refraction material with both mounted in a fairly large eye size frame. This will not only provide a vehicle to explain the thickness of a high minus correction to the patient, but also gives them a comparison to decide whether the additional expenditure is justified in using the newer, harder materials.

SPECIAL OPTICAL CONSIDERATIONS

It is helpful to note whether the base curve of a lens normally provided for a given prescription would clear the eyelashes in the frame chosen. Sometimes it is necessary to digress from the best possible prescription base curve to a steeper one in order to allow for eyelash clearance. Base curve changes between lenses, as well as maximizing and minimizing thicknesses of lenses, can also be helpful in reducing some of the effect of anisometropic prescriptions. Laboratories should be advised not to change the base curves found in the old prescription of presbyopes that are +2.00 sphere or greater in power because adaptation problems often occur. These possibilities are often overlooked in the daily routine of prescribing.

Another special lens possibility that can help the visual function of the patient is the slab-off in anisometropic prescriptions. There is a fine-line in trying to weigh the benefits of special prescriptions such as slab-offs versus the cost of producing that lens; yet, many patients can be helped by your thoroughness.

APHAKIA

Aphakic patients offer a challenge for the doctor when attempting to arrive at the most accurate prescription possible. The doctor should carefully explain the visual distortions that are going to be experienced, and the large magnification effect due to the strong lenses. Special attention should be made to the vertex distances both during the examination and when adjusting the glasses. A trial lens over-refraction of a present prescription or a close diagnostic lens prescription is helpful in arriving at an accurate prescription. This will also often reveal the acceptance of more plus merely because of the tendency of the elderly to not keep their head firmly placed against the phoropter. Showing and explaining the difference in a single cut versus lenticular design lens is a must in dealing with aphakic patients, and demonstration lenses can be very helpful.

Trial lenses can be a significant benefit when used over an existing prescription to demonstrate to a patient his new visual performance or to double check the accuracy of the lens prescription.

STYLE VS. COMFORT

A frame may be beautiful on a patient's face, but if it does not feel good or stay adjusted, the doctor has an unhappy patient on his hands. Discretion must be used in advising patients regarding frame choices. A good stylist will be tactfully candid with the patients choosing unattractive frames. Even though a patient walks out pleased with a poor choice, a negative comment from family or friends or a chronic adjustment problem will destroy that satisfaction. Sound advice from the stylist may decrease the incidence of hindsight regret. It is also in the best interest of the office to make patients look as attractive as possible since this will affect the decisions of others on where to seek visual care. When selecting frames, a patient wants to find a style that is becoming and appropriate for the fashion of the time. However, many attractive frames can be in poor taste or be very unattractive when united with the lens prescription. Probably the most frequent problem patients encounter when picking up their glasses is the unsightly edges of thick lenses that are a result of choosing a frame that was too large for their prescription.

Patients' complaints to the office are often, "I can't wear these" and "they slide down" implying that the doctor made a mistake. What they really mean is "they are too heavy", "I don't like the frame", "appearance", etc.! Counseling patients to select smaller eye sizes, carefully explaining why you are doing so, can be helpful in satisfying those patients at dispensing date.

Rimless designs are often popular, but should be discouraged when the edges are thick or extra thin. Careful consideration should be given to every frame selected as to the pressure it may create upon the bridge of the nose when combined with the lens.

Proper bridge fits and temple adjustments are of paramount importance in making a frame feel comfortable on a patient's face.

A discussion about selecting a frame that would make eyes appear wider apart (when the PD is narrow) can be helpful in creating a cosmetic illusion. Choosing frames that will not create excessive prism demands while getting the prescription ground on PD can also make the glasses more attractive. Counseling the patient to consider the added weight of picking heavier, more massively built frames can also be appreciated when combining the weight of heavy lenses. The materials must be strong enough, yet complement the lenses, regardless of their weight or thickness.

Certain lenses such as no line multifocals, etc., have limited uncut lens diameters that will limit the eyewire size chosen. A compromise of the proper pupillary distance will make adequate visual performance impossible.

Spring hinge frames can be beneficial in many circumstances for comfortable fit and for flexing at the temples when hit accidentally. However, the patient should be advised in advance that there is a maximum amount of side tension that can be placed on a spring hinge type frame if he should prefer the fit to be extra tight on the side of his head.

Selecting frames that have too narrow a frame PD can create difficulties in adjustment to a wide face. The temples will have to be spread too wide and stress on the hinges can cause future breakage.

Sometimes a patient will complain of excessive cheek touch or space between the frame and the cheek because the style of the frame chosen was improper in relation to the pantoscopic angle. Good balance in this area is an important point to be considered, and is especially important in strong prescriptions. If the pantoscopic angle is improper, unwanted cylinder is also induced into the prescription.

PROPER ADJUSTMENT

Having chosen the proper lenses and frame, a good adjustment at dispensing can save many heartaches for the office staff and sore ears and noses for the patients. Common reasons for glasses adjusted too loose are temples adjusted or sized too long. Temples bent in too soon before the widest part of the skull is reached, and insufficient amount of wrap around behind the ear can cause slippage. Sore ears are often a result of the bending of the temple too far forward of the ear causing a pressure point at the top of the ear, or a lack of conforming of the temple to the contour of the skull behind the ear. A sore nose is usually a result of selection of a bridge that is a different contour from the shape of the nose, or the adjustable pads have not or cannot be adjusted properly.

Care should be taken in heating frames to be sure that the surface is not blistered or dulled as a result of too much heat, or the frame marred because of the sticking of beads from the warming pan. To make good adjustments to a frame, the proper tools and facilities are necessary, and instruction in their use should be made to all office staff who deal with adjustments or dispensing of glasses.

VERIFICATION

Thoroughness in the examination and communication with the patient will be of no value if the final prescription is not adequately checked and verified when it returns from the laboratory. Careful attention to surface defects of lenses can also reduce patient dissatisfaction. Nothing can be more embarrassing to the doctor and disheartening to a patient than to later discover they were not made according to the prescription, or that the glasses were inadvertently switched with those of another patient after verification, and dispensed . . . even to the point of assuring the patient that the blurred vision will disappear as soon as he adapts to the new Rx. Patients with strong prescriptions and older patients often have a hard time adjusting to new prescriptions. It is often advisable to encourage them to wait until the next morning to start on their new glasses which you are dispensing today.

Sometimes the ophthalmic benefits of contact lenses are overlooked in arriving at a patient's best visual correction. Patients should be informed as to the advantages of contact lenses, particularly as they relate to better peripheral vision, image size, improved visual corrections that could result in amblyopia if wearing glasses, and the elimination of cosmetic problems created by strong prescriptions.

Careful consideration must be taken into account regarding the vertex distance between contacts placed on the eye and glasses 13mm in front of the eye.

Attention to every detail in a visual analysis is important, yet failure to follow through with the same preciseness in filling that prescription, whether it be glasses or contact lenses can result in a dissatisfied patient.

Successful optometrists are those who pay attention to the little details. What seems small to the doctor may be a mountain to the patient, and should be regarded from the patient's perspective.

Chapter **17** | # Selecting Frame Suppliers And Laboratories

There are several questions to consider when selecting frame suppliers and laboratories. Do the frames have a warranty? What is the length of the warranty? How much paper work is involved to realize the warranty? What amount of time is required for delivery? If a company is local, can it provide a frame that day or the next? What is the suppliers' policy on returned frames? If an office has a frame for a month and it appears it is not going to move, can it be returned for credit on other frames which will fill a need? Is there a consignment inventory? Will they bring in frames on inventory allowing the office to buy only frames for replacement? Will they send a requested frame to the office for a patient to try without obligation? Is the laboratory a full service lab? Does it supply frames, make repairs, supply a variety of lens sizes and types? Knowledge of all services available from a lab can eliminate lost hours in practice.

In addition to careful selection of materials, quality workmanship must be demanded. Securing top quality requires an assistant who checks all work done by the lab. Scratches on frames and lenses should not be accepted. The lens prescription must be within ANSI–Z80.1 standards. (See regulations at end of chapter.) Improper frame alignment or tints not matching the color ordered constitute a reject. Defective glasses or contact lenses should be replaced by the lab.

The cost factor is ever present. Are the prices equitable to another lab doing the same work with the same quality? Concern over charges should not take priority over quality. It is a wise investment to have a little more expensive lab fee than to sacrifice quality. Conversely, higher prices do not always mean better quality. One must be discerning.

Of growing importance to the doctor is the awareness of miscellaneous or hidden charges. These hidden charges can be such things as edge polishing, different center thickness, different base curves, oversize blanks, and prism for P.D. Often things of this nature are overlooked in the prescription cost resulting in a lab bill more expensive than were the the charges quoted to the patient.

Often there are discounts for large volumes or early payments. Some labs will provide a discount to doctors for patients purchasing more than one pair of glasses.

It should be established whether or not the lab will charge for prescriptions that must be remade due to doctor change or a patient's inability to adapt to a prescription. Some labs have a reduced charge for a doctor's do-over.

Again, one of the most valuable sources of reliable information is talking with other practitioners to learn what kind of lab service they are receiving, and whether their quality standards are consistently met.

It is the duty of the labs to keep the office informed of the latest trends and technology available. New developments taking place in the industry should be communicated to the office. This can happen only with a good working relationship with the lab representative. If the representative does not work cooperatively with the doctor and office staff, it will be difficult to receive consistent quality service. The office also needs someone available at the lab for communications in daily service and particularly in problem situations.

Any laboratory or manufacturer chosen should be supportive of the profession of Optometry. That support is obvious in such ways as funding scholarships to colleges of Optometry, supporting educational meetings, or by providing speakers for doctors, as well as sponsoring informative seminars. Support of the Optometric profession is usually an indication of what kind of support and respect the lab will show to an individual practitioner.

All of these considerations are important not only for the beginning practitioner, but for the veteran as well. It is easy to continue using the same labs without re-evaluating the many factors discussed in this chapter. All doctors should use opportunities such as convention exhibits to acquaint themselves with the reputation, the services, and fee structures of other labs.

Many offices find an in-office finishing laboratory beneficial. Statistics must be evaluated as to how many pair of glasses are ordered each year that could have been produced or finished in your laboratory. Then costs of equipment, labor, office space, supplies and lens blanks must be determined. If quality and service time can be significantly improved and the expenses at least break even, a finishing lab would be beneficial to the practice. Personnel to run the laboratory must be well trained and quality oriented. Inadequate personnel training is usually the most common reason for failure.

The laboratory can cut and edge lenses, produce tints, polish edges of plastic lenses, temper lenses and repair frames. Some offices have complete surface and finishing laboratories. This is a very expensive venture and most offices do not have the volume to justify the expense.

FRAME INVENTORY

The prudent doctor has a plan for frame inventory and is constantly aware of its content. The modern frame inventory is composed of the styles and types of frames that meet the specific and individual needs of the practice. Knowledge of the latest trends and designs in eyewear, as well as fashion, is essential. The frames need to be up-to-date and have appeal to the different types of people who may be visiting a particular vision care office. This creates the need to analyze the practice population by age, sex and lifestyle. For example, seeing people primarily over the age of 65 years of age will dictate a different type of frame inventory than an office serving patients 20-35 years old.

Trends in fashion and special features of eyewear are projected in the modern office. If a trend develops on a particular type of frame, the public will search it out. In order to constantly change and update the inventory, frames should be used from the inventory rather than always ordering. This will make it possible to be constantly buying new styles. Patients will appreciate knowing they will not see a number of other people with the same frame in the community served by their doctor.

The one constant reminder in approaching frame inventory is quality. It must be the best. Working with sub-standard materials provides untold problems for the patient, as well as the office, and the doctor will become known as one who provides poor quality.

Excellence in services and materials will develop clientele who return and refer new patients. An alert should be sounded on "special" frame deals. They are usually frames that are discontinued, or a cheap import of which repair parts cannot be ordered. They can cost more money in future problems than the present savings are worth. Other doctors in the area are information sources to identify the best frame supplier, the ones who will give good service, and the ones who will honor their agreement.

CONTACT LENS INVENTORY

Contact lenses are now a major part of most practices. The doctor must decide which lenses will be used and how many the office will inventory. Most of the larger contact lens companies consign lenses to offices who use enough of their lenses to justify the expense of consignments. For this reason it behooves the doctor to limit the number of companies from which lenses are ordered.

When contact lenses are stocked in the office, lost and damaged lenses can be replaced immediately. In most instances, lens fittings and trial wear are possible on the initial visit. Most successful contact lens practitioners agree that having lenses available saves time and adds a service the patients appreciate.

The authors have listed lens types in order of priority which might be inventoried in the office.

TYPES OF CONTACT LENSES TO INVENTORY

1. Your first company preference for minus soft contact lens –0.50 to –6.00 diopter in .25D increments
2. O_2 Permeable firm contact lens Base Curve Range 7.40 mm to 8.40 mm Power –0.50 to –6.00 diopter in .25D increments
3. Your second company preference for minus soft contact lens –0.50 to –6.00 diopter in .25D increments
4. Your first company preference for plus soft contact lens +.50 to +6.00 diopter in .25D increments
5. Your first company preference for minus extended wear lens (with the new lenses reaching the market, this may become the first lens to stock) –0.50 to –6.00 diopter in .25D increments

6. Bifocal soft contact lens

7. Toric soft contact lens

8. Aphakic soft contact lens +12.00 to +18.00 diopter (this lens may need to be moved up in priority if you practice in an area with an older population)

9. Add to the power ranges in each category listed above

With new lenses rapidly becoming available, this listing can become obsolete quickly. Inventory the lenses that are used the most, yet are cost effective to have in stock.

INVENTORY CONTROL

A system should be used to keep track of how many lenses are used and how many remain in stock. An assistant should be responsible for monitoring stock and ordering lenses as needed. Each stock lens should have a specific slot so that empty slots can be counted and compared to the number of lenses that have been used. Records must be kept of lenses ordered, lenses rejected due to defects and lenses replaced on warranty.

Guidelines should be established as to how empty vials will be stored and for how long. There should be an office policy regarding the cleaning and sterilizing of lens stock, how it should be done and when. Storage of lenses can be organized according to brand and the powers arranged from weakest to strongest.

A logical pattern for overall organization of lenses would be a shelf or tray(s) for minus soft daily wear, minus soft extended wear, plus soft daily wear, 0_2 permeable firm, etc. Organizing the lenses in an orderly fashion improves stock control and saves time when looking for lenses. Chapter 4 on "101 Facts That Every Doctor Should Know" has diagrams for contact lens storage cabinets.

Contact lens inventory control is complicated with the best manual system. Computer programs can ease the burden and also show which lenses are in stock from any terminal in the office. The receptionist can key in the lens needed when a patient calls for a replacement and tell him immediately if the lens is in stock. The contact lens assistant can run a report listing lens replacements needed. She can compare lenses used with the lenses in stock. If the total numbers do not correlate, some lenses are missing and need to be accounted for.

All businesses which carry inventories normally have inventory control guidelines. The optical services provided by a doctor's office is a business and frames, cases, solutions and contact lens inventories should be managed accordingly.

a. ANSI Z80.1 STANDARDS

The provisions of the Z80.1-1979 recommendations, in contrast to the Z80.1-1972 standard, are no longer stated as minimum standards but rather as quality goals for lenses prepared by laboratories for individual prescriptions.

For further detailed information see "American National Standard, recommendation for prescription ophthalmic lenses (ANSI Z80.1-1979)," American National Standards Institute, Inc., 1430 Broadway, New York, New York 10018; the May 1979 issue of the American Optometric Association Journal, which is largely devoted to ophthalmic standards, and a paper by M.W. Morgan, O.D., Ph.D. Ophthalmic standards, guides or goals, Canadian Journal of Optometry 41(3):129–137 (September–October), 1979.

The following table summarizes the ANSI Z80.1-1979 tolerance goals for ophthalmic lenses.

Lens Characteristic	Tolerance
1. REFRACTIVE POWER	
Sphere	0.00 to 6.50D $\pm$0.13D $>$6.50D $\pm$2%
Cylinder	0.00 to 2.00D $\pm$0.13D 2.12 to 4.00D $\pm$0.15D $>$4.50D $\pm$4%
Cylinder Axis	0.125 to 0.275D $\pm$7° 0.500 to 0.750D $\pm$5° 0.975 to 1.500D $\pm$3° $>$1.625D $\pm$2°
Addition	For distance lens powers 0.00 to 8.00D $\pm$0.13D For distance lens powers $>$ 8.00D $\pm$.18D
2. PRISM	
Single lenses	1/3 △ in any direction (Placement error of 1mm)
Mounted lenses (provisional)	
Vertical	1/3 △ imbalance (Placement error of 1mm in levels of major reference points)
Horizontal	2/3 △ imbalance (Maximum of 2.5mm difference in horizontal placement of lenses)
3. SEGMENT LOCATION	
Single lenses	+1m of specification, horizontal and vertical
Mounted lenses (provisional)	
Vertical	Within 1mm
Horizontal	Within 2.5mm of specified near interpupillary distance
4. THICKNESS	$\pm$0.3mm of specifications
5. BASE CURVE	$\pm$0.75D of specifications
6. WARPAGE	1.00D except within 6mm of eyewear.

*From American Optometric Association Journal, May 1979, p. 550

b. ANSI Z80.2-1972.

The following tables summarize the ANSI standards for contact lenses.

Table 1

Prescription Requirement for Corneal Lenses

(All measurements are made in the air with lenses in an air-dried state.)

Parameter	Tolerance
Diameter	±0.05mm
Posterior optic zone diameter	
Light blend	±0.1mm
Medium or heavy blend	±0.2mm
Posterior central curve (base curve) radius	±.025mm
Posterior secondary, intermediate, or peripheral curve width	
Light blend	±0.05mm
Medium or heavy blend	=0.10mm
Posterior secondary, intermediate, or peripheral curve radius	±0.1mm
Refractive power	
+10.00D to -10.00D	±0.12D (Notes 1, 2, 3)
More than ±10.00D	±0.25D
Prism power (measured from the geometric center)	
If lens power is:	
+10.00D to -10.00D	±0.25 △
More than ±10.00D	±0.50 △
Cylinder power	
less than 2.00D	±0.25D
2.00D to 4.00D	±0.37D
greater than 4.00D	±0.50D
Cylinder axis	±5°
Toric base curve radii	
△ r 0 to 0.20mm	±0.02mm (Note 3)
△ r 0.21 to 0.40mm	±0.03mm
△ r 0.41 to 0.60mm	±0.05mm
△ r 0.60mm	±0.07mm
Bifocal refractive power addition	±0.25D (Note 2)
Bifocal segment height	-0.1m to +0.2mm
Center thickness	less than ±0.02mm (Note 4)
Edges	As specified
Anterior peripheral curve radius	±0.2mm

Anterior optic zone diameter	±0.1mm
Optical quality and surface quality	No bubbles, striae, waves, inhomogenieties, crazing, pits, scratches, chips, lathe marks, or stone marks
Color	Pigment inert and uniformily distributed

Note 1: If the lens base curve and power errors are cumulative (that is, base curve and lens power errors both add plus power or both add minus power to the refractive correction) the cumulative error shall not exceed 0.25D.

NOTE 2: The cumulative errors in power between the right and left lenses shall not exceed 0.25D.

NOTE 3: Symbols used are as follows:
D = diopters
△ = prism diopters
△ r = difference between radii of principal meridians

NOTE 4: The algebraic differences in thickness error between right and left lenses shall not exceed 0.02mm.

Table 2

Prescription Requirements for Scleral Lenses

(All measurements are made in air with lenses in all air-dried state.)

Parameter	Tolerance
Outside diameter (size)	±0.5mm
Posterior central curve (base curve) radius	±0.03mm
Refractive power	
+10.00D to -10.00D	=0.12D (Notes 1 and 2)
More than =10.00D	±0.25D (Notes 1 and 2)
Prism power (measured from the geometric center)	±0.25 △
Cylinder axis	±5°
Center thickness	±0.03mm
Edges	Well rounded and polished
Anterior central curve radius	±0.01mm
Surface quality	Free of cutting rings, scratches, polishing rings, etc.
Transition	As specified
Fenestration	As specified
Clearance	As specified ±0.02mm

NOTE 1: If the lens base curve and power errors are cumulative (that is, base curve and lens power errors both add plus power or both add minus power to the refractive correction) the cumlative error shall not exceed 0.25D

NOTE 2: The cumulative errors in power between the right and left lenses shall not exceed 0.25D.

Chapter 18 | Computers For The Optometric Office

Even at the time of the writing of this book many people are saying that someday, maybe in ten years or so, computers will become a reality for optometry. The fact is they are a reality now. There are some offices that are completely computerized virtually eliminating the normal use of records and paper that is customary in optometric practice.

There are a number of basic advantages when using a computer. The following are some of the reasons for using a computer system:

(1) Time efficiency: A definite asset to a busy office is having the ability to retrieve information at the push of a button and to input information at the speed of typing or faster.

(2) Accuracy: One of the problems that can occur in an optometric practice is transposing information, such as prescriptions, patient addresses, telephone numbers, etc. When utilizing computers, once they are programmed correctly they will always reproduce correctly.

(3) Better patient communication: As the number of patient families increase in a practice, it gets virtually impossible to communicate with each family by typing individual letters on different subject matters related to vision care. When utilizing computers and automated printers, personalized letters can be sent on office letterhead discussing virtually any subject desired.

(4) Personnel Problems: Since personnel turnover in an optometric staff is a serious matter, a computer can help resolve this

problem to some degree since it actually fulfills many of the functions of assistants. Since the computer never (at least rarely) gets sick, pregnant, or has a family crisis, etc., there is a reliable assistant substitute present at all times in the office.

(5) Better Statistics: One of the problems of keeping accurate statistics in a practice is the ability to consistently gather data in an accurate way. Computers automatically gather whatever statistical information is requested by the program in the system. Forgetting to record or count activities or deleting information is never a problem with a computer.

(6) Filing Space: As practices grow an added problem in addition to the need for more regular space for handling the patient is the filing space required. Patient records, family journals, and all accounting activities are stored within the memory of the computer. All storage is kept inside a small circular disk and the large areas of records that are normally maintained along a given wall and counter area are no longer necessary.

(7) Impressive PR Tool: Patients are accustomed to being exposed to computers in the business world, but are very surprised when they see them in an optometric environment. Not only does it speak to them of the advanced state of the art which you, as an optometrist, have reached, but it also shows your desire to provide the most complete and up-to-date visual care possible.

There are four basic components to a computor:

(1) The computer remote terminal (CRT) is the video keyboard where the information is displayed and put into the system. CRT's are available with varying degrees of complexity or functions. Some have built in memory (smart terminals) while others have very little or none (dumb terminals). There are also many added features and function keys on some models that less expensive versions do not have. The more advanced CRT's permit more sophisticated programming to be done resulting in faster and more complete programs.

(2) There is a storage device that maintains all of the information in a way that it can be retrieved upon demand. There are two basic types of storage used: one is a floppy disk system where "phonograph like" inserts are placed in the computer to operate specific programs for the

office, and the other is a fixed hard disk storage method which permits different programs to be run simultaneously at a much faster speed. The storage ability of the computer is rated by megabytes of storage. A megabyte is a million bytes of information storage.

(3) The third component is called a processor, and this is the electronic portion of the computer that contains the ability to synchronize and process the information between the CRT and the storage disk. It is rated by units of "K" memory. The more elaborate and complex the program, the more "K" is required to run it.

(4) The fourth major component is a printer. In order to obtain a hard copy of information in the computer, a printer is required to type out the information contained. Letters, records, patient histories, financial information, receipts, etc. can all be generated with the printer.

Word processing is a basic task performed by many computers or automatic typewriters. They involve sending a "canned message" to a patient or target audience that appears to be personalized specifically to them and is individually typed by the computer printer. The quality of the typed message varies with the speed and quality of the printer used. As with typewriters, there are different printing heads, such as dot matrix, or daisy wheel, etc., which affect the speed and quality of the printing.

One of the most fundamental word processing activities is sending recall notices. These messages may speak of a patient's own individual problems such as being nearsighted, farsighted, astigmatic, presbyopic, in need of a health check, contact lens check, etc., and the importance of their keeping that appointment. Recall notices can be sent on either stationery or post cards depending upon the impression the optometrist wishes to impart. The computer is a natural for keeping track of when the patient is to return for future care. That time can be set for any given period such as one month, twelve months, eighteen months, etc.

The recall can even be automatically assigned to each patient according to the age and by whatever criteria the doctor prefers. When a specific case is different, the date is merely changed manually. For any given month the computer prints a list of the patients due to be recalled that month and then individually types a letter to each one of them specifying the reason they are to return. If the patient fails to return for their regular check up time, a missed recall program can be activated at any time, such as four months after their check up time, and another recall letter sent reminding them of their need to come in for an examination.

Other types of word processing are the sending of thank you letters — both for new patients and for referring new patients. Periodic newsletters can be sent to all patients or a target group only. Welcome letters to a patient prior to the appointment date can also be easily sent. Birthday letters can be sent to specific age groups within the practice. Past due letters, with a personalized message, can be very effective with delinquent accounts.

Service agreements on contact lens care can be generated within the office, as can any kind of special instruction sheet.

An appointment book can be very confusing when the patient load is heavy and numerous changes have been made. Regular problems encountered are incomplete information, overlooked openings, inconsistent information, overbooked days, missed appointments not noted, the problem of moving from one page to another, and the general overall look of disarray that is present. A computer allows the receptionist to see in a very concise way the appointment opportunities that are present on any given day. It will also be possible to see the types of openings that are available and will not only keep track of whether that appointment is kept but will note whether that patient has missed appointments previously. It is also possible to integrate the recall appointments with the scheduling system so that an appointment time can be automatically saved and assigned. This would, of course, require a higher frequency of changed appointments that were not convenient or timely for a patient, but this is easily accomplished by function keys on the CRT which move the appointment information from one slot to another.

One of the most frustrating areas of optometric practice is dealing with patient records. The pulling, preparing, filing, and locating records which can be in numerous different locations, require a great deal of an assistant's time. All of this information, including the case histories, examination data, prescriptions, patient instructions, etc., can be stored conveniently and retrieved with the use of the computer. Most of the information keyed into the CRT is done by utilizing the ten key section of the keyboard. As an example, when recording some of the most common symptoms of discomfort in the computer, the doctor looks at a number of coded options: 0 = none; 1 = burning; 2 = itching; 3 = tired; 4 = red; 5 = dry; 6 = tears. If the patient reports symptoms of burning and red eyes, the doctor would merely key in a #1 and #4 and the computer would automatically write in the actual words burning and red.

When the patient arrives for the first time in the optometric office, an account number is assigned to that family and specific patient. An assistant can load into the computer any questionnaire information, preliminary tests performed, the old prescription being worn, etc. With a CRT in the examination room, the doctor can add any additional case history and load the examination findings as they are taken. On all patients, a history screen is maintained that accumulates pertinent information over a period of several examinations and displays it all together, such as all past prescriptions, tensions, fields, keratometer readings, and special comments. Another screen maintains similar information for contact lens histories. Any instructions given to the patient and the final prescription, is then recorded, whether it be for glasses or contact lenses. After the stylist completes the styling procedure, she loads the additional frame information and sees that the final prescription is recorded in the computer.

When the frame selection is complete, the stylist can determine the charges. Most of the usual and customary fees are loaded by pushing one function key and is called "batch loading". The additional special charges are then added. Another function key records the pay arrangements agreed upon by the patient. Those arrangements and the fee breakdown is printed on the receipt. The payment is received and the patient is given the receipt. The computer's adding machine capabilities eliminates the possibility of misaddition of the patient's fees. If the visual care is not paid in full when the glasses or contact lenses are dispensed, the computer will send a statement at the appropriate time, calculating any delinquent charges and writing an appropriate collection message depending on the age of the account. When the delinquent account reaches a predetermined age, the message "turned over to collectors" is automatically inserted and a printout given to the optometrist of those patients needing such action.

Because FDA regulations require that each patient be given a copy of his Rx, this information is automatically printed on the receipt.

This virtually eliminates the possibility of any patient leaving the office without a prescription.

Monthly, quarterly, and yearly information is automatically computed and printed giving the doctor information regarding his gross, fee breakdowns as required, number and types of examinations rendered, number of contact lens patients, number of frames that were used, number of bifocals, trifocals, soft contact lenses, oxygen permeable contact lenses, etc. The amount of statistics accumulated can be endless, yet accurate when utilizing the abilities of a computer.

The ordering of laboratory prescriptions can be a delight in comparison to writing out the orders or calling them in by telephone. Merely by punching a button, each prescription written for the day can be typed out by the printer and itemized by individual laboratory, as well as a separate order for frames by supplier that need to be ordered that day. This eliminates the transposing errors involved in writing prescriptions and the problem of forgetting to order the prescription. The computer can be programmed to keep track of where the jobs have been sent and how long they have been there. Periodic printouts can be solicited to see what jobs need to have additional follow up.

A computer can be very helpful in the bookkeeping and payroll areas of an office. When a statement is received, the information is keyed into the computer. It then will print checks for disbursement and record the information in the proper areas of the general ledger. Monthly reports made include balance sheets and profit and loss statements. Payroll checks are also printed by the computer and information kept on a monthly basis, as well as quarterly. This information is used to make deposits to IRS as well as to make the quarterly reports. At the end of the year, the culmulative amounts will be printed on W2 forms to be distributed to the employees and the IRS.

Each evening at the close of that day's business, **all** information that has been put in the computer is transferred to a backup disk for safekeeping in another location. This prohibits losing information by malfunction, storm, theft, etc. since there is always at least two copies of all information.

As with everything else,there are some disadvantages to owning a computer. Since they are expensive initially, their maintenance is also expensive. Service agreements are available and vary from company to company.

There are monthly and yearly licensing and software fees for program maintenance and updates. This must be considered when attempting to evaluate money savings to the practice. Also, not to be ignored is the possibility of system failure either from weather, hardware, or software. A contingency plan must be ready to be put into effect until the system is back in operation. This normally means reverting back to "doing it the old way". Most of the time, the programmer can program over the telephone to alleviate these failures, so that downtime on the computer is minimal.

Two companies that are presently in the forefront of optometric programming are "Professional Computers" and "Chips". The system that included all the criteria discussed in this chapter and which met the needs of our office was the hard fixed disk program by "Professional Computers". This system permits many different programs to be run on different terminals simultaneously. They utilize Wang hardware and their programs include all the major aspects of optometric practice.

Although we are in the midst of the computer age, professional offices are just beginning to take advantage of the resources available. Computers are available in all sizes and degrees of sophistication. Just as important as the equipment itself is the skill and availability of the programmer. He is the key to making computers work for you!

Chapter 19 | Third Party Vision Care

HARRIS NUSSENBLATT, O.D., M.P.H.

Vision care plans are special benefit packages that provide for vision examinations and eyewear for eligible persons according to the policy's provisions. Coverage is generally provided for routine examinations, frames and lenses, limited contact lens services and materials, and occasionally vision therapy or low vision services.

Health insurance plans, including vision care plans, base their reimbursement mechanisms primarily on whether the policy is an indemnification or full service plan. Indemnification plans are plans that have a schedule of benefits with a maximum dollar amount that the company will pay the patient (beneficiary) for the service. The plan may specify that it will pay up to a specific amount for a vision examination, or for a frame, and payment will generally be made directly to the patient. The patient may, if he or she chooses, receive the payment directly from the insuror or may assign the benefit (sign a release authorizing the insuror to send the payment directly to the practitioner). Full service (prepaid) plans are designed to pay providers directly and are usually tied to a panel of providers. A practitioner can agree to join the panel of providers in which case his/her name is given to potential patients. If a practitioner (provider) is a panel member and the patient desires services, then the cost of the service to the patient is fully covered. If the practitioner is not part of the panel, then the patient can still receive services from the practitioner, but payment is made according to a schedule which usually requires the patient to pay the difference between the schedule and the actual cost of the services. From the practitioner's viewpoint, however, agreeing to be a member of the panel usually requires the practitioner to provide his/her service for a reduced fee according to a previous agreement. In other words, by agreeing to be listed as a panel doctor, the practitioner agrees to accept assignment on payments from the carrier.

Payment to practitioners for covered benefits is handled by companies in a number of ways. One way is to pay the usual fee for services wherein the practitioner bills the company and the company sends reimbursement. This, however, is not the norm and, in fact, few insurers will reimburse practitioners this way. Reimbursement mechanisms are usually based on a percentage of the billed fees in relation to other doctor's charges for the same procedure in the same area. Insurers will calculate a reasonable charge, a customary charge, and a prevailing charge and will use these charges to determine the amount to be sent to the practitioner. The customary charge is the median billed charge for a specific procedure during the previous calendar year. If a practitioner changed fees over the year, then the charge that is at the 50th percentile will be the customary charge for the year, not the actual billed charge. The prevailing charge is often the 75th percentile of the distribution of all provider customary charges in a given area during the previous calendar year weighted by the number of times each provider billed for that service (Medicare modifies this somewhat by also calculating a Medical Economic Index and relating the prevailing charge calculation to this index). This charge takes into account the provider's charge in relation to other practitioner's charges for a procedure as well as the experience of the practitioner in delivering the service. The reasonable charge (maximum allowable charge) is the lowest of the provider's actual billed charge, customary charge, or area's prevailing charge and is usually the charge that is actually paid to the practitioner for a percentage of the reasonable charge.

The determination of charges to be paid by carriers to practitioners is often complicated and varies from carrier to carrier but, in general, each carrier develops a profile of charges by services for each practitioner. These profiles are based on what each practitioner has submitted for fees for covered services and are used when carriers update payments to practitioners. New practitioners to a community, therefore, must develop profiles over time which are then used as a basis for future payments. All practitioners, new or established, should bill for services based on their actual fee structure and should not send in a lower fee under the assumption that the carrier will only pay a percentage of the true fee. Even though the practitioner will receive only a percentage of the actual billed charge, the billed charge will be used in the future to adjust payments to the practitioners.

VISION BENEFIT PLANS

The number of vision benefit plans has increased significantly over the last few years and now covers close to 18 million people. The proliferation of these plans has resulted in confusion to many practitioners who must deal with a variety of plans each having different coverages and payment mechanisms. The American Optometric Association has listed what it considers to be appropriate guidelines for vision plans that practitioners can use to evaluate plans when deciding whether or not they wish to participate. The AOA Guidelines focus primarily on the plan's structure and reinbursement mechanism. Benefits should ideally provide the full scope of examination, diagnosis, and treatment services and patients should have the freedom of choice of practitioners. Any options that are included, such as tints or oversize lenses, should be available to the patient at the provider's usual and customary charges and exclusions should be clearly identified and periodically reviewed for benefit inclusion. The ideal program should not have any co-insurance or deductibles but, if present, should be only for materials and not for examinations and related procedures. Payments for services should be prompt and current and should not be different for different types of providers or for panel or non-panel providers. Practitioners should also have the freedom of choice of labs for the lab work and not be limited to certain labs by the plan.

In addition to these guidelines, plans should have a mechanism for identifying patients who are eligible either through a confirmation form the patient can bring to the office or toll free phone confirmation. It is also advisable that the plan permit the use of a universal claim form rather than a plan specific form and materials covered by the plan should be covered without regard to manufacturer or place of manufacture. There should not be any arbitrary requirements placed on lens changes such as visual acuity or prescription changes and the plan should have optometric consultants to settle disputes between practitioners and carriers as well as a mechanism where the provider can obtain information concerning the program quickly and easily.

Vision benefit plans are currently provided by insurance companies, Blue Cross/Blue Shield, or Vision Service Plans. Insurance companies such as Prudential, Aetna, Metropolitan Life currently underwrite and administer vision plans for a number of large companies such as General Motors, Bell Telephone, Maytag Co., and the Bendix Corp. Blue Cross/Blue Shield has also begun offering vision plans even though Blue Cross/Blue Shield is not an insurance company. Blue Cross/Blue Shield consists of independent nonprofit tax exempt membership corporations that provide protection for hospital care and medical and surgical care in limited geographical areas. While they are supervised by state insurance agencies, they do not have the same restrictions placed on their operations as insurance companies and normally operate differently from most insurance companies. As an example, Blue Cross/Blue Shield usually contracts directly with providers for services by a schedule and do not normally have indemnity plans. There are about 70 different Blue Cross/Blue Shield organizations across the country, each of which covers a specific non-competing area from other Blue Cross/Blue Shield plans.

Vision Service Plan (VSP) is another organization established to provide vision care services. VSP was set up about 25 years ago primarily by optometrists as a result of the lack of basic vision and optometric coverage by traditional medical insurance plans. Most of these medical plans did not (and still do not) cover routine eye care whether it be for general examinations, eyewear, contact lenses, or vision therapy. VSP, then, was a mechanism to provide this coverage through an independent nonprofit corporation usually sponsored by optometrists. Most plans initially established during the 1960's and 1970's were established on a state basis but more recently these state plans have consolidated under regional areas in order to more effectively provide coverage. Practitioners, in most plans, must belong to a panel and requirements for joining the panel vary from plan to plan. Most plans cover annual examinations as well as eyewear as needed. Services not covered under the plan can usually be provided to the patient on a private patient basis. The VSP is marketed to employer groups and eligible patients obtain an eligibility form and a list of panel members from their employer. They can then choose the practitioner they wish to see from the panel and present the eligibility form at the time services are provided. If the patient does not select a practitioner from the panel, then reimbursement is made according to a fixed schedule. Panel providers must accept the payment from VSP as payment in full for the covered service. A directory of VSP can be obtained by writing to the national office at 1000 Peres Rd., Suite 280, St. Louis, MO 63131.

Vision benefit plans, whether offered by insurance companies, Blue Cross/Blue Shield, or Vision Service Plan all have a number of components with which practitioners must be familiar. Each plan will specify eligibility, benefits, options, exclusions, benefit frequency, co-payments/deductibles, panel participation or nonparticipation, and reimbursement mechanisms. Plans generally cover the employee, spouse and eligible children (usually children up to age 21 or 25 if they are living at home or going to school). Some plans extend coverage to retired employees and their dependents as well as surviving spouses and their dependents. Benefits usually include a vision examination every 12–24 months, frames every 24 months, and lenses. Each policy will have different requirements as to frequency of use and some have limits on frame types or lenses unless the patients pay the difference. Lenses normally covered are clear first quality lenses though some policies will cover sunglass prescription lenses while others will not. Exclusions normally include such items as non-prescription lenses, medical or surgical treatment of the eyes, drugs or other medication, or specialized procedures such as low vision services and aids. Contact lenses are usually covered for aphakia or when medically necessary. Cosmetic contact lenses are usually allowed, but payment is limited to a maximum amount (usually $35.00–$50.00).

The practitioner has a number of options available to him when receiving payment from patients. If he is familiar with the plan, he may submit the patient's claim with the patient's signature authorizing the company to pay the practitioner. When payment is received, the practitioner may then bill the patient the difference between the received amount and the total cost, provided the plan permits this type of billing. This is not an efficient way to be paid since it often takes a number of weeks before payment is received from the carrier and then it will probably take more time to receive payment from the patient. Another way is to have the patient pay the bill. The practitioner can complete the patient's claim form with payment to be made directly to the patient. This is preferable to the first option as it removes the practitioner from interacting with the carrier. The disadvantage is there is extra work on the practitioner's part in completing the claim form for each patient.

The ideal way to handle claims is through the use of a universal claim form as an office fee slip. The claim form is actually an office fee slip that is designed for submission to insurance companies. The fee slip is written as usual except a diagnosis and treatment are written on the fee slip. The patient then submits a copy of the fee slip with the claim form (which the patient can complete) and payment is made directly to the patient. This is the preferred method as it decreases office paper work, insures payment from the patient prior to claim submission, does not require a practitioner to be part of a panel nor require the practitioner to remember all details of all vision plans he/she deals with.

MEDICARE

Optometric services under Medicare are presently limited to the coverage of eye health evaluations for aphakic patients and the dispensing of aphakic prescriptions. When Medicare was originally passed in 1965, optometric services were allowed for any covered service when authorized by a physician. In 1967, however, the Social Security Administration questioned the optometrists' ability to perform any service beyond refraction and dispensing. It was not until 1976, when an HEW study reviewed the role of optometric services under Medicare, that optometric services were recognized and the Secretary of HEW recommended to Congress that optometric services be approved for aphakic care. Legislation approving these services did not pass Congress until December, 1980 and became effective July 1, 1981. The aphakic amendment authorizes payment to optometrists for all optometric services for aphakic patients (except for the refractive portion of the examination) and eyewear or contact lenses for aphakic patients. Practitioners who intend to submit Medicare billings must register with the fiscal intermediary in the state in which they will be practicing. The fiscal intermediary is an agent for the Federal Government who has agreed to handle claims processing and reimbursement procedures for the Government. In most cases, the intermediary is the state Blue Cross/Blue Shield organization though some states utilize insurance companies. The name of the particular company to contact can be obtained from your state optometric association, local practitioners (physician or optometrist) or from the local Social Security office. The company will send the practitioner an application to be filled out and then will issue a provider number, claim forms, and information on how to submit claims. Since each state has a different claims processing procedure, the procedure for submitting claims must be carefully reviewed but there are a few factors that are common across all states.

A practitioner has the option, under Medicare, of accepting assignment or not accepting assignment. If a practitioner accepts assignment he/she is telling the patient and Medicare that he/she will accept whatever Medicare approves as the total charge and will not bill the patient for the difference between the actual cost of the services and Medicare's approved charge. The practitioner may still collect, when accepting assignment, the deductible from the patient, the 20% co-insurance up to the Medicare approved charge, and any services delivered that are not Medicare approved (such as refractions). Medicare will send payment directly to the practitioner. Accepting assignment often is of benefit to indigent patients and insures that the practitioner will receive some payment (though often not the total) from patients. The primary disadvantage of accepting assignment is that the practitioner is not able to collect the full fee but must accept the Medicare approved fee and often does not know how much Medicare will pay until the check arrives. Since patients must meet a calendar year deductible (currently $75.00) and then are responsible for 20% of the covered services, practitioners will at best receive only 80% of the approved cost and at worse will have the full deductible deducted from the fee and then be paid only 80% of the remainder. As an example, the practitioner who accepts assignment in the case of a patient who has not met his yearly deductible will receive $15.00 as payment in full from Medicare for services billed at $125.00. If the total fee was $125.00 of which Medicare approved $94.00 (75% of the total fee based on UCR formula) then Medicare will subtract $75.00 from the $94.00 and then pay only 80% of the resultant $19.00 ($15.00).

The patient is still liable for the deductible ($75.00) and the co-insurance of $4.00 (20% of $19.00) but it is often extremely difficult for the patient to understand this liability. If the patient had previously met the deductible, the practitioner would collect 80% of the approved charge of $94.00 ($75.00) from Medicare and could collect the co-insurance of 20% of $94.00 ($19.00) from the patient. The practitioner could not collect more than $94.00 in this example from both sources if he/she accepts assignment. If the practitioner does not accept assignment then the patient is responsible for paying the total fees and can then submit the bill to Medicare which will then send the patient whatever amount they will be reimbursing. In the example above, the patient would be responsible for the total fee of $125.00 and Medicare would send the patient $15.00 if the deductible had not been met or $75.00 if the deductible had been met (80% of $94.00). Many practitioners will often waive the co-insurance portion of the patient's fee if they accept assignment and collect what Medicare pays them as payment in full as long as the patient has met the deductible for the year. If the patient did not pay for services in full at the time they were delivered, then the practitioner must still collect the balance from the patient.

Routine eye examinations (refractions) are not covered under Medicare and if billed to Medicare will not be paid. Every intermediary has a list of procedural codes which list the code and procedures acceptable for payment. Methods for billing Medicare will depend on whether or not the carrier has procedural codes for eye examinations without refraction or complete eye examinations. It must be clearly indicated on the claim form whether or not services being billed also include a refraction. If the services do include refraction, Medicare will assume that 20% of the total fee is for a refraction and will deduct that amount from the total cost prior to calculating payment. If the services being billed do not include a refraction, a statement to that effect must be included on the claim form otherwise Medicare will deduct the 20%. The patient is responsible for paying the refractive portion of the examination though some practitioners, again, will waive this portion of the fee if they are accepting assignment.

Patients may submit claims for Medicare payment through forms in practitioner's offices or by picking up claims forms from any Social Security office. The practitioner should submit the claim if he/she will be accepting assignment, otherwise the patient should submit the form. The patient will need an itemized bill showing the date and place services were received, the charge for each service, the doctor or supplier, the patient's name and Medicare number, and the diagnosis; which should all be attached to the claim form. Patients may accumulate bills from many doctors, submit them as a group, or submit them whether paid or not.

The need for private insurance to cover the gaps in Medicare coverage has increased over the last few years due to rapidly rising co-payment and deductibles and many patients now carry supplemental coverage for services not covered by Medicare. These should be pursued with the patient as these policies will often cover the deductibles and co-payments for covered optometric services.

MEDICAID

Medicaid, Title XIX of the Social Security Act, is a program of medical assistance for persons receiving federally aided public assistance. It is a state administered and state controlled program (as opposed to Medicare which is federally administered and controlled) though most of the funds come from the Federal Government. Individuals the states must cover in this program fall into one of four categories; Aid to Families With Dependent Children (AFDC), Blind, Totally and Permanently Disabled, and the Low Income Elderly over 65 (states can also cover the medically indigent if they so desire). Vision care is considered optional and is up to the state to determine whether or not it will be covered.

The exceptions to this are eye examinations, eyeglasses, hearing aids, and some dental care for children eligible for the Early and Periodic Screening, Diagnosis, and Treatment Program (EPSDT). EPSDT is a preventive health screening and treatment program for children under age 21 who are eligible for Medicaid. This program will pay for periodic screenings for children and treatment for discovered conditions. Though the treatment is limited to the amount, duration, and scope of services covered under the state's Medicaid plan, payment is authorized for eye examinations and eyeglasses. This means that Medicaid, through EPSDT, will pay for examinations and eyewear for children under the age of 21, even if Medicaid does not cover the same services for adults.

Since the Medicaid program is a state administered and state run program, eligibility, claim submission, covered services, and reimbursement procedures will vary from state to state. Practitioners who desire to be included in this program should contact the agency running the progam for information on obtaining a provider number and claim forms. In most cases, the state welfare agency has primary jurisdiction in running the program though it often contracts with the state health department in providing screening services. In many cases, the state will also contract with a state fiscal intermediary who will actually do the claims processing. The appropriate agency to enroll in the Medicaid program can be obtained from the state optometric association, a local health practitioner, or the state welfare department.

As in other governmental third party programs, Medicaid claims require the practitioner to submit for services according to a specific procedural code, and payment normally follows the usual, reasonable and customary guidelines for optometric services. Many states that cover eyewear will pay only the material costs of the eyewear plus a dispensing fee and some require the submission of lab invoices to verify material costs. Medicaid requires practitioners to accept assignment on covered services which means that the practitioner must accept the payment from Medicaid as payment in full for services rendered and cannot bill the patient for the difference between what Medicaid paid and the actual fees billed to the program. In the eyeglass program, the practitioner must show the patient frames and lenses that are available from the program at no charge to the patient, but most programs permit the patient to pick out more expensive eyewear or add options (such as tints) if the patient pays the extra fees. Some states have restrictions on changes in lens prescriptions so that the program will only pay for eyewear every two years or only if there has been a specific power change in the prescription (such as more than +0.75D change). Contact lenses are usually covered only if that is the only way to correct a defect or if needed for a medical condition such as keratoconus and usually requires prior authorization from the carrier before fitting.

Financial And Tax Planning In The Optometrtic Practice

Chapter 20

GALEN TAYLOR, C.P.A.

The complexities of today's financial world for the business professional make it imperative that a financial plan and organization be developed in order to meet one's personal and economic goals. The reasons for the complexities in a professional healing arts practice is due in part to the legal complications which have stemmed mutually from government regulations and public demands that professionals exercise due care in their performance of services; also, advancing technology in the health care field has had a tendency to change and complicate the practitioners method of operation. Coupling these factors with high inflation and increased exposure to taxation at higher earning capabilities has caused the optometrist more concern. The impact of the inflationary trend can be explained by the fact that in 1950 a comfortable income was an annual amount of $12,000; those same dollars in 1980 translate to a range of $40,000 to $50,000. While inflation has been rampant driving up all costs across the board in a proportionate manner, one of the areas that the growth has been more than proportionate is in the area of the impact of income taxation. The tax structure was initially developed in 1913, and since that time has had only minor overall reform as it relates to inflation. Due to the fact that the system is based on a progressive tax rate structure (a method whereby higher tax rates are charged as the base of income increases), efforts to control tax impact through means of tax planning, improved record keeping, interpretation of financial feedback, and seeking the professional advice of bankers, attorneys, insurance agents, and accountants is mandated more than ever before.

This discussion will therefore begin by giving consideration to the broader aspects of what financial statements are, and how they relate to today's practice. The term "financial statement" is a term that is used in today's business world in a rather loose fashion that can mean different things to readers. The most common elements of a financial statement are the balance sheet and the income statement. There is also used by the more sophisticated investors and analysts what is called a "statement of changes in financial position;" however since it is basically irrelevant to this level of presentation, this statement will not be explained.

THE BALANCE SHEET

The balance sheet is the basic tool by which lenders and financial analysts measure the overall profitability, flexibility, liquidity, and successfulness of a business enterprise. A balance sheet is measured as of one specific date rather than covering a period of, for example, twelve months. The balance sheet breaks down into three major divisions; the first is called **assets,** which represent those items that are used as an accumulation of the resources or profitability of a business. This most commonly consists of cash, accounts receivable, equipment, and real estate. The other two divisions are **liabilities** and **equity** (or net worth). Liabilities are those claims against assets that are made by creditors. This will usually be found in the form of accounts payable, payroll taxes withheld, and notes or mortgage payable. The equity or net worth of a business is the amount of capital or resources contributed to that business by the owner, plus an accumulation of the profits that are undistributed.

THE INCOME STATEMENT

The income statement differs from the balance sheet in that it is a summary of the profitability of a business for a short time period, most commonly twelve months or less. The income statement might be illustrated as a chapter that relates to an overall book of many chapters; the specific chapter shows or measures only the income and expenses for a given time period. The professional uses the income statement primarily as a measurement tool to historically summarize income and expense areas that can be further analyzed to make decisions and better manage one's practice. It is common to acquire statistical information from a given trade or profession, and to compare the industry norms or standards to what is happening in the individual practice. This way better decisions are made which will ultimately result in higher profitability and achievement of designated goals.

RECORDING INCOME AND EXPENSES

The last aspect of an overall introduction is a basis of recording income and expenses. This can be done by two methods or a hybrid method that is in between the two basic methods. The first, and most commonly used method, is called the **cash basis** of financial statement presentation, which reflects the financial activity as the transaction takes place. More specifically, income is recorded as the fee is received and expenses are recorded at the time the disbursement is made. The other extreme in reporting financial statements is called the **accrual basis** of reporting. This method reflects income as it is earned, not when it is collected, and reflects expenses as the service is performed or the goods have been received, not when paid. A hybrid method is a form that might take some attributes from the first method and some from the second method.

TAXATION

Individual income taxation was initiated in the year 1913 in an effort for the public as a whole to provide additional sources of revenue to fund the services and goods provided by the federal government. The basic premise used in establishing laws was one primarily concerned with the capability of generating revenues, not establishing equity or equality in the rules for taxation. Income taxes are computed by tables that are based on a progressive tax system, i.e. the higher the base of income to be taxed the rate of taxation increases faster.

INCOME TAX

There are several types of taxes which one should be familiar. The first type of tax is income tax. This tax is an accumulation of the items of taxable income, less the business and other income reducing expenses, less the itemized deductions and personal exemptions, leaving an amount called taxable income. This is the amount upon which the tax computation is made.

SOCIAL SECURITY TAX

Closely related to the basic income tax is the self-employment (or social security) tax. This tax is based on the net earnings from self-employment income and amounts to a rate of approximately 10%. This is the tax which is paid into the social security tax system to fund its benefits. As a taxpayer gets into a higher tax bracket, he may find himself exposed to a liability for minimum or alternative minimum tax. This is a tax on certain investing or tax sheltering activities, and after a small exemption is charged a rate of 15%, it is added to the regular income tax.

GENERAL TAXES

The final general taxes to be covered in this overview are gift and estate tax. A gift tax is based on the amount of transfer of assets to another individual; it is a progressive tax and is calculated on an annual basis after an exclusion of $10,000 per donee (the person receiving the gift). Estate tax is the final tax on the net accumulation for a taxable estate. It is calculated basically on all the assets owned or accumulated during the person's lifetime, less debts and administrative expenses of the estate, and finally reducing the estate by the transfer to a surviving spouse, if any, and a specific flat exemption.

DEDUCTIONS AND CREDITS

Now some of the specific terminology used in discussing tax and tax planning should be understood. There is a significant distinction between the effect of a deduction and a credit. A deduction is an item which reduces the income which will be taxed, thereby reducing the final taxable income. It gives an economic effect in accordance with the amount of a tax bracket percentage that would be used for the financial computation. An income tax credit is an item which has a direct dollar for dollar reduction of income tax. Some of the activities that give rise to an income tax credit and an explanation of those activities follows:

1. Investment tax credit — This credit is the result of the purchase of new or used equipment. Equipment having a life of three years but less than five years qualifies for the credit to the extent of 60% of the total expenditures. Equipment having a life of five or more qualifies to the extent of 100% of the expenditure. The qualifying expenditure receives a credit in the amount of 10% as a direct offset against the tax liability. The qualifying expenditures for equipment are rather broad, but it does not necessarily include all expenditures. Buildings and building improvements are basically excluded from receiving a credit for their expenditure, except for the very limited area of old building rehabilitation expenditures. These types of expenditures receive credit only if the building is at least 30 years old and would receive an increase credit if 40 years old.

2. Jobs tax credit — This type of expenditure relates to the special credits being given to offset the income tax liability for hiring certain types of employees. The employee characteristics relate specifically to certain veterans, specific age groups of youths, young people affiliated with certain employee training programs through public schools, and other individuals certified by specific welfare departments.

3. Other miscellaneous credits — In general, other credits that may affect most taxpayers are for contributions to candidates for public office, credit for child and dependent care expenses, and residential energy credits.

It should be somewhat apparent that the benefit gained from a credit will exceed those benefits of a deduction. For example, a taxpayer in the 35% tax bracket would receive, for a $1,000 expenditure, a tax benefit of $350. The same $1,000 credit would reduce taxes dollar for dollar. In summary, the above illustration shows an approximate tripling of benefit for the $1,000 credit as compared to the $1,000 deduction.

TAX PLANNING METHODS AND TECHNIQUES

Since it is evident that in one's earning lifetime there will be a necessity of paying income taxes, the process should be followed of determining some corresponding techniques in an effort to reduce the amount of income tax liability as much as possible. The primary means to accomplish this is by means of what would be considered "leveling" or an income smoothing process. In other words, sharp increases or decreases in taxable income over a period of time will incur a larger total tax liability than the same amounts taxed proportionately over the years at an even growth level. This result is due to the undesirable effects of a progressive tax system, which, once again, charges an obligation at a higher rate with the increased amounts of taxable income.

TAX BRACKET

The term "tax bracket" has been used several times previously. At this point, consideration should be given to the term "tax bracket". Essentially, increases in taxable incomes are calculated on a base amount plus a percentage of the excess up to the next base amount. The base usually differs by an amount ranging from three to six thousand dollars. The excess over the base relates to the percentage which we commonly describe as a tax bracket. In reality this percentage is not a contract that applies to all taxable income, i.e. taxable income of approximately $12,000 might have a tax base of $10,000 and the excess $2,000 over that might be taxed at a rate of 21%. The combined liability does not equate to the same overall percentage of the taxable income. The concept of tax bracket is important in considering alternatives for expenditures, or the consequence of receiving additional income. More specifically, one should be aware of the possible consequence of earning one dollar additionally, and this is where the percentage concept becomes noteworthy.

THE TECHNIQUE OF TIMING

The timing element of receiving income or making expenditures has an important role in tax planning. Income is controlled more in areas that do not primarily relate to activities within a practice other than at year end. To elaborate on this, the collection efforts might be decreased or taking additional time off would be considered advisable late in the tax year. Other areas of income for which the timing or deferral of their effect comes into planning consideration is for sales of real estate, stocks, or other assets. Deductions can have a consequence due to the opportunity of prepaid expenses late in the year or even possibly making loans to fund the ability of prepayment. Consideration for this type of planning would relate to specific events occuring in one year that would not or should not occur in the prior or subsequent year. Some examples of these would be the possibility of an inheritance, sale of investment land, sale of an interest in a business, marriage or divorce, or the return of an investment in a tax shelter such as an oil well.

INCOME SPLITTING

Income splitting is a tax planning technique that takes into consideration the differences in tax brackets for which the income would be taxed. This allows using the progressive tax rates more to the taxpayer's advantage since the lower income would result in a overall reduced tax rate. Income splitting is a method to divide the income by a legal means so that a portion of the income is taxed to another person or entity leaving a reduced amount of taxable income for the individual controlling the overall income.

Some methods of accomplishing income splitting would be by incorporation of a business, forming a family partnership, setting up a trust, using sale and lease back of building or equipment between a taxpayer and his children or others, and use of various deferred compensation and retirement plans.

TAX SHELTERS

Probably the most significant area of tax planning in the last several decades has been in the area that is normally referred to as tax shelters. Motivation for this usually relates to the necessity of deferring income, the possibility of converting ordinary income into capital gains income, multiplying tax relief through use of loans (leveraging), all of which are directed possibly toward a mismatch of income and expense. The preliminary indication of a need for investing activities in this area is when a taxpayer approaches the 40% or higher income tax bracket. Therefore the need for seeking investment opportunities of this nature is normally after the practice has had several years to grow and develop.

INVESTMENTS

Investment activity, whether motivated strongly by tax savings or for income production reasons, should be evaluated more closely using the following criteria:

1. Relative risk — The risk inherit after the investment has been made for the possible return of investment, whether it is a high return or otherwise, must be weighed. There is always the possibility in areas of high risk that no recoupment of the full additional investment would occur. Careful analysis should be made in determining whether the overall consideration is one of high risk, low risk or lying somewhere in between. A few of the factors that help determine this are the location of the investment, the expected returns on investment by the type of industry as a whole, management enterprise, amount of competition, and the overall business viability; in other words does it make good business sense? The ultimate goal should be slanted toward the less risk exposure relative to the investment.

2. After-tax costs — Measurments should be made of the actual economic outlay for the investment. This is measured by the amount of gross investment times the expected tax deduction that

will be generated by the expenditure; this sum should then be multiplied by the expected current income tax bracket, which results in the tax savings. Finally, the tax savings should be deducted from the gross expenditure resulting in the after-tax cost. Further, one should be aware that some investments result in as high as a 100% write-off in the year of expenditure to a low range of only five to ten percent write-off. Assuming an investment would result in a 60% write-off in the year of payment, and that the taxpayer is in a 40% tax bracket in that same year, the tax saving for this investment would be 24%; the remaining after-tax cost would be 76%. Once again, there is a very wide range of tax benefits to be gained and these may be increased by use of loans or leveraging as mentioned previously. Very often the amount of tax write-off will correlate with the degree of risk as mentioned in number one.

PLAN DEVELOPMENT

After consideration has been given to the above factors an overall plan should be developed setting forth the various stages for financial planning as it relates to the commencement and development stages of a practice. Some of the considerations that would be recognized are the personal needs, the amount of capital available, the expected amount of equipment needs, the expectation of real estate purchases for personal residence and possible office building, and the growth for the practice. Beginning with needs for personal housing, one should consider present family size and the possibility of later additional housing needs; obviously there will be economic restrictions on this in today's market for real estate, which is quite expensive. Most lending institutions relate mortgage approvals to annual income, and monthly housing payment to monthly income. The approval is further complicated by changes that occur in a new practice concerning the production and net incomes which hopefully will be rapidly increasing. Again, this expectation of a financial outlay will have to be correlated to the needs of the practice, both initially and as growth takes place.

The need of a new practice will depend upon one of the two alternative methods of commencement. One alternative is to start a practice "cold turkey", that is setting up an office where none has previously existed. The other is to purchase an existing practice and/or be associated with a mature doctor who will retire in the near future. The needs in the new practice will be more significant from a capital needs standpoint than in acquiring an existing practice. Consideration must be given to the physical office, as to whether it may be rented, purchased or negotiated with an option to rent with a later purchase at a predetermined amount. Additionally the needs for equipment as it will relate to the expected number of examination rooms, layout of office, availability of used equipment, and the possibility of having accumulated some equipment previously must also be considered.

BUYING VS. LEASING EQUIPMENT

Often a practitioner is faced with needs of acquiring additional equipment to match or generate growth in his practice. The question will ultimately come up, "should I buy or lease the additional items?" Frequently the factors will at first glance appear to weigh more heavily on the leasing of additional equipment; this is due to the reduced cash outlay at the beginning of the transaction, and the potentially lower monthly payments as compared to borrowing the money to buy equipment. Certainly a decision of this nature will have some variation in the individual circumstances, but usually three major factors will weigh more heavily in favor of buying the equipment. They are as follows: profit motivation for the lessor, benefits of depreciation, and advantages of investment tax credit.

To explain these areas more explicitly, the profit motivation by the lessor is inherent in the transaction in order for the lessor to make the equipment available. This will tend to increase the cost slightly, as there are risks that the lessor will assume in addition to the profit factor. These risks can be assumed by the purchaser and an elimination of the profit can be obtained by an outright purchase of the equipment.

Flexibility relates to the comparison of the write-offs through means of depreciation as compared to the deductability of lease payments. Federal income tax laws allow a deduction for lease payments and as such there is no tax planning opportunity in that the lease payments are set up by contract, and will have to be made at set amounts on a monthly basis. In contrast to this, there are several depreciation alternatives available which will more directly correlate to an individual's personal income tax situation. Obviously with this additional tax planning tool, the net cost in the equipment may be reduced.

Investment tax credits are available for purchasing equipment. This takes place at the time of purchase, and reduces the cost of acquiring the equipment. When an item of equipment is leased, the investment tax credit may or may not be available to the lessee; the lessor has the right to make the election of retaining the investment tax credit for his own benefit, or elect to "pass through" the investment tax credit to the lessee. Normally, if the lessor elects to pass through the investment credit to the lessee, it will increase the amount of the monthly lease payments.

Emphasis again should be placed on the specific facts and circumstances each time equipment is being considered for expansion purposes. While there will be no predetermined choice, the usual benefits will accrue to the purchase of the equipment as pointed out.

The final stages of the plan development relate to the needs of an office. The needs are determined principally by location and its proximity to the market place. It has been rather favorable for doctors to be located adjacent to or near other medical service offices. This space may sometimes be more expensive than other space; however, the value or cost of the space normally will correlate to the increased or decreased practice growth opportunity. Again the alternative has to be selected for renting or purchasing space for the office needs. The significant drawback about the purchase is normally the arrangement relating to the down payment. While the simpler approach is to rent space, the disadvantages to this in the early stage of practice are the increasing cost of property, and the restriction on the expansion of the office that will be encountered due to the control of the adjacent space by the real estate owner (lessor). The possible compromise of these situations is the lease–purchase arrangement whereby the doctor will initially lease the office space with the option to purchase the space at a negotiated amount. Present income tax laws are most favorable toward property ownership due to the fact that a 15 year life for depreciation purposes is allowable; this compares to the previous forty or more year life that was required for depreciation purposes by the Internal Revenue Code.

SEPARATION OF EQUIPMENT FROM PRACTICE

As discussed earlier, a frequently used tax planning technique is by means of separating or splitting taxable entities. A very useful specific application of this technique is by means of a partnership or sole proprietorship that is separated from the incorporated practice. This technique will achieve a splitting of taxable entities that can save taxes in several ways. To develop this concept, the general tax flow of an equipment-purchase cycle should be understood. When the equipment is purchased, there is usually initial tax losses that will avail tax savings. In the separate proprietorship or partnership, these losses will flow through to benefit the doctor, while if these same benefits were in the corporation, where the tax bracket is lower, the benefit derived would not be as useful. Accordingly in the separate entity after several years have passed the related tax sheltering has for the most part become minor or in fact a tax burden, the ownership can be shifted to other family members to generate new tax benefits. This accomplishes advantages both from the standpoint of the use of family members who are in lower tax brackets, and at the same time generating income to that family member to relieve the economic obligation to that member on behalf of the business owner. This type of transaction is receiving much more scrutiny from the IRS and should be done so in a careful manner so as to protect the tax benefits. Otherwise the transaction would be restored with the elimination of the advantages gained.

BUILDING OWNERSHIP

Many practices often grow to the point that it is a consideration for the doctor to evaluate acquiring his own building. This is beneficial from the standpoint of an equity buildup in the ownership as compared to the lack of such attributes in an office building lease. If the building is owned within a sole proprietorship or partnership, there is no basic difference whether the building is owned "within or without the practice." However, if a practice is incorporated, then the tax planning opportunity exists by means of owning the building as a separate sole owner or in a separate partnership. The advantage of this stems from several factors.

In the later years of a practice, frequent consideration is given to selling the practice. A good control and security in this transaction is the possibility of selling the practice first, and then a few years later, selling the building. This can be accomplished much more easily if the building is already in a separate entity rather than in the professional corporation. If the building is in the professional corporation, the practice can be sold without the building; but a corporate liquidation would have to take place which is more complicated than an outright transfer of stock from the selling doctor to the one purchasing. Additionally, the sale of the building will generate capital gains, which is much more exempt from significant taxation at the individual level than that of a corporation. To be more specific a corporation enjoys capital gain benefits best when there is a noncapital gain annual income of $100,000 per year or more. Usually this amount of profit would not be left within a professional corporation for the doctor in any single year. Therefore, the taxation at the individual level would be more beneficial, as it would never be taxed at a rate greater than 20% of the gain. There will be other considerations that have to be evaluated when a final decision is to be made about who will own the building, but in most circumstances the factors will tend toward the individual or partnership ownership.

RETIREMENT PLANNING

The matter of planning for retirement from the practice is a consideration which should be integrated early in the overall financial plan. This is due to the fact that some income tax laws are very favorable to this type of expenditure, and with inflation and increasing standards of living the funding requirements are now somewhat higher than in previous years. Retirement planning expenditures can be divided more or less into two basic areas; the first area is the individual retirement account (IRA) for which a maximum $2,000 per year can be contributed in behalf of the practitioner. In addition to this, if the spouse has a salary or other earned income, a $2,000 annual contribution may be made for the spouse also. The maximum annual contributions are not limited as a percentage of income, but are limited by the net income dollar for dollar; in other words, if a taxpayer had earnings of $1,200 in a year this is the maximum amount that can be deposited into an IRA.

After the practice has developed to the point that there is the availabilty of more funds for investment, larger amounts may be deposited into a Keogh plan, which is a pension plan for the self-employed, or to a corporate pension plan. The amounts that may be contributed into a Keogh plan are 15% of annual earned income up to a maximum of $15,000 under current tax law. For a corporation the amount that may be contributed may vary depending upon the type of plan, but one of the more common approaches is a contribution of 15% of salary. The disadvantages of the increased amounts that may be contributed to the Keogh or corporate plan coverage must include all eligible employees. This differs from the IRA in that only the owner or employees of his own choosing need to be covered.

Another aspect of retirement planning is consideration of the attributes that it has in common with other tax shelter activities. More specifically the retirement plans achieve the ultimate goal as described earlier in the terms of relative risk and after-tax cost. The relative risk to which this activity is exposed is virtually non-existent, while in terms of after-tax costs the amounts invested are currently 100% deductible. Other tax shelters such as oil and gas investments, real estate investments, equipment leasing investments, and mining developments give rise to higher degrees of risk and in most cases lower annual tax deductions.

OTHER TAX PLANNING OPPORTUNITIES INCORPORATING

After much of the financial planning has been done, and the practice has been operating rather profitably for several years, many doctor-taxpayers take advantage of another facet for potential major tax planning by means of incorporating the practice. Incorporation is a method of tax planning that should be utilized only when there are several existing conditions for which advantage of lower tax rates can be used. There is no hard and fast rule that will mandate incorporating. Usually, it will be advantageous to incorporate when one of the following occurs: the individual tax bracket of the doctor approaches the 40 to 50 percent range, the amount of debt service (note payable and other obligations of the practice) is significant, or the doctor wishes to make use of the larger contribution limits that are available on corporate pension plans as opposed to the IRA or Keogh plan. In order to more fully understand the benefits available to the incorporated practice a description of the advantages are as follows:

1. Debt service — While the practice has been growing and expanding, it is likely that some of the necessary funding has been financed through banks or other lending institutions. The debt that is retired is funded through future profitability: these profits are "locked in" profits of the corporation and therefore are taxed. The corporation tax bracket normally will not exceed 20% which is somewhat less than the bracket for an individual.

2. Capital buildup — A corporation can accumulate working capital which is much like the net income that gets locked into a corporation, again at the lower tax rates. The capital must be accumulated in order to support the growth of the practice. This is because of the necessity to pay the increasing overhead that usually is incurred before the collections increase.

3. Employee benefits — While the sole proprietor is not considered his own employee for income tax law purposes, he is an employee of the corporation. Therefore there are several benefits which will be available for the employee, some of them on a nondiscriminatory basis, which can be used. Examples of these are forms of term life insurance, medical reimbursement plans, employee gifts or awards, and tax free death benefits in limited amounts.

4. Additional Retirement Plan Contributions — As previously discussed, higher limits are placed for annual contributions into a corporate pension plan than those limits placed on the sole proprietor or partnership plan. It is not uncommon to contribute as much as $20,000 or more per year into these plans. While other benefits are available which will promulgate tax savings, the basic concepts have been mentioned.

5. One opportunity for tax savings, that happens only in the year the corporation is formed, occurs by the shifting or deferral of income through selection of the fiscal year. It should be kept in mind that individuals file income tax returns based on a calendar year basis, and that corporations may select whatever fiscal year is desired. By use of this a one time savings can frequently be made in this transitional period.

As with other areas of tax planning there are some drawbacks to operating as a corporate entity. This relates primarily to the formality required in a corporation, i.e. the setting of salaries to be paid at regular intervals and the necessity of not writing personal expeditures. The other disadvantage relates to the possibility of a dividend. Dividends are distributions of profits from a corporation which are not tax deductible; correspondingly, the dividend is taxed twice. This is usually circumvented by use of bonuses or investment and tax sheltering expenditures.

Again it should be emphasized that incorporation is a matter relative to the fact and circumstances individually. The tax rate differential becomes important in that corporations pay taxes on the increments of income as follows: the first $25,000 net income at 15%; the second $25,000 net income at 18%; the third $25,000 net income at 30%; and the fourth $25,000 net income at 40%; any net income over $100,000 is taxed at a rate of 46%. Individual tax rates differ from the standpoint that instead of four stairstep levels, the tax brackets change every $3,000 to $6,000 as mentioned previously. For example, taxable income of approximately $12,000 is taxed on the base at just over $500 plus 16% of the excess to $16,000; $25,000 of taxable income will be taxed for $4,000 on the base plus 29% on the excess up to $30,000: $60,000 of taxable income will be taxed approximately $18,000 plus 49% of the excess up to $85,000.

As can be seen, the differential in rates comes into play in a more significant manner the higher the individual's net profits are from the practice. Care should be taken to consult a qualified tax advisor about this matter when considering incorporation of the practice.

STARTING YOUR PRACTICE

Brief mention of starting a practice with regards to purchasing or starting a new practice will be made. The primary benefits of the purchase of an existing practice are the readiness of patients and immediate cash flow, the organization that has already been accomplished, and the overall business structure that has been established. The drawback of the practice that is purchased is the possible obsolescense of equipment, routines and procedures that patients are accustomed to and the reluctance to change (even if improvements can be made by change); and from a tax standpoint some goodwill (blue sky) is involved in the purchase, which is not tax deductible.

The other option for starting a practice is opening a new office "cold turkey." This approach invariably entails more financial uncertainty concerning expectations of need, growth, and suitability of location. The advantages are the ability to select more carefully the equipment, to plan the office layout and set up systems which can constantly be improved, the reduced need for cash flow as an immediate payout to a former owner, and more tax advantages, benefits and planning flexability.

SUMMARY

The matters discussed previously in this chapter should be considered as an overview for financial and tax planning. Consideration should always be given at the important decision making times during the growth of the practice for consultation with appropriate advisors. This normally will consist of a banker, insurance agent, attorney, and an accountant. Choosing this team is usually a difficult task due to the fact that there is little experience in dealing with consultants previously. A good approach in seeking these consultants would be to discuss your needs with other practitioners who already have established relationships on a satisfactory basis. One should talk to several professionals in these areas to ascertain a compatibility of personalities and operation philosophies. To be more specific, this entails the overall needs for the practitioner as it relates to the questions he has in developing and improving his practice, the specific consultation he needs, when they should communicate and the availability of the consultants. Other factors that should be discussed are the costs for services provided, and an understanding of operating philosophy which could range from aggressive to passive.

It is essential that feedback be obtained by means of the financial statements, employee relations, patient relations, statistical data, etc. The feedback must be assimilated, measured, and evaluated so that more improved decisions can be made in managing your practice. Combining the feedback, practice experience, and professional advice will enable the doctor to achieve his goals in a more efficient manner.

Chapter 21 | Brainstorming - Idea List

The dictionary defines brainstorming as "stimulating the imagination of a group by stating every solution that comes to mind." This chapter is intended to bring together a potpourri of thoughts and information that add unique touches to make patients feel "special" and the doctor appear "successful."

1. Decorate the reception room for different seasons and holidays.

2. Offer coffee or soft drinks to patients waiting.

3. Use hard back bound photographic books in the reception room. (eg. New England, Rockies, Wildlife, etc.)

4. Have a telephone available for patients to make calls.

5. Keep the office clean and uncluttered.

6. In large multi-personnel offices, assistants and doctors should wear name tags.

7. Personalize desk signs for assistants.

8. Assistants should always "praise" their doctors.

9. Display diagrams of the eye and normal fundus in the examination rooms.

10. Bookshelves should be full of books. (They do not have to be new.)

11. Diplomas, plaques, and awards should be displayed professionally.

12. Photograph album in reception room. Pictures of staff and equipment with explanations of duties and functions.

13. Bulletin board — pictures of patients and articles about patients, staff, and doctors.

14. Prizes for kids in a treasure chest.
    a. balloons
    b. pencils
    c. pencil grips
    d. rings
    e. coloring books
    f. small toys and trinkets

15. Gumball machine — pennies available.

16. Seymour Safety stickers or smile faces. (Children)

17. "Captain Goodsight's" coloring books. (Children)

18. Pin-on buttons — for adults and children, especially during holiday seasons.

19. Puppets to decorate exam room and to use during testing.

20. Mechanical toy above screen at end of exam room as fixation point for children.

21. Cartoons — slides or 8mm projector.

22. Exam chair booster seat for children.

23. Toys or books in exam area for children to play with while Mom or Dad is being examined.

24. Laminated near point cards.

25. Fitting contact lenses from consignment inventory on the initial visit saves time and reduces patient loss from shopping prices between visits.

26. Antiques and quality artwork used in the office decor are also good investments that set the office apart from other offices.

27. Trophy companies are good sources for signs needed in the office. Gold plated plaques can be engraved or ink inlaid.

28. Magazines should be screened as much as possible since even the "reputable" magazines occasionally have articles and pictures inappropriate for professional office.

29. Send candy or presents to key patients and other doctors at Christmas. (Always have them delivered to their office so other people will see.)

30. Send special gifts to patients who refer several patients.

31. Send birthday cards, newsletters and thank you notes.

32. Patient recall of your name is enhanced when it is printed on all literature.

33. "Professional sign" in the reception room to describe services that are offered.

34. An employee bulletin board communicates articles or messages to assistants.

35. Regularly schedule office meetings — even if you only have one employee.

36. The person who answers the telephone should project a SMILE.

37. Reprint articles that you have written.

38. Stationery is a reflection of you and the way you practice.

39. Audio-visual equipment for patient education and instruction.

40. Telephone messages should have date, time, and who took the message.

41. Custom packaged kits for contact lens supplies.

42. Displays for contact lens products.

43. Give plastic tweezers for soft contact lens handling. They can be purchased inexpensively in quantities.

44. Make sure employees understand office policies and abide by them. Policies should be in writing!

45. The telephone should never ring more than three times before someone answers.

46. Patients should never have to wait more than 15 minutes without someone giving them individual attention.

47. If one measures anything — performance will increase. Example: If the receptionist is asked to count the number of exams per week the number of exams will automatically increase because she is being evaluated.

48. Plastic erasable marking boards in the examination rooms.

49. Good plastic models of the eye.

50. Efficiency of the office can be enhanced when the office and telephone is staffed during the noon hour.

51. Every patient should be wearing an imaginary sign that says, "Make me feel important!"

52. Try to take care of the specific problem that brought the patient to the office.

53. Have definite credit policies and professional signs to explain them.

54. Business cards which have space on the back for appointment times.

55. An explanation sheet for new multifocal wearers.

56. Lens cleaning tissues for glass lenses.

57. Liquid cleaners in sample sizes for glass and plastic lenses.

58. Patient interview/information sheets. It should contain visual requirements, history, visual changes and financial arrangements. Child and adults forms should be available.

59. Pictures in the pre-testing and examination area to help explain tests performed. (Fundus pictures, anterior pictures, cross-section schematics, etc.)

60. Literature to explain vision functions
    a. vision reports
    b. AOA pamphlets
    c. cataract booklets
    d. BVI pamphlets
    e. contact lens information pamphlets
    f. visual precautions sheet

61. Samples of lenses made in various types of frames and prescriptions.
    a. high-minus in rimless — edges polished
    b. aphakic lenticular lenses and aspheric lenses
    c. sample scratch resistant plastic lenses
    d. photogrey lenses with ultraviolet light to show darkening process.
    e. flattop 25mm and 35mm bifocal and trifocals
    f. executive bifocal and trifocal
    g. progressive addition lenses
    h. samples of tints and engravings

62. A laminating machine to laminate glasses warranty cards, contact lens emergency cards, business cards and contact lens service agreement cards.

63. Carousel projectors in the exam rooms to show slides while the internal exam and retinoscopy are performed. Patients enjoy slides taken by the doctor.

64. One inch round colored paper dots from an office supply can be used to stick on old contact lens vials to identify the patient, date and eye. Patient files may also be coded with the dots to specify pathology, contact lenses, etc.

65. New patient welcome letters explain office procedures and your concern for them.

66. Progress letters sent four to six weeks after eyeglass dispensing or after a contact lens patient has been dismissed finds problems and shows concern.

67. A survey card can be enclosed with the progress letter and lets the patient evaluate the office.

68. A logo on the stationery adds "class" and helps the patient identify correspondence from your office.

69. All stationery, recall cards, newsletters, etc. need consistency — color, print, paper quality, and logo.

70. Bulk postage rates can be used for large mailings to reduce cost.

71. Postage meters improve mailing efficiency for offices with large volumes of mail, however, the overall cost may be slightly greater.

72. An answering machine can record messages when the office is closed. The sound quality of the instruments vary. Buy the best.

73. A large calendar at the front desk can be used to note employee days off, vacations, appointments with lab representatives and educational meetings.

74. Thank you letters to referring patients and professionals show appreciation. Change the letter format frequently.

75. Printed fee sheets for contact lenses, service agreements and

visual training reduces explanation time and assures coverage of all items.

76. Color coded record tabs help in filing, pulling and locating misfiled records.

77. See sales people on a scheduled basis rather than at their convenience.

78. Smocks make good coverup uniforms for assistants. They can often be personalized with names, logos, etc.

79. An alternative to a uniform is to color coordinate dress each day. Example: — Monday — Navy blue and grey.

80. An organizer rack on the wall in the exam room can hold all the loose, miscellaneous items.

81. A magnetic wall mounted bar can hold lab tools.

82. Clips, hooks, or trays outside exam rooms to hold records.

83. A broom holder will hold the Burton lamp.

84. A credit card addressograph is needed if credit cards are accepted.

85. Rubber stamps for checks and deposits can be made at an office supply inexpensively.

86. Use old contact lens vials with color coded caps to fill non-used holes in the storage trays. At the end of the day inventory can be evaluated at a glance.

87. A contact lens modification unit saves time and adds flexibility to contact lens fitting.

88. A Sharpie pen may be used to mark soft contact lenses. It lasts 2-4 weeks, this enables a patient to easily develop a routine.

89. Instruct your local police and ambulance squads (para-medics) in the removal of soft and firm contact lenses.

90. Rough hands may lead to scratches on silicone lenses, therefore instruct these patients to use a Q-tip and the palm of their hand when cleaning lenses.

91. Have suction cup contact lens removers available for emergency situations.

92. Use flippers for contact lens over-refractions.
    Power Suggestions: Top flipper +0.50, +0.50
        Bottom flipper -0.50, -0.50

93. Check the edges on all firm contact lenses that can be modified. Rough edges might not be visible, but patients can feel them.

94. Measure pupil in dim illumination when fitting contact lenses. A recommended method is to use an ophthalmoscope on low illumination. Obtain a red reflex thru the pupil and with the use of a mm ruler situated under the pupil shine the light on the ruler and measure the size of the red reflex.

95. Print contact lens identification cards with your business card on the opposite side.

96. To measure specifications of soft contact lens, pat dry with tissues.

97. When removing thin soft lenses, advise patients to place one drop of saline in their eye prior to removal.

98. When fitting X-Chrome lenses, use a brown tinted lens on other eye to enhance effect and make more cosmetically desirable.

99. Breath freshener (sugar free) should be available for use by doctors and staff . . . particularly after meals. It makes close encounters with patients (ophthalmoscopy or insertion of contact lenses) a more pleasant experience.

100. Staff should identify themselves by first name when answering the telephone.

101. Addressing patients by first name is usually acceptable to young patients.

102. Elderly patients are generally not offended if the doctor calls them by the first name but expect staff to use their surname.

103. The staff should always address the doctor as Dr. (surname) in the presence of patients.

104. Doctors must decide whether to address staff by first name or surname in front of patients and make this an office policy for consistency in name tags. Some offices like the informality of first names and consider the surname too stuffy.

105. Golden Rule of Brainstorming:

    "Creative imagination is the best ideal of all."

PRINTED SAMPLES AVAILABLE

Packets of materials are available at a minimal cost. A contact lens material packet contains soft and firm instruction booklets, blink pamphlets, service agreement information, etc. A packet containing recall letters, multifocal instructions, patient information sheets, progress letters, survey cards, etc. is also available. For more information write to:

Rx for Success
6912 E. Reno, Ste. #101
Midwest City, OK 73110

Any comments or questions concerning the material in this book is encouraged and may be sent to the above address.

Chapter 22 | Gems Of Wisdom

SUCCESS

Success can be measured in many ways. In every group, however, there seems to stand alone a small percentage who are the "elite". These are people recognized by their peers as being the leaders, and in turn perceived as successful. Optometry is no exception. There are indeed, practice leaders who exemplify the word "success".

It has been our opportunity to interview some of these leaders of Optometry. The following question was posed to each of these successful practices.

"If you had to start in practice again in a new city with no equipment and very little money, how would you do it?"

The following are their replies (Note that the first two replies are authored individually by partners of the same practice).

DRS. DENNIS KUWABARA AND STANLEY J. YAMANE
Waipahu, Hawaii
Dr. Dennis Kuwabara

In starting a practice in a new city, the first task should be to develop some type of "Plan of Action." A plan detailing a step by step method is essential, because it demands careful consideration of how to proceed and within what sort of time frame this task must be completed. Time is an extremely important factor. In many instances it can mean the difference between success and failure. For example, most telephone companies have deadlines for inclusion into their white and yellow pages. If you miss this date, you would not be listed for the whole year and this would mean no one would be able to locate you in the telephone directory. Without a listing, you might not be able to obtain patients through this most often used reference resource. Not having much money complicates this plan and therefore requires that the approach be systematic and methodical to be successful. This "Plan of Action" should be concerned with the following: Determination of need, location selection, establishment of credit, office equipment, and development of community image.

The best way to determine the need for optometric services is to conduct a personal survey of the various communities within the city selected. Little cost would be involved if you are willing to do the footwork. This survey should include a census of the community, population growth statistics over the past 10 years, economic stability of community, and the number of health care practitioners (especially optometric) within the community. All of these would affect the success of a new pratice in the community. Data can be obtained by contacting local optometric societies/associations, civic groups (Jaycees, Lions, Kiwanis, Rotary), businessmen's groups, Chamber of Commerce, community associations, Better Business Bureau and realtors.

Having decided upon a particular community within the city selected, you must now select a suitable location for the practice. If you consider need to be the primary factor in selecting your location, you can expect to be successful. On the other hand, if you are more concerned with an aesthetic location which may be away from those who need your optometric services, you can expect that your success will be hindered considerably. Locating your practice where you are needed is probably the fastest way to develop not only a successful practice, but one that is satisfying as well. The key to finding a suitable location with the shortest period of time is to work closely with a reliable, professional, and busy realtor. This individual will be able to tell you and direct you to the location you need to set up your office. A realtor with any experience can, through personal records, detail what locations have proven to be good and which have proven to be poor choices. If you are able to develop good rapport with this individual, you may be developing an outstanding referral source. Realtors are constantly working with people relocating into the area and are usually asked for referrals of all sorts. People needing optometric care could easily be referred to you since your realtor has worked with you and wants to help you get established. Do not overlook this potential referral source. Your office location should be readily accessible by mass transit, have ample parking stalls, situated on the ground floor or be accessible by elevator (essential for geriatric/wheel chair patients), in a high foot traffic area, near other health care practitioners, and have adequate floor space (1,000 square feet minimum). Since you have limited finances, you will definitely not be able to afford a location that satisfies all the above considerations. In light of this, you must weigh the importance of each, and the amount of money you will need to put into the office. Always remember that this may not be your first and last office. You cannot dismiss the fact that you may need to relocate in the near future. Only by being and working in the area for awhile can you make the determination whether this will be a suitable location for you for years to come. Do not make the mistake of trying to make the impossible decision of finding the office of your dreams at this time. With the economy the way it is, the population base could shift quite rapidly and what was once a desirable location might now be a poor one.

With an office location secured, the task of obtaining financial assistance is your next major consideration. You need to sit down with a banker of a full-service bank that is near your office. Dealing with the bank manager is preferred. Do your homework before you even sit down with anyone. Have your projections outlined, detailing your anticipated income and expenditures. With the economy forcing the foreclosures of many businesses, your desire to set up a new business will come under a great deal of scrutiny. Having no collateral, you will not be a good financial risk. All that you can do is to sell yourself. The leverage that you have is that you will be bringing dollars to this bank and that you will do all of your financial business with them exclusively if they provide you with the necessary financial support. A good banker will be able to advise you as to the best course to follow and the most favorable interest rates for your particular needs. The banker, like the realtor, has worked with many individuals and is likewise a good referral source for you. You will need the services of a competent certified public accountant, insurance agent and attorney at this point if you are to establish a practice that will be successful. Consider selecting these individuals not only on the basis of competency, but on their age. If these individuals are of the same age as yourself, you can anticipate not only growing old together, but having similar ideas and attitudes.

Assuming that you now have the financial support, you are now faced with the proposition of equipping the office. The three areas that are involved are: professional equipment and supplies, office equipment and supplies, and office staff. The basic design can be decided upon with the assistance of the American Optometric Association slide presentation on office designs or the major optical equipment manufacturers. A two eye lane construction should be seriously condsidered. It allows for patient preparation in one eye lane, while the doctor works with another patient in the other eye lane. It also allows for expansion . . . room for another doctor in the office. Initally, one of the eye lanes should be fully equipped with the most "durable" equipment that can be obtained with the limited funds available and the other lane equipped with an acuity projector and special testing equipment. Leasing of equipment with limited funds would be the only way to obtain good equipment with a minimum of cash outlay. Since you will be using your phoropter, chair and stand, slit lamp, and keratometer on a daily basis, you should consider getting the most durable and yet aesthetically attractive. As for the professional supplies, such as the hardware items like frames and your contact lenses, you should consider getting them on consignment. Again this will not incur a great deal of cash outlay and yet you would have the lenses and frames you would need for your patient. The arrangement for optical frame consignments can be worked out with your local lab. As for the office equipment, the basic necessities are an electronic correcting typewriter, a telephone answering device, an electronic calculator, a plain bond copier, and an efficient pegboard accounting system. With a good electronic correcting typewriter, you can generate professional looking office forms and with your copier you can print large quantities of them and other office hand outs. As for the staff, initially two optometric assistants are desirable . . . one to manage the office and the other to assist with the patient. If full–time assistants are not feasible, you should consider part time help. Local college students or housewives make excellent part time assistants if they are trained properly. Time should be set aside each week for office meetings and for in-office training of the staff.

The most important consideration at this point is to develop a good community image. This boils down to basic public relations. This is an ongoing proposition. You need to sell yourself and your service to the community. You will have a successful practice, if the people in the community are aware of your existence and your willingness to help them. Without a good community image, you will not be able to generate the patient flow you will need to be successful. The way to get exposure is to get involved. You need to join organizations in the community (Jaycees, Lions, Kiwanis, Rotary, etc.). The only consideration here is that you should join an organization that you believe in and that you can support. You must be willing to devote what time you have to the organization in an earnest manner and not be there only because you want the exposure. In the long run, your efforts will reap the rewards. Besides the standard office opening announcements, consider sending out a mass mailing of a newsletter about your practice, writing articles on vision for a local community paper, developing in-office literature and possibly getting interviewed on your local radio or television station. Another way of developing an identity in the community is to patronize all the shops and stores. Whenever possible use a credit card or a check in paying for merchandise for further reinforcement of your identity and your profession. Attend seminars on practice management and learn what others have done to enhance their professional image in the community and to build a more efficient practice. In general, patients come to the practice as a result of recalls, referrals from patients or others, and third party programs. In a new practice, recalls would not be available to you (unless you purchased an existing practice of someone that was retiring or relocating). Your work in the community will generate new patients for you; but one other avenue may be to go after third party contracts. Working with large businesses or unions in the area you may develop some form of a third party program, where you provide your services for a reduced fee based on volume. Go after professional referrals from health care practitioners. Introduce yourself and your services to these individuals. Having expertise in the field of contact lenses, low vision, vision therapy, or industrial vision can be a means of obtaining referrals from these individuals. One final means of obtaining patients is to tailor your office hours for their convenience. Having evening hours by appointment or opening the office when others are closed (for example, Saturday and Sunday) is an excellent way to provide optometric services for those with unconventional work schedules.

The measure of success one attains is directly related to the amount of effort expended in obtaining it. Don't expect to be a winner unless you really want to be. Optometrists are trained health care professionals, who are educated to perform their services to a high level of efficiency, but when it comes down to the management of their practices, many fail miserably. Optometrists need to realize that they must be businessmen as well as clinicians. Being a listener has its attributes. Listen to those who have successful practices and you will learn that they did it through sound business procedures. The more we can listen to those conducting practice management seminars, the better our practice will become. So attend these seminars whenever possible. Always remember to conduct yourself in a professional manner, both in dress and speech. If you present yourself as a professional, you will be treated like one. Most importantly, make yourself available to your patients. They are the life blood of your practice and without them you have nothing. Having a telephone answering device on your office telephone, or an answering service, or a private pager are excellent means of being accessible to your patients. Finally, do the best you can for all your patients and treat them as you would a family member. Always provide the best in optometric care for your patients, because they expect nothing less from you. Attitude is the key to success.

DRS. DENNIS KUWABARA AND STANLEY J. YAMANE
Waipahu, Hawaii
Dr. Stanley Yamane

If I had to start a new practice again tomorrow in a new city with no equipment and with little capital, I would first do a comprehensive study of areas that showed a critical need for a new optometrist. While some areas today are over saturated, there are areas that do need more optometrists. I would want to be sure that there existed a current need as well as a long-term need for an optometrist, as frequent moves would be undesirable. I would temper the data gathered by other factors such as desirability of the area to my family and myself.

After determining a geographic area, I would seek the counsel of a real estate consultant who was familiar with the town to find a location that would be suitable for an optometric practice. I would want to locate near other health care professionals. I would want to be near major mass transit lines and easily accessible from all areas. I would want ample parking facilities available. Being new to the area, I would prefer to have good frontage to passing foot traffic if possible.

I would hire an architect to work with me on the design of the office to assure that it met the necessary building codes and to involve the general contractor who would be doing the actual construction of the office. I would be somewhat spartan in the furnishings but plan it with multiple lanes with the concept of having the practice grow and develop over the years into a multiple optometrist practice. I would want at least 1,500 square feet as a minimum for office size.

With little capital, I would seek to lease all of my instrumentation going with the best and latest available. Starting out in a new area, one wants to quickly establish a reputation as a new, up-and-coming practitioner utilizing the latest procedures and instrumentation.

I would seek out the services of the best health-specialty employment agency to screen for necessary personnel. They can assist in finding competent help without the hassles of attempting to screen everyone and allowing you to pick from a number of competent candidates. Later, I would attempt to hire from among my patient population as the practice grows.

I would establish rapport with the banker of the largest bank close to my office location assuring him that I would handle all business transactions with his branch. In return, I would ask his assistance in securing financing through conventional and government-guaranteed sources to finance my practice. I would make use of the Small Business Administration in developing a practice portfolio to present my "case" to the lending institution to help assure a positive response.

To promote my practice, I would start with conventional announcements in all the printed media informing the general public of my practice opening. I would join many of the civic and service organizations to meet many of the influential leaders in the business and civic areas. I would become active in all of my optometric professional groups and seek to gain leadership positions in them. I would use periodic mailings to my patients informing them about new developments in eye care field. Further, I would establish an "eye care family" attitude towards all in the patient "family" being sure to thank each patient who referred a new patient to me for eye care. If I had established a specialty area or area of special interest with optometry, I would make it known and seek to develop it fully.

I would devote a lot of my "spare, open" time to training my staff to be the most competent personnel in any practice around. I would develop the necessary forms to make sure that the "paper flow" through the practice was done efficiently. I would live and shop in the same geographical area as my practice so that I got to know the community well and to allow those in the community to meet and know me. I would pay for everything by check, if at all possible, as this requires the sales person to verify who you are and allows them to get to know you as an individual.

I would make an effort to get to know my optometric colleagues in the area as colleagues and friends rather than as competitors. I have learned over the years that there is always more than enough business for all and that working together helps to strengthen the professional image of optometry. By getting together, it would allow each of us to know how the other is practicing and what the current standards are within our community area. Much can be done if the group can work together to build a better image for the profession during special observances such as "Save Your Vision Week."

I would be sure to conduct myself in a professional manner both in and out of the office. Realizing that professional people are constantly being scrutinized by the general public, I would want to be sure that my actions reflected the mature manner befitting of a Doctor of Optometry.

I would seek out the services of the best certified public accountant to be sure that my books are kept correctly, the best full–service insurance agent to be sure that I am adequately protected from undue risks in all areas, and the best attorney to be sure that all legal documents I need to sign are properly written and in my best interest.

I would make myself available to my patients and let them know that I do so because I do care about them and their vision problems. While establishing regular office hours, I would be sure that my home phone number is easily accessible to them. I would also establish a 24–hour answering service for those times when I am not home and have it tied to a paging unit that would allow me to be reached without any difficulty at any time.

I would try as early as possible to establish a multiple doctor practice feeling that it would help to strengthen the practice and to assure patients of better care. It would allow members of the staff to sub–specialize if they desire to do so. It would also allow for better coverage when one wants to take vacations or is away on a business trip or ill or injured. Group practice, while it sacrifices some independence, also allows for greater purchasing power of supplies and the sharing of expensive instrumentation by a number of practitioners.

DRS. PAUL FARKAS, T.W. KASSALOW, AND BARRY FARKAS
Practice Limited to Contact Lenses
New York, New York
Dr. Barry Farkas

1. Location of Practice — goals
   a. Well-trafficked
   b. Easily accessible by car or mass transit with ample and convenient parking available
   c. Size, socioeconomic level and age of potential patient population should be consistent with desired patient population and specialty goals
   d. Area should have at least 10 years devoid of major socioeconomic or industrial upheaval.

2. Equipment
   a. Buy the best from both a functional as well as aesthetic standpoint. Old, substandard or standard instrumentation has no real trade value later on, so you may consider the purchase of quality instrumentation an investment. The best proven investment is in yourself.
   b. Equipment can be leased, but then you're merely supporting a third party. Basic opthalmic instrumentation doesn't change much, so, if at all possible, seek to own your equipment.
   c. Equipment and contact lens companies know well the difficulties in starting a private practice. Most of them will provide financing to get and keep your business. Don't be shy — ask for their assistance.
   d. Always strive to work with the most technically modern and advanced opthalmic materials possible. It will pay dividends in the future.
   e. Stationery should be consistent with your desired professional

image. Be sure it lists professional degrees and specialties and is ample to cover your day to day needs.

3. Personnel

a. Hire staff who best typify your goals in practice and who complement your strengths and weaknesses. Your employees are, from day one, a reflection of you and they should be able to communicate on an equal level with your patients.

b. Even for the new practitioner, it is important that the office has ample staff coverage, even when the doctor is not in. Again, consider it an investment in the future.

c. Be prepared to pay your staff higher than the going rate. You get what you pay for. A good employee will more than make up the difference in getting prospective patients in the office and keeping your present patients satisfied.

d. When hiring, give prepared tests for administrative and typing skills. Look for the career-minded individual. Life is always easier when dealing with a 'professional.'

e. Use all available job market vehicles to run ads in your area. The more applicants, the better your resultant staff will be.

4. Financing the New Practice

a. Borrow the maximum amount possible from banks, family and loan institutions while interest rates are down. As your practice grows these amounts, which presently seem enormous, usually become insignificant.

b. Seek outside, part-time employment to support your growing practice. If selected properly, these positions will not only bring in extra income, but sharpen your clinical skills and knowledge.

5. Building Up a New Practice

a. Acquire a sub-specialty that is either lacking or needed in your area.

b. Personally visit as many M.D.s, O.D.s, opticians, pharmacists, etc. as possible in your area. They will know why you're there and help you more than you would expect if you are humble, impressive and perform services that they do not.

c. Make it known to professionals in your community that you are willing to take on difficult cases or patients. If you are successful, more patients will follow.

d. There is an art to advertising without advertising. Be the first in your area to contact local newspapers, television, radio, magazines, etc., when new developments become available, or even just to let them know what it is that you do.

e. Join as many productive organizations as possible to build a patient base consistent with your goals in patient population.

f. Be sure to have office hours at times most convenient for your patients, when others may not. This may include early mornings, late evenings, Saturdays and Sundays.

g. Be sure to have a good answering service or recording machine.

Summary

1. Be special! We, as optometrists, are generally unaware of the miracles of sight that we perform.

2. Talk to your patients. Tell them what you are doing and why, as much as possible. It is easier to work with patients when you are working together. Friendly patients will also be much better referral sources.

3. Fees should be either very low or very high for your area. Practitioners who charge middle-ground prices are generally squeezed out.

4. View each patient as a potential referral source. Extend every courtesy that you would to your very best friend. Do everything possible to satisfy their needs or requests. That extra effort will pay dividends in the long run.

DRS. C.L. McEACHERN, WAYNE M. CANNON AND MICHAEL C. McCLAY
Columbia, South Carolina
Dr. Wayne M. Cannon

1. What type of life style do you want?

2. What kind/size of city or town do you want to live in?

3. What hobbies and other interests do you have?

4. Do you want to practice solo or in a group practice?

5. Are you interested in some type of institution environment, i.e., VA, schools, military, HMO, etc.

After these and I am sure many other questions have been answered — and the answer is to start a practice in a new city, I feel the following should be done:

1. Talk with as many providers of vision care in the area as possible — the more the better! Do not pay a lot of attention to what they say as to the need for additional practitioners, but observe the office, the personnel, the equipment, etc.

2. Evaluate the location of all providers of vision care. The best way is to get a map of the area and mark where they are located using different colors for optometrist, optician, and ophthalmologist. One area of the city that is not well covered may be evidenced from this.

3. The type of practice that is desired (professional, specialty) should determine the location to some extent. Then decide if a mall location, a professional office building, a free standing building is best for the type of practice desired.

4. Equipment can be bought from a variety of sources. I would start and see if anyone in the optical field has any used equipment they want to sell. Also check with the state association. Many times they have a list of equipment that is available and will be aware of someone who has some equipment. Usually this will provide the best buys for equipment. The other obvious source is equipment companies. There seem to be a lot of companies in the equipment business. Get at least three or four to make bids on the equipment.

5. Office furnishings — Many optical and equipment companies carry this type of equipment. There are many commercial companies available locally. Again get three or more bids.

6. Financing can be acquired through several sources. Many equipment companies will carry the loan themselves. With deregulation of the banks, interest rates are negotiable. Go to several banks and savings and loans and let them make a proposal.

7. Personnel — 1. Check with the Board or State Optometric Association. 2. Check with the local doctors and labs. 3. Placement companies. 4. Advertise in the newspaper. 5. Check with friends and relatives.

We are aware of no "secret" ways to success and can only attribute our success to persistence and hard work. However, we will elaborate on several common sense factors that we feel have allowed us to become effective in reaching our goals.

First, write down what it will take to make you (and your wife and family) happy. For example: Do you insist upon living in a metropolitan area, beach town, your specific home-town, etc. How much money will it take to keep you happy? How hard are you willing to work? How much time off do you want? How much priority do you place upon recreational time and activities? After you have listed your goals, prioritize them realistically. It should become more apparent to you what steps will be necessary for you to attain these goals.

DRS. PAUL W. THIELKING, DANIEL D. HINSON, WILLIAM A. BOETLER AND DAVID W. HANSEN
Des Moines, Iowa
Dr. David W. Hansen

Starting a business or a profession such as optometry is not a unique decision on the part of the individual. Thousands of new ventures are started each day throughout the country. With these new enterprises there are some that fail and some that excel.

The optometric practice must start with a self-discipline comprised of emotional involvement and technical expertise which enable the individual to first serve the patient, second, his profession, and third, his family and himself. If at any point in time this order is changed or reversed, the outcome of helping the patient will be easily recognized by all, especially the patient. That is why the goals and philosophy of starting a practice must start with a well-planned outline which ultimately considers the most optimum health welfare for the patients. Once the plan is developed and organized, the details, including location of the office, equipment, type of practice (partnership, professional corporation, or solo practice), financial assistance, and community loyalty, enables the Doctor of Optometry to achieve his designed future success.

An optometric degree and state license only allow us the privilege to serve mankind. Total dedication in all areas of optometric practice and community health welfare are mandatory to insure this privilege.

I truly believe that under most circumstances, successful practitioners from around the country could move to different geographical areas and become successful. These individuals stand out among their peers whether they be in an urban setting or in a rural outlying area. Because a successful practice can be developed at any geographical level, the optometrist should first decide upon the environment that suits him and meets his family's needs.

Geographic location is very important for the starting optometrist. Systematic research should be analyzed regarding the quality of optometric care, lifestyle in the community, and general socioeconomic conditions. Rural agricultural industry complemented with manufacturing and business is generally important for a stable economy. All of these are important factors in selecting a location. Many geographic areas of rapid growth provide unstable, transitory occupations, so therefore are extremely poor locations. I personally feel that small to medium size cities provided an excellent opportunity for most graduates.

In selecting the mode of practice, one has to know himself. Not everyone is a partnership candidate. However, I believe that a group partnership offers the recent graduate the opportunity to help the practice as well as benefit from past experience and the expanded financial resources which are available. Most partnerships are involved with sub-specialties which allow the new graduate to blend his newest research knowledge with the established clinical mode of practice. Many times there is a void in a sub-specialty which can be filled to benefit the practice and the patients of the community. A young doctor interested in vision therapy going to an area without this sub-specialty can expand the scope of practice as well as generate the confidence of the new community.

Once a location and mode of practice have been selected, it is now time to concentrate on the specific optometric equipment and business tools necessary to function in an efficient optometric practice. Since most graduates are required to purchase hand instruments while in school, the next phase involves major investments including chairs, stands, phoroptors, microscopes, visual field instrumentation, tonometry equipment, etc. In order to be successful, one has to look successful to his patients. It is not necessary to buy "Rolls Royce" equipment when starting, but one should remember that major instruments last for many years and should be quality items. If they can be properly financed as a package, it will be a lasting investment for the future.

It is important for optometric students to familiarize themselves with and use various manufacturers' equipment in order to determine the advantages and disadvantages of each one. Also, when graduating from school, the new practitioner should establish specific instrument priorities. For a general optometric practice, the new practitioner will need the mandatory equipment consisting of a comfortable chair, instrument stand, phoroptor, biomicroscope, tonometer, visual fields equipment, vision skills equipment, binocular indirect ophthalmoscope, a keratometer, and projector. The most important tool of the above mentioned instruments in my opinion is the biomicroscope. The biomicroscope should allow the new practitioner the advantages of comfortable vision for himself. Superior optics and illuminations also aid the doctor in identification of the patient's problem. Quality of the instruments must not be compromised when deciding which instrument package is financially feasible. Once the practitioner is established, automated refractors should be budgeted to aid his efficiency and provide better examination for the patients.

The initial cost of instrumentation in starting an optometric practice is frightening and, to say the least, very expensive! The new graduate should consider purchasing or leasing as alternatives for his instrument package. I strongly feel that combination of both is an advantageous method whereby the doctor has monthly payments set aside for buying instruments on a fixed rate and a leasing program which enables him to maintain an adequate cash flow for laboratory bills, for contact lenses, ophthalmic products, business supplies, overhead and salaries.

One should choose financial consultants who will aid in maintaining leverage with middle-of-the-line philosophies, not too radical and not too conservative. In a group practice, the financial advisors are usually well established and know the philosophy of the office and, therefore, help the new doctor with his personal needs.

Of all areas of optometric practice, the most challenging and rewarding involves an area which is seldom talked about in optometry schools. The training and selection of optometric assistants is a key and integral part of a successful practice. Assistants, both male and female, are the backbone of service and dedication of our offices. It is the assistants who represent the doctor's integrity and technical knowledge and his commitment to the health and welfare of patients in the community. Assistants should be well groomed, knowledgeable, and willing to dedicate themselves to better health care. They should be genuinely interested in the patients and the practice growth. The doctor's desire to obtain superior vision for his patients should also be shared by the assistants.

An efficient office, starting from the first phone contact, is easily recognized by most people. It is important for the patient to proceed through the office in an organized manner. The receptionist's "ability to receive" patients and conclude their appointment efficiently and pleasantly is reflected in the patients' enthusiasm to refer other patients without hesitation. A referral is the highest form of compliment from a patient. Ancillary personnel are an integral part of the referral process. An unpleasant, uneducated assistant can cost you many referrals. Generally I feel that sub-specialties produce more optometric referrals than general practice. However, it is not necessary for all optometrists to be involved in a sub-specialty. Vision therapy practices generate more optometric referrals because of the unique benefit to the patient.

Low vision can be considered in the same category. Contact lenses, on the other hand, are fit by many doctors and technicians, so other factors enter in, including economic, for our patients. Limited contact lens practices generally are difficult to start unless associated with an optometric group or unless the doctor has been in general practice for a few years and decides to switch his total emphasis towards contact lenses. Therefore, I feel that functional vision and vision relating to learning problems offer the newest graduate an opportunity to fill a void which unfortunately is in most of our communities. Working with schools and community involvement will lead to speaking engagements, vision screening, and parent-teacher conferences and staffings, which allow the new optometrist an avenue for further exposure.

Generally optometric care should be uniform throughout the entire career of the optometrist with the exception of progressive changes to benefit the patient, both in instrumentation and provision of services. The last patient you see before retirement should be treated as well as the first patient who enters your new practice.

Optometry is a very gratifying profession which allows us the opportunity to work with basically healthy people, to improve existing health care, and to lead an economically comfortable life. It is therefore important for the Doctor of Optometry to thank his patients for allowing him to serve as their doctor. Thank-yous are always appropriate and especially necessary when referrals are guided towards him. We should never be too busy to thank our patients and friends for their loyalty and confidence.

Involving ourselves with our patient's welfare will encourage our desire for new knowledge through optometric continuing education, certification, sub-specialty work, and interest in new modes of efficient optometric practice to expand in all areas including the above mentioned areas. Once a practice is growing, it is also important for the doctor or doctors to continually stimulate their practice by bringing in new associates. A perpetuating practice gains the confidence of the doctors involved as well as the community. Self image and the ability to project it is recognized by everyone.

DRS. DANIEL KLAFF AND MURRAY KLAFF
Bellaire, Texas
Dr. Daniel Klaff

If I had to get started **again**, (and had the knowledge I have now), right to the bank I'd go. Banks are most willing to loan money for a good client, but before I'd go, I'd decide on the location. Bankers consider location one of the (if not the most important) essentials in loans, and the location , between the major bank and post office on a busy street. I'd stay away from downtown, choosing suburbia. Bankers want to know the exact amount you want to borrow, including living expenses. No banker wants approximate figures either. They want information about leases, proposed income, fixed expenses, living expenses, salaries, and pay-back.

As for equipment, I still consider, for a man with no money, that good used equipment, sent to the paint shop for brightening up, is good sense.

Of course, I would not turn down an invitation from an established O.D. to join his practice. This is ideal for some young men out of school with no money and no equipment.

When I got out of school, there were no practices around large enough to support more than one O.D., but now there are plenty. So it certainly is a viable opportunity for young O.D.s to visit these larger practices and make themselves available for either hire, or associate. And for the comfort and security of not having to worry about getting patients, or laying out any money, I'd sure work for a lot less than in commercial practice, just to stay where the 'good guys' are.

In cities where there are optometry colleges, teaching part time and practicing part time are common . . . and you get the best of both worlds.

Sometimes young O.D.s practice in their own office part time and in another office also part time. Nothing wrong there.

Patients always come from contact. Making yourselves known is important. The best patient is one you meet out of the office. Joining civic, church, synagogue, and doing volunteer work always pays off. It pays off in tremendous satisfaction in that the work you do is worthy and appreciated, and if it's done for that reason then, it's proper. But along with this good work, comes contacts with people who may indeed choose you as their O.D. when the time comes for their needs. Visiting other offices and letting your special talents be known are important too. After all, with specialization today, all of us cannot be really good at everything. Some O.D.s and M.D.s need to be referring their complicated cases to others.

In the beginning however, you must decide on that basic philosophical approach to optometry. Are you going to have a quality practice or a quantity practice? And once you make up your mind, it is much easier to map out your game plan.

A patient said to me just a few days ago, that when she inquired where to go for her contacts, one of our patients said to her, "Go to the Klaffs, they sure are nice over there". I still contend, regardless of talent and instruments, if you give patients what they want, they'll come in droves. And what's that? It's what we all want from people we deal with. Respect . . . Love . . . Care . . . Honesty . . . and a proper fee. Not a cheap fee necessarily, but a proper one, and in most cases that is rather substantial to make a good living.

DR. ROBERT MORRISON
Harrisburg, Pennsylvania

If I were to begin my career in optometry in a new community with no financial backing, what would I do?

This question is a lot easier to answer at this time in my career than when I first started out . . . for I have the advantage of profiting from my experiences and knowing now what doesn't seem to work and what probably does. Respectfully, let me list what I believe to be some key factors that I would suggest be considered as meaningful to a new practitioner.

1. Group practice . . . I would suggest that this be entered early in one's career to benefit from the knowledge and experiences of associates.

2. Recognize your weaknesses as a practitioner and resolve to eliminate them through education and practice.

3. Seek out experts in the field — correspond, visit and communicate, exchange ideas and share techinques.

4. Share your knowledge with others . . . be available for lectures within your community and your profession.

5. Specialize . . . I would select a specific field of optometric care and actively pursue competence in that area.

6. Dare to do it differently. Innovation can be challenging and rewarding. Think progressively!

7. Computerize as early in a practice as you can afford it — it is wonderfully effective and an efficient way to practice.

8. Make the most of your opportunities . . . seize upon the good things that happen in your career.

9. Become an active part of your community — not only as a practitioner but as a person.

10. Build a pleasant image in your practice, in your community and in your profession. Be proud to be an optometrist!

11. Be benevolent — share your good fortune with others less fortunate.

12. Play it low key — let your deeds speak louder than your words.

Finally, I would work at being a good practitioner and offer my best effort to every single patient who entrusts his/her vision to me.

Specialty Practices

We are in an age of specialization. As the profession of optometry becomes more and more complex, there will be more specialty practices.

The following are interviews with optometric specialists in two different fields, and their impressions and advice toward specialization!

DR. ROBERT KOETTING ASSOCIATES
Practice Limited to Contact Lenses
St. Louis, Missouri

If I had it to do over again, I wouldn't change a thing, but twenty years ago few people would have foreseen a successful future for the non-dispensing optometrist. Indeed, when I limited my practice to contact lenses, I joined ranks with the medical refractionists, price house O.D.s and a small selection of assorted misfits who felt that there was an honorable future in the contact lens field.

The idea doesn't seem so farfetched any longer, and so far as I am concerned, a contact lens practice is "first class" optometry. For the most part, contact lenses are a luxury and contact lens patients are a cut above the average, but there is more to it than that.

Anyone can wear glasses and patients **expect** them to work without giving the matter any more thought, but contact lens patients are happy and enthusiastic. The optometrist is rewarded by a degree of problem solving satisfaction which is rarely achieved in any other facet of practice. The personality improvement found in young teenagers or the joy of youth returned to a presbyope is exceeded only by the gratitude of an aphakic who regains the wide world of binocular vision. Patients with keratoconus, high school athletes, wall flowers, twelve diopter myopes — all love contact lenses.

I've never enjoyed dispensing. The happiest day of my life was that when I first told a little old lady, "I'm sorry that your ear hurts, but I won't be able to adjust your glasses — please see your optometrist!"

Developing a specialty practice takes time. After all, there are only a certain number of people who will wear contact lenses so that patients are drawn from a substantially larger population segment. The new practitioner must mark time for a while and develop experience, probably in association with someone in a large practice.

Ultimately, the best source of new patient referrals in contact lens practice, like general optometric practice, will be those satisfied and enthusiastic patients who send friends and relatives to your office. During the intervening years while this group reaches a practical density, sources of immediate referral in quantity are essential. The three best are non-contact lens fitting optometrists, ophthalmologists, and opticians followed closely by members of the same three groups who are fitting a limited number of lenses and willing to refer problem cases. Don't be afraid to ask!

The optometrist whose practice is limited to contact lenses will find a surprisingly cooperative relationship here because these practitioners are anxious for help from a non-competitive colleague.

Even the most commercial optician is happy to refer problem contact lens patients without hope of compensation if he can be certain that they will not end up in the shop of another optician. If a patient returns for his next pair of spectacles or sunglasses, the referral source will be doubly pleased.

Contact lenses are a luxury! They must be fitted in appropriate surroundings. Adequate equipment is important, of course, but patient impression may mean even more in a practical sense. Use new or professionally reconditioned instruments only.

Office equipment must look good without the slightest suggestion of homemade or amateur adaption. On the other hand, having the very latest or most expensive model is not significant to the patient. Remember that not one patient in a thousand knows anything about your phoropter but every one of them knows how much your furniture is worth. A good quality electric typewriter on a first class desk will mean much more than one thousand extra dollars spent for a deluxe refractor. No one respects the doctor's frugal attributes when he outfits his reception room with his mother-in-law's old dining room chairs. They don't even care if the saving is passed along to his patients.

As in other phases of optometric practice, the contact lens specialist can get along with fewer than 1,000 square feet but only under the right circumstances. An ideal starting office should have about that much space. Avoiding high rent areas, in my opinion, is a serious false economy. A few hundred dollars spent on a better location fifty feet away may well be worth every cent of it. Floor space can be overpriced, of course, but the laws of supply and demand apply in real estate as everywhere else. You generally get what you pay for.

The decision to own one's own building is an individual matter. I would not practice in a building unless multiple specialities were represented. The prestige of being there with other doctors is important and referrals usually compensate for the added cost.

Someone once asked Willie Sutton, the famous robber turned author, why he robbed banks. His reply was to the point and applicable, "because that's where the money is!" A contact lens practice must be located in a community where people can afford contact lenses. Go first class!

A final word of caution on this subject involves avoiding communities that "have an opening for an optometrist". Assuming that community is not without an optometrist because the last one there has died or retired, a new graduate would be well advised to look elsewhere. The grave of any professional practice is a very clear omen. Avoid the place.

An old story I've told many times concerns the man who bought a stove and seated himself comfortably before it saying, "now if this thing works I am going to buy some coal". Optometrists too often take this same position and here I repeat the importance of having the right attitude. If you know where you are going and the type of practice you want, you will have a pretty good idea of the equipment and personnel required to maintain that practice. Waiting until the dollar volume "justifies" purchase of first class equipment and inventory represents a foolish economy. The limits of practice are set by what you think you **are** and not by what you may someday become.

Capital is available from many sources. Using your own or your family's is a great idea if you have it. If you are not that fortunate, and most of us aren't, establish immediate contact with a local bank, being sure that you can "float" for a year. Talk it over with the loan officer (some advocate going right to the president) and be prepared to answer questions in a straight forward manner, but don't use up borrowing power on equipment. You can lease instruments or arrange extended payments with the seller. Laboratories will often assist by providing extended payments and consignment arrangements so that you can keep an extensive lens inventory with a relatively small investment.

A good CPA or business advisor is not a luxury. This is a basic expense and will cost less than you might think because the accountant will expect to be better repaid as your practice grows and as you can afford it. Seek professional financial advice in the same way you seek help in other areas. Talk to successful professional people in the community. Seek their opinions and referrals.

Human nature has not changed remarkably during my years in practice. New optometrists are now, as they were then, anxious to dig in and get started. I find no fault with this enthusiasm but if you aspire to an optometric specialty or limited practice (and I will be eternally grateful for having made this decision) please take your time.

To say that one's attitude is more important than specific details may appear to be dodging the issue. There is, nevertheless, no cookbook answer. Backplanning is essential.

Decide upon the type of practice you want — the patient volume, the general physical description, the location, etc. and **behave** as though you are a part of that practice now because you really **are**. In no time at all you will find that you have stopped wasting your efforts. You will be meeting and talking to professionals who can help you build. You will be taking courses and buying instruments that will aid you in your chosen specialty. You will find yourself and your wife and your friends wearing contact lenses and talking enthusiastically about them to other people. You will feel so secure in the goal-oriented attitude that each step will fall into place because you won't be wasting time on distracting activities.

DR. DONALD J. GETZ
VISION THERAPY SPECIALIST
Van Nuys, California

A newly licensed optometrist has many choices to make in determining the direction his optometric career is going to take. In restrospect, the choice I made to specialize in vision therapy has provided me with a rich, fulfilling and exciting life.

A vision therapy practice is both fun and exciting. There are too many people in the world who do not enjoy what they do for a living. I have never met an optometrist involved in vision therapy who did not enjoy what he was doing. It offers diversity since you are using different therapeutic techniques from day to day and from year to year. You are always on the threshold of new knowledge and it remains a challenge and a source of constant interest.

There is nothing magic about establishing this kind of practice. The major prerequisites are a love of people (especially children), an outgoing personality and a lot of enthusiasm. It would be very helpful to spend approximately one year working for an optometrist who specialized in vision therapy so that additional therapy and practice–management skills can be learned.

I am often asked, "what is the minimum equipment necessary to start a vision therapy practice?" The minimum equipment necessary is generally what you already have in your office for testing purposes.

All that is needed are the proper concepts, the knowledge of what you are trying to accomplish and a moderate degree of imagination. I feel that too much emphasis has been placed on equipment and this conveys to the patient and to the optometrist that elaborate instruments do all the work. We must not lose sight of the concept that the patient is primarily responsible for learning involved in vision therapy. Vision therapy is what optometrists do **with** people, not **to** people.

Vision skills that are learned in the artificial, stationary environment of most instruments do not carry over to the dynamic, constantly changing environment of real life. Therefore, skills should be taught in real space. The minimum number of instruments that are necessary can be obtained consequently, for a very small investment (under five hundred dollars).

Getting started in a vision therapy practice involves many factors. First of all, you must be able to recognize a possible vision therapy patient. Strabismics are relatively easy to recognize, but the child with a visually related learning problem is a bit more subtle. The main thing is to take a thorough history and really listen to what the patient and his parents are saying. There are specific behaviors which may indicate the presence of a visual problem and these possible behaviors should be investigated. After a thorough visual analysis is completed, an attempt should be made to correlate the visual findings to the specific behaviors discovered during the history. I found it very helpful in building my practice to get out into the community and do a lot of public speaking. Service clubs, PTA's, etc., provide golden opportunities to get your message across. It was also helpful to get on the telephone with teachers and principals to report your analysis of patients at the conclusion of each examination.

It is a common misconception that a large amount of space is necessary to build a vision therapy practice. Although my current office is 3,000 sq. ft., the practice was built in an office measuring approximately 600 sq. ft.

There are many rewards that come from a successful vision therapy practice. To make a crossed eye straight is an exciting accomplishment. To see a child go from very poor grades to very good grades is also quite exciting. Everyday, you can observe both children and adults achieving much closer to their respective potentials. This can be seen in their academic, vocational, avocational, and athletic performances.

In addition, the financial rewards can be as high or higher than in any other aspect of optometric practice. One of the main advantages is that vision therapists can be employed so that many patients can be cared for at the same time. In the general practice of optometry, usually only one patient can be seen at a time.

There is still one other major advantage of this type of practice. It has allowed me to spend a large percentage of time away from the office lecturing and touring around the United States and Europe. In most optometric offices, not only does a vacation cost money, but production in the office usually ceases while the optometrist is away. In a properly functioning vision therapy practice, the therapy continues even while the optometrist is away from the office.

Milton Eger, O.D., the editor of the Journal of the American Optometric Association, stated in a recent issue that, "the future of the profession lies in two areas — the use of drugs and in functional vision and that we must become as knowledgeable as we can in these areas because every year the visual information demand increases."

We, in optometry, are the only hope those children, teenagers and adults have to perform to their maximum potential and it is, indeed, exciting and fun to fill such a great need.

Appendix A | **Office Policy Manual**

FOREWORD TO OFFICE POLICY MANUAL

Welcome to our staff! We hope you will enjoy your work.

This policy handbook has been prepared in order to inform you about what to expect from us, as well as what we, in turn, will expect from you. It is our intention to make the office run more smoothly and efficiently by teaching everyone their obligations and responsibilities.

Please read the entire manual. It will answer a lot of questions you have concerning your position.

SALARY AND RELATED BENEFITS

1. Semi-monthly pay checks will be given on the 15th and the last day of each month.

2. Withholding tax and social security will be taken out of each semi-monthly check.

3. A uniform allowance may be given each month for uniforms, payable at the end of each quarter. This will be discussed with you at the time of hiring.

4. A Christmas bonus will be given if you have been employed for a period of three months at the time.

5. Three weeks vacation (15 working days) after working one year (includes sick leave and all personal business leave).

6. Five vacation days are available after three months employment to use for sickness or as needed.

7. After one year, a percentage of the gross salary will automatically be put into a trust fund. If your employment terminates, a sliding scale determines how much of the accrued trust fund you will receive, depending on the number of years employed. The purpose of the trust is to encourage extended years of employment.

8. Salaries will be reviewed at six month intervals. Periodic salary increases are important to you and it is also an indication that you are doing a satisfactory job. This does not mean that salaries will be increased at each review or that you are doing a poor job if there is no salary increase.

PERSONAL OFFICE POLICIES

1. Our expectation is that your personal appearance be neat and clean.

2. Name plates will be issued and should be worn at all times so that the patients can be familiar with your name.

3. Smoking is bad for your health and ours. If it is necessary to smoke, please do it when not in the office.

4. Please confine all eating and drinking to the lab.

5. Employees will be provided with free vision care. Lenses, frames, and contact lenses will be provided at invoice cost.

6. The immediate family of employees will receive free vision care. Frames and lenses provided at invoice cost.

7. We know that personal phone calls are sometimes necessary, but please try to limit the calls to only essential ones.

8. At times, employees moonlight at other jobs. When you accept this position, you must consider this job as your first obligation.

9. Your positive attitude and cooperation when working on the office team are expected to be your most important attributes.

10. Staff meetings will be on the second and fourth Tuesday of each month. Suggestions are welcome at these meetings.

11. Uniform tops will be furnished by the office and slacks will be furnished by the employee.

12. Parking needs to be in the back row of the back lot or in the lot to the west as parking spaces are limited.

WORKING HOURS AND TIME OFF

1. Working days will be Monday through Friday, 8:00 until 5:30.

2. When the employee desires to terminate services, the doctors would appreciate two weeks notice.

3. The holidays this office will observe with pay are:
   a. New Year's Day
   b. Memorial Day
   c. Independence Day
   d. Labor Day
   e. Thanksgiving
   f. Christmas Eve
   g. Christmas Day

4. After three months probation period, five vacation days will be available to use for sickness or as needed.

5. Three weeks of vacation (15 working days) will be earned after one year of employment. A notice of when the vacation will be taken should be given one month in advance as a minimum. After three years of employment, vacation time will be increased to four weeks annually. We would prefer that vacation time be taken in months other than July and August, and when convenient, when one doctor is off, also. Conflicts in vacation time will be assigned by seniority. Dates when you will be gone should be placed on the calendar in the front office.

6. Extra work days will be paid on a daily basis comparable to the monthly salary of the employee.

7. Days traded with other employees tend to upset normal office procedure. If it is necessary to trade days, arrangements should be made well in advance with notice being given to the doctors.

8. Employees are urged to attend educational seminars related to the duties of that employee. If during regular office hours normal pay will be given. Otherwise, only fees, meals, lodging and travel will be paid.

9. Borrowing money or giving advances on pay checks can create difficulties. This office will give no advances or lend money on time.

GENERAL OFFICE INFORMATION

1. A list of suggested telephone procedures and phrases will be available at the business desk.

2. When taking appointments, it is necessary to receive the patient's address, telephone number, age, type of service wanted and whether they are a new or former patient.

3. The doctor will write or dictate a rough copy of necessary reports. The assistant can then type and prepare them for mailing after the doctor has made any necessary correction.

4. The receptionist is to keep track of petty cash and inform the doctors when the supply is running short.

5. All employees are welcome to and encouraged to use books from the doctor's personal library. If there are any questions concerning terms, procedures, or office problems, please do not hesitate to ask questions.

6. All records from the past six to ten years are kept in the open filing holders in the business office. After ten years, the records are inspected and either stored or destroyed.

7. Employees will find it more interesting and can give the patient more information if they are familiar with optometric terminology. A list of common optometric terms will be available.

8. When dissatisfied patients enter the office, the assistant is to take them as soon as possible. In most cases, they are complaining loudly and the reception room is a poor place for them to be. Listen courteously to their problems and tell them we will do everything we can to help. Verify all parameters on the prescription to see if we missed something. If not, the patient should be moved to a separate room and the doctor will then see the patient and discuss the problem.

9. A list of preferred colleagues for referral will be at the front desk.

10. Emergency information about each doctor and employee will be listed at the business desk.
    a. Home telephone number
    b. Telephone number at spouse's place of employment
    c. Personal physician's number
    d. Emergency, fire department and police department telephone numbers
    e. Name and telephone numbers of nearest relative

11. A list of all lab numbers is located in our lab area.

12. When helping a patient and something is ordered **or** you cannot finish with the patient, make a note of what has been done and what needs to be finished. Then initial it and put it on the front of the record.

13. Professional Courtesies — Doctors 20%; Doctor's Family 10%; RNs 10%; Ministers 10%, except doctor's minister; Parents of Assistant 20%; Brothers and Sisters of Assistant 10%; Children of Assistants not living at home 20%; no reduction to the spouse's family.

14. The doctors will keep records of vacation time and leave taken without pay by each employee.

15. The doctors will assign responsibilities to each assistant:

    (1) Preliminary Testing Assistant

    (2) Stylist

    (3) Lab Tech

    (4) Receptionist

    (5) Contact Lens Assistant

    (6) Bookkeeper

    There may be times that those responsibilities will have to be covered by fellow workers.

JOB DESCRIPTION AND OFFICE ROUTINES

1. It should be understood that at times it is necessary to cover for fellow workers when they are busy handling other chores or are off duty.

2. List of employees and their responsibilities.

RECEPTIONIST

a. When the office is opened, make sure all doors are unlocked. The office should be prepared for the daily routine and the reception room put in order.

b. Appointments should be taken promptly and courteously. If the schedule is full and a patient wants an appointment as soon as possible, the name should be put on a list and the patient called if an opening becomes available. Confirmation calls will be made to the patient two days in advance of the appointment. Information to be obtained when making an appointment for a patient include: **age, telephone number, address, new or former patient status, contact lenses or regular exam.**

c. A list of the time needed for vision analysis, contact lens fitting, contact lens progress and consultation will be at the front desk for easy consultation when taking appointments.

d. When the patient arrives he/she should be greeted with a smile. The registration form is then handed to the patient with appropriate explanations. Upon completion of the form, assigning an account number and entering the information into the computer terminal, the patient is ready to be seen by the screening assistant.

e. Quoting fees over the telephone is to be on a restricted basis only. If the patient insists on knowing, he should be told the basic fees with an explanation that this can vary depending upon which tests are needed.

f. The doctor should be consulted when a patient is tardy or drops in. If he wants to fit them into the schedule, he will make that decision.

g. The doctor will change the normal recall period if the need is warranted. Otherwise, the recall is set on a standard age related scale.   (Children _____ months); (Age 18-40 _____ months); (Age 40-50 _____ months); (Age over 50 _____ months).

h. A list of fees is to be placed within easy access and all assistants should be familiar with them.

i. When mail and deliveries arrive, it should be sorted, opened and directed to the proper people.

j. After payment the proper entries concerning the patient's account should be recorded. The record should then be filed.

k. Be familiar with optometric terminology and be able to have an intelligent conversation with patients regarding optometric care.

l. At the end of the day, the business should be closed out and a deposit made.

m. The telephone recorder should be turned on and the program for the end of the day completed on the computer.

OPTOMETRIC ASSISTANTS

a. Upon arrival, the assistants are to turn on the instruments and prepare the refracting rooms for the patients.

b. The styling and dispensing rooms should be checked by the assistant assigned to the area to see that all frames and tools are in order.

c. When the patient arrives for an examination, the assistant or receptionist is to check to see that the proper information is in the computer.

d. The assistant then meets the patient and, depending upon the age, carries out certain procedures:

 1. Titmus visual skills are to be run on children under age 14.

 2. Spectacles being worn are to be verified.

  a. Checked on the computer lens analyzer in minus cylinder form with a printout.

      b. Power of "Add", if present, type and height of bifocal.

      c. Tint of old lenses is to be recorded.

   3. Color vision, near acuities, amplitude and pupillary distance are to be taken in the skills room.

   4. Blood pressure, tonometric readings, fundus photographs and glaucoma fields screening will be taken on all patients above the age of 30.

e. The patient is seated in the examination room. The case history is completed. Distance acuities and keratometry are taken. The spectacle prescription is loaded in the phoropter and the computer.

STYLIST

a. When the patient and doctor return to the styling area, the stylist will help with styling and filling out the prescription form. Also, a fields test may be needed at this time.

b. The fees for the patient will then be determined and the stylist will explain the payment schedule. The fee for services and material charges will be explained and the charges put into the computer terminal in the styling area.

c. Copies of insurance forms should always be available. It is necessary that the stylist and insurance assistant be able to complete and handle mailing of these forms.

d. At this time, the prescription is ordered.

CONTACT LENS ASSISTANT

a. The contact lens assistant will teach insertion and removal to contact lens patients. The doctor will give instructions on the procedures the assistants are to perform.

b. Contact lenses received are to be verified for correct parameters.

(Firm and oxygen permeable lenses)

   1. Ascertain power on lensometer

   2. Determine overall size and optical zone diameter from the hand magnifier.

   3. Check for scratches on the surface of the lens.

   4. Base curves should be within three points and center thickness checked.

   5. Lenses are to be checked for correct color and whether the right lens is dotted.

c. The contact lens assistant is to keep track of contact lenses ordered, contact lens inventory, the contact lens file, VIP expirations, damaged soft lenses, warranties and the old vials.

d. Lenses being worn by new patients or former patients need to have the parameters verified at the time of their examination.

e. Polishing and modifications of firm or oxygen permeable lenses when needed.

LAB ASSISTANTS

a. The lab assistant needs to follow this check list for checking a new prescription:

1. Power and Prism — tolerance posted in lab

2. Proper tint

3. Proper segs, heights, segs level

4. Scratches

5. Lenses tight in frame

6. Frame adjusted and in good condition

7. Proper frame and size

b. When lab deliveries are made, the lab assistant should verify prescriptions. She should inform patients if glasses do not arrive on schedule.

c. Call patients when the glasses are ready.

d. When dispensing, the lab assistant needs to adjust the frame, explain possible adaptation expected with the new prescription, clean the lenses, put the patient's name in the temple, select a case, provide tissue lens cleaners for glass lenses, explain the care of the lenses, and make sure the fee balance is paid.

e. Help confirm appointments.

f. Keep track of inventory of cases, repair parts, etc. in lab.

g. Keep track of repairs ordered, frames ordered, prescriptions not being picked up.

OFFICE CLOSING

a. At closing time, the instruments in the lab and examination rooms are to be turned off. All trash should be emptied and rooms put in order. Lights are to be turned off and all instruments are to be checked to be sure they are off.

b. Lock doors and set thermostats to the proper night temperature for the season.

OPHTHALMIC INSTRUMENT PROCEDURES

1. Lensometer — used to verify prescriptions of the glasses and contact lenses.

    a. Place lens in holder, concave surface down. Turn wheel on the right side until green lines start to focus.

    b. Turn the dial on the left side of the instrument until the three thin green lines are clear and straight. Take the reading from the side dial.

    c. Reduce plus by turning the side wheel forward until the three separated lines come into focus. The difference between the first reading and this reading is the amount of cylinder in the lens.

    d. The reading on the left dial gives the axis of the cylinder in the lens.

    e. Axis readings will be from 0 degrees to 180 degrees.

    f. The red numbers on the side wheel are minus and the white numbers are plus.

    g. Complete instructions on using the lensometer will be given to new assistants.

2. Pupillary Distance (P.D.) Scope — measures the distance between the center of the pupils.

    a. Have the patient look down tubes at the black circles.

    b. Take the reading from the reticule directly under the center of the pupil. This is the pupillary distance for the left eye. Push the lever down and take the reading on the right eye.

3. Vision Tester — Used to test different visual function skills of the eye. An instruction booklet is provided with the instrument for complete explanation of procedures.

4. Blood Pressure Reading:

    a. Patient should be in a sitting position. Roll the sleeve up and wrap the cuff above the right elbow.

    b. The cuff is pumped up and the stethoscope pad is placed on the inside of the arm at the elbow. Pressure is applied until a beat is no longer heard. Pressure is slowly released by opening valve on cuff until a beat is present (top reading, systolic). Pressure is then released until a beat is no longer heard (bottom reading, diastolic).

5. Tonometric Testing — a test for glaucoma by measuring the pressure in the eye. This procedure will be demonstrated as it cannot be adequately explained.

6. Visual Fields — this is an auxiliary test which will be demonstrated.

7. Use of laboratory tools for frame adjustments and repair will be demonstrated. Also, books on dispensing and adjustments will be available in the library.

8. Humphrey Lens Analyzer — A computer that checks the lens prescription. Proper use will be demonstrated.

9. CRT — Computer terminal — input station for the computer. At some terminals only certain programs can be used. At the front desk and lab all programs can be used, and only programs one through eleven can be used at other terminals. A procedure manual will explain the programs and functions of the CRT.

Legal Documents For A Partnership

Appendix **B**

A statement was made earlier in this book that a partnership is much like a marriage. This analogy must be carried further to remind professionals that with marriage also goes the possibility of annulment or divorce! The partnership must be structured so as to deal with each of these possibilities if disharmony arises among the partners.

In the documents that follow, you will note a legal method to deal with all of the following situations plus many more as well:

1. What happens if the partners have an unresolvable disagreement? How is the partnership dissolved? (Employment Agreement)

2. How do you dissolve the partnership when one of the partners wants to retire? (Stock Purchase Agreement)

3. How do you determine temporary or permanent disability? (Stock Purchase Agreement)

4. What if one partner justs wants to relocate in another area (not retire) and wants out of the partnership? (Stock Purchase Agreement)

5. What guidelines are set for vacations, sick leave, and educational meetings? (Employment Agreement)

6. How do you determine what the practice is worth? (Contract for Sale and Purchase of Stock and Certificate of Agreed Value)

7. With the death of one of the partners, how does the deceased shareholder's estate get paid for its portion of the practice? (Stock Purchase Agreement)

8. What guarantee is there that money will be available to purchase the deceased shareholder's portion of the practice? (Stock Purchase Agreement)

9. How much of an employee's total compensation can be put in an "Employee Profit Sharing Plan"? Does all money put into the plan immediately belong to him? What circumstances will permit you to draw out contributions made in your name? (Employee Profit Sharing Plan)

The following legal documents are only examples and should be modified in consultation with an attorney to meet the specific situation under consideration.

1. Promissory Note

2. Employment Agreement, Drs. Senior and Junior, Inc.

3. Contract for Sale and Purchase of Stock

4. Certificate of Agreed Value, Drs. Senior and Junior, Inc.

5. Stock Pledge Agreement

6. Stock Purchase Agreement, Drs. Senior and Junior, Inc.

7. Summary Plan Description: Employee Profit Sharing Plan

8. Office Lease Agreement

When entering a partnership agreement, an attorney specializing in professional partnerships needs to be consulted. Each state has different laws which determine how the legal documentation is formulated. The following documents are examples only and are not all inclusive for professional partnerships and corporations.

PROMISSORY NOTE

$ Amount   Date

FOR VALUE RECEIVED, the undersigned, A. Junior, O.D. (herein called "Maker"), promises to pay to the order of A. Senior, O.D. (herein called "Senior"), the principal sum of _____ Dollars ($ _____), payable in twelve equal semi-annual installments, commencing _____ , of $ _____ each, principal sum, together with interest from the date hereof on the unpaid balance at the rate of _____ percent (_____) interest, per annum, payable with each payment of principal installment, and at a rate of _____ percent (_____) per annum after maturity.

The Maker shall have the right after January 1, 19 _____ , to prepay in whole or in part, without penalty, any installment or installments hereof. Any such prepayment shall be applied against the next ensuing installment or installments of principal so as to reduce the amount thereof payable on the due date thereof.

Both principal and interest shall be payable to senior personally or at such place as the holder may from time to time designate in writing delivered to the Maker.

To secure the payment of this Note and the indebtedness evidenced hereby, the Maker has executed a certain Stock Pledge Agreement dated _____ , whereby a security interest is created in one thousand five hundred (1,500) shares of Voting Common Stock of A. Senior, O.D., Inc., a corporation, in favor of senior as the secured party (Pledgee). A breach of the terms and conditions of the Stock Pledge Agreement on the part of the Maker hereof (the Pledgor under the Pledge Agreement) shall constitute a default under this Note and at the option of the holder hereof the entire remaining unpaid balance of the indebtedness hereby may be declared to be immediately due and payable in full.

In the event of a default in the payment of any installment of principal or interest due hereunder or the failure of the undersigned to perform, or a breach of any provisions of this Note, the holder hereof may, at its option, declare the entire remaining unpaid balance of the indebtedness evidenced hereby to be and become immediately due and payable.

The Maker and endorser hereof severally waive demand, protest and nonpayment, and agree that the maturity hereof may be extended from time to time and renewal notes accepted without notice.

Executed on or about _____ to be effective from and after _____ .

———————————————————
A. Junior, O.D.

DRS. SENIOR AND JUNIOR, INC.
EMPLOYMENT AGREEMENT

THIS AGREEMENT, is made and entered into by and between Drs. Senior and Junior, Inc., hereinafter called "CORPORATION", and A. Senior, O.D. and A. Junior, O.D., hereinafter collectivey called "OPTOMETRISTS";

WITNESSETH:

CORPORATION agrees to employ OPTOMETRISTS for the performance of professional services in connection with CORPORATION'S practice of optometry in (City, State), and OPTOMETRISTS agree to accept such employment and to perform such professional services on an exclusive and full-time basis for the CORPORATION, upon the following terms and conditions:

1. **Qualification to Practice Optometry.** OPTOMETRISTS represent that they are duly licensed and otherwise qualified to practice optometry in the State of _____ . OPTOMETRISTS further represent and warrant that while employed under this contract, they will practice the best optometry that they are capable of performing, considering their personal ability, the extent of their professional training and their experience.

2. **Effective Date and Term of this Agreement.** This Employment Agreement shall be deemed effective at _____ a.m., _____ , 19_____ . The term of employment of OPTOMETRISTS is for one year beginning from such effective date. This Agreement and the terms of employment shall continue in force and effect during the year and hereafter on a year-to-year basis, unless sooner modified or terminated by either party hereto as hereinafter provided.

3. **Termination by Notice.** Notwithstanding that the term of employment is for one year, either CORPORATION or OPTOMETRISTS may terminate this Agreement at any time by giving to the other party not less than ninety (90) days prior written notice of effective date of such termination. OPTOMETRISTS shall be entitled to their regular compensation to the date of termination. From and after the effective date of termination, neither party shall accrue any further rights or obligations under this Employment Agreement.

4. **Termination by Death of OPTOMETRIST.** If either OPTOMETRIST, or both, should die during the existence of this Agreement or any successor agreements, the CORPORATION shall pay their widows, or if none, their Estates, the full compensation that is owed to them under Agreement as of through the end of the month in which the death occurred. Upon completion of such payment, the CORPORATION shall have no further obligation to said OPTOMETRISTS, their widows, Estates or heirs, under this Employment Agreement.

5. **Compensation.**

(a) CORPORATION shall pay each OPTOMETRIST reasonable compensation for his services. It is contemplated that during the existence of this contract, between OPTOMETRIST and CORPORATION, all its income, after paying all reasonable and necessary expenses, will be insufficient for the CORPORATION to retain any significant income or surplus. Therefore, each OPTOMETRIST agrees to take as his compensation for his services, a percentage of net income of the CORPORATION which is set opposite his name:

DR. JUNIOR: From _____ , ___ % net income of the CORPORATION after paying all ordinary and necessary expenses of the CORPORATION **but** such annual compensation shall be reduced by the amount of $2,000.00, which shall be retained by the CORPORATION.

DR. SENIOR: From _____ , ___ % net income of CORPORATION after paying all ordinary and necessary expenses of the CORPORATION **but** such annual compensation shall be reduced by the amount of $2,000.00, which shall be retained by the CORPORATION.

(b) It is agreed by the parties hereto that the percentage of net income to be paid to each OPTOMETRIST as annual compensation for his services shall be based upon the following schedule of percentage: (Percentages listed below are only examples)

Year	Dr. Junior	Dr. Senior
19 _____	30%	70%
19 _____	30%	70%
19 _____	35%	65%
19 _____	35%	65%
19 _____	40%	60%
19 _____	45%	55%
19 _____	50%	50%

Said percentages represent the percentage of net income to be paid by the CORPORATION to each OPTOMETRIST on an annual basis after paying all ordinary and necessary expenses of the CORPORATION **but** such annual compensation shall be reduced by the amount of $2,000.00, which shall be retained by the CORPORATION.

(c) As used herein, the term "net income" means the taxable net income of CORPORATION, determined on a cash basis in accordance with generally accepted accounting procedures, after deducting for any contribution made to any Employee Deferred Compensation Plan, if any, but before the payment of any compensation to the OPTOMETRISTS and before the payment of any corporate income taxes.

(d) Each OPTOMETRIST may, during each calendar month that he is employed by the CORPORATION, be paid a monthly salary as an advance against his compensation under this Agreement.

Such advances shall be deducted from the compensation otherwise payable to each OPTOMETRIST and shall be subject to required withholding FICA taxes. Each OPTOMETRIST has an absolute right to the above sums, monthly, without regard to earnings of the CORPORATION.

(e) The payments of compensation under this contract shall be made not less frequently than quarterly, provided more frequent payments may be made with the approval of both OPTOMETRISTS.

6. **Annual Accounting Review.** Within not more than ninety (90) days after the end of a taxable reporting year of the CORPORATION, there shall be an annual accounting review completed which shall establish the amount to be paid each OPTOMETRIST under Paragraph 4 hereof. Any adjustments in payments made to OPTOMETRISTS for the preceding year shall be made within (30) days after delivery to all OPTOMETRISTS of copies of the review. Unless written objections to the review are delivered to the CORPORATION within thirty (30) days after its delivery to all OPTOMETRISTS, the annual review shall be deemed finally accepted and binding on all parties hereto. A written objection made by an OPTOMETRIST to the review shall be resolved by unanimous action of all other OPTOMETRISTS who are parties to this Agreement, which decision shall be binding and final. If a unanimous decision cannot be reached, the OPTOMETRISTS hereby agree that the dispute or matter shall be submitted to and settled by arbitration. Notwithstanding the above provisions, if no review is undertaken within ninety (90) days after the close of the taxable year of the CORPORATION, each OPTOMETRIST shall be deemed to have accepted his compensation as it was paid to him as being in accordance with this Agreement.

7. **Vacation and Sick Leave.** Each OPTOMETRIST shall be entitled, during the year of employment, up to _____ (_____) days of vacation time and to an additional _____ (_____) days sick leave time without loss of compensation. Time spent on temporary active military duty shall be counted as vacation time. During an OPTOMETRIST'S first year of employment relationship, any time off to attend professional meetings taken by said OPTOMETRIST shall be counted as vacation time, except for _____ (_____) days spent attending the State of _____ annual convention, which shall not count under the limitation of this paragraph. If either OPTOMETRIST should

take excess vacation or sick leave time, it shall result in his compensation being reduced on a day-by-day basis, using a formula of _____ (_____) working days to a month. If either OPTOMETRIST'S employment is terminated during the employment term, he shall not be entitled to receive or to be compensated for any unused vacation or sick leave time.

8. **Representations and Warrants.** The CORPORATION represents and warrants to OPTOMETRISTS that during the employment period: (1) OPTOMETRISTS shall receive other fringe benefits normal to this type of employment, considering the practices of other similar types of employers, and the standard of the trade area of the CORPORATION, (2) the CORPORATION will provide and pay for malpractice insurance protection on OPTOMETRISTS, for their benefit and for the benefit of the CORPORATION, (3) the CORPORATION, at its expense, will furnish office space and all necessary equipment, supplies and medicines to permit OPTOMETRISTS to carry out the duties of their employment and shall pay all national, state and county optometric association dues of the OPTOMETRISTS, (4) the CORPORATION annually will pay for each OPTOMETRIST, the actual expense of the registration at one professional seminar approved for the employee to attend and the round trip expense of a commercial airline ticket to the place of the meeting. All other expenses of the meeting will be borne by the OPTOMETRIST personally as a condition of employment imposed on him by the CORPORATION. In connection with the above, the CORPORATION will establish and pay for a health insurance program and a medical benefit reimbursement plan for the benefit of the OPTOMETRISTS and their lawful dependents, and a profit sharing plan with funding for the OPTOMETRISTS and other employees at the level of fifteen percent (15%) of basic compensation.

9. **Announcements, Professional Records.** All patients treated by OPTOMETRISTS during their employment with the CORPORATION shall be treated and recognized to be the CORPORATION'S patients. All patient records on patients treated by OPTOMETRISTS shall be the property of the CORPORATION.

10. **Automobile.** Each OPTOMETRIST shall furnish and use his own automobile as may be required in connection with his employment but shall be reimbursed by the CORPORATION for all operating expenses and repairs that do not exceed _____ .

11. **Binding on Assigns.** This Agreement shall be binding upon the parties hereto, their heirs, successors, executors, trustees, administrators and assigns.

12. **Alterations.** The Employment Agreement shall remain in full force and effect without change, except a change which is reduced to writing and signed by the parties including both employees. However, Paragraph 5 of the Employment Agreement may be altered by the parties by action taken at general meetings of the directors in which amending action is taken and specifically referred to as such.

IN WITNESS WHEREOF, the CORPORATION and OPTOMETRISTS have executed this Agreement on _____ to be effective from and after _____ .

CORPORATION:

(SEAL)

ATTEST:

_____
A. Junior, O.D., Secretary

OPTOMETRISTS:

DRS. Senior and Junior, Inc.

an _____ corporation

By _____
A. Senior, O.D., President

_____
A. Senior, O.D.

_____
A. Junior, O.D.

CONTRACT FOR SALE AND
PURCHASE OF STOCK

THIS AGREEMENT, made and entered into by and between A. Senior, O.D., hereinafter called SELLER, and A. Junior, O.D., hereinafter called PURCHASER:

WITNESSETH:

For and in consideration of the mutual covenants and promises herein made and exchanged, the parties hereto agree as follows:

1. **Sale of Stock.**

(a) A. Senior, O.D. will sell and deliver to A. Junior, O.D., and A. Junior, O.D., will pay and purchase from A. Senior, O.D., one thousand five hundred shares (1,500) of the Voting Common Stock of A. Senior, O.D., Inc., a (State) corporation. The total price to be paid for such shares of stock is _____ Thousand Dollars ($_____), which shall be paid in accordance with the provisions of Paragraph 2 below:

2. **Payment of Purchase Price.** PURCHASER shall pay the total purchase price owed to the SELLER in accordance with the following schedule of principal payments:

1. $ _____ on July 1, 19 _____   7. $ _____ on July 1, 19 _____
2. $ _____ on January 1, 19 _____   8. $ _____ on January 1, 19 _____
3. $ _____ on July 1, 19 _____   9. $ _____ on July 1, 19 _____
4. $ _____ on January 1, 19 _____   10. $ _____ on January 1, 19 _____
5. $ _____ on July 1, 19 _____   11. $ _____ on July 1, 19 _____
6. $ _____ on January 1, 19 _____   12. $ _____ on January 1, 19 _____

with simple interest payments commencing from the date hereof with each principal payment of _____ percent (_____ %) per annum on the unpaid balance. PURCHASER shall have the right after January 1, 19 _____ , to prepay any part or all of the purchase price to SELLER without penalty.

3. **Default.** If the PURCHASER fails to make any payment of principal or interest in accordance with the schedule of payments set forth in the above numbered Paragraph 2 hereof, or if the PURCHASER dies or terminates his association with the CORPORATION as a full-time professional employee, for any reason, or does any act which subjects the shares of the Common Stock of the CORPORATION being purchased herein to be subject to being purchased by the CORPORATION or any other shareholder under the terms of a Stock Purchase Agreement in effect at any time hereafter between the CORPORATION and the PURCHASER, SELLER may, at his option, declare and accelerate all remaining sums due and payable on any note given by the PURCHASER to the SELLER in connection with the purchase of stock pursuant to his Contract to become due and payable immediately in full and the same shall bear interest thereafter at the rate of _____ percent (_____ %) per annum, until paid in full, and enforce his security interest in the one thousand five hundred (1,500) shares of Voting Common Stock pledged in a certain Stock Pledge Agreement executed herewith by the parties hereto.

4. **Transfer of Stock.** At the time of the closing, SELLER shall execute and deliver all necessary stock certificates, assignments of the original stock certificate and do such other acts or actions reasonably required for accomplishing a complete transfer of the stock of the CORPORATION to the PURCHASER in compliance with the intent of this Agreement and a certain Stock Pledge Agreement executed herewith. The PURCHASER hereunder shall at the same time execute a promissory note for the purchase of the stock and do any and all such other acts or actions that may be reasonably required in order to further the intentions of this Contract. PURCHASER further covenants to execute and deliver all shares acquired under this Contract (1,500) to be held pursuant to the terms of a separate Stock Pledge Agreement as collateral for this contractual obligation, with such shares to be released from the pledge and returned to the PURCHASER, when his obligations under this Contract are performed in full.

5. **Stock Purchase Agreement.** The PURCHASER agrees and understands that the stock was subject to a Stock Purchase Agreement, originally dated _____ , 19 _____ , which is to be replaced by a successor Stock Purchase Agreement executed between the PURCHASER and SELLER and dated _____ , 19 _____ . Said successor Stock Purchase Agreement or any agreed successors thereto shall remain in force and effect for so long as the PURCHASER and the SELLER are stockholders in the CORPORATION.

6. **Binding on Assigns.** This Agreement shall be binding upon the parties hereto, their heirs, successors, executors, administrators and assigns. The Contract further contains the entire agreement between the parties and any executory agreement hereafter made shall be ineffective to change, waive, modify, discharge or terminate this Contract unless such executory agreement is in writing and signed by the party against whom enforcement is sought.

IN WITNESS WHEREOF, the undersigned have executed this Agreement on or about _____ to be effective from and after

_____ .

CORPORATION: *A. Senior, O.D., Inc.*

                            By _____
                            A. Senior, O.D., President

(SEAL)

ATTEST:

_____
Mrs. Senior, Secretary

SELLER: _____
                            A. Senior, O.D.

PURCHASER: _____
                            A. Junior, O.D.

CERTIFICATE OF AGREED VALUE
DRS. SENIOR AND JUNIOR, INC.

The undersigned, pursuant to the provisions of paragraph 10 of a Certain Stock Purchase Agreement, having an effective date of _____ , do hereby agree and specify for all purposes of said Purchase Agreement, that the value of all the issued and outstanding shares of capital stock of Drs. Senior and Junior, Inc., is as follows:

(a) In the event of a death of a shareholder while this Certificate is in effect, the book value of all of such capital stock is $ _____ , and the book value for the shares of the deceased shareholder shall be determined by prorating this total value to all of the issued and outstanding shares; and,

(b) For all purposes of the Stock Purchase Agreement, other than when the death of a shareholder occurs, while this Certificate is in effect, the book value of all such capital stock is $ _____ , and the book value for the shares held by each shareholder shall be determined by prorating this total value to all of the issued and outstanding shares.

The value is signed, to be effective from _____ , and for a period of _____ (_____) months, or until it is sooner amended or modified, by the unanimous action of the undersigned.

CORPORATION:

Drs. Senior and Junior, Inc.

By _____
A. Senior, O.D., President

(SEAL)

ATTEST

_____
A. Junior, O.D., Secretary

_____
A. Senior, O.D.

_____
A. Junior, O.D.

STOCK PLEDGE AGREEMENT

THIS AGREEMENT, made and entered into by and between A. Junior, O.D., PLEDGOR; A. Senior, O.D., PLEDGEE; and A.N. Attorney, Inc., ESCROWEE;

W I T N E S S E T H :

Recitation. PLEDGEE has sold to PLEDGOR One Thousand Five Hundred (1,500) shares of Voting Common Stock of A. Senior, O.D., Inc., a (State) corporation, under the terms and provisions of a "Contract for Sale and Purchase of Stock", dated _____ , 19 _____ , and have evidenced the obligation created thereby a certain Promissory Note dated the same date, in the principal amount of _____ . It is the intent of these parties to further secure the performance of the Contract and said Promissory Note and to this end, the shares of stock of the PLEDGOR have been directly issued in the name of the PLEDGOR and delivered, and PLEDGOR in turn has executed an assignment of such shares separate from certificate and delivered such shares and the assignment to the ESCROWEE.

Warranties. PLEDGOR now further warrants to PLEDGEE, and agrees:

(1) That he owns said shares free and clear of any claim adverse to the interest of the PLEDGEE. That by this Agreement, PLEDGOR creates a security interest in said shares in favor of the PLEDGEE. That if any breach by the PLEDGOR occurs in the Contract for Sale and Purchase of said Stock, dated _____ , 19 _____ , or in the said Promissory Note dated the same date referred to above, the PLEDGEE, without notice may declare all obligations of the PLEDGOR under said Contract and Promissory Note due and payable and may enforce his security interest in the actual shares of stock pledged hereunder, in any legal manner, including, but not limited to selling all or any part of said pledged stock at public or private sale, with or without advertising or notice, and the PLEDGEE shall be eligible to bid on or purchase such stock or any part thereof without limitation or restriction. PLEDGOR further expressly waives the right to receive notice of demand of performance from the PLEDGEE and waives the right to receive notice of sale of stock, if PLEDGOR materially breaches the covenants of said Contract for the purchase of stock or the covenants of the Promissory Note referred to above.

(2) If a sale of the stock occurs under this Pledge Agreement, then the net proceeds derived therefrom, after paying all reasonable costs incurred in connection with the sale, shall be applied against the contractual indebtedness of the PLEDGOR and thereafter any excess shall be paid to the PLEDGOR.

Delivery to Escrowee. The PLEDGOR and PLEDGEE mutually agree that the Certificate for the Stock of the PLEDGOR covered by this Pledge Agreement shall be delivered to ESCROWEE for safekeeping, and in order to perfect the PLEDGEE'S security interest in said shares of stock. If a breach of either the original Contract for the Sale and Purchase of said Stock or in the Promissory Note referred to above, or both, occurs, upon demand by the PLEDGEE, such shares shall be delivered by the ESCROWEE to the PLEDGEE. If PLEDGOR fully performs in accordance with the Contract and the terms of the Promissory Note, upon the demand of the PLEDGOR at the expiration of the contractual term and after payment in full of all principal and interest due under the Promissory Note, the stock shall be delivered by the ESCROWEE to the PLEDGOR, free of the provisions of this Pledge Agreement.

Voting Rights. PLEDGOR retains all right to vote the stock of the Corporation while it is subject to this Pledge Agreement. All dividends or other benefits arising out of the ownership of such stock shall be paid and delivered to the PLEDGOR unless previously thereto there has been a material breach of the Pledge Agreement by the PLEDGOR.

Separability. If any provision of this Agreement is invalid or unenforceable, it shall not destroy the validity or enforceability of the remaining provisions of this Agreement.

Attorney's Fees: If any party hereto breaches this Agreement, the injured party shall be entitled to receive the damages provided by law, plus a reasonable attorney's fee, court costs and all other costs directly incurred.

Binding on Assigns. The obligations of the PLEDGOR shall be binding, and the benefits to the PLEDGEE shall inure to the benefit of their respective heirs, executors, administrators, trustees, guardians, successors and assigns.

Notification to ESCROWEE. The ESCROWEE does hereby acknowledge that upon execution of this document he has received notification of the PLEDGEE'S security interest in the shares of stock pledged herein and holds such as a bailee under _____ of the State Uniform Commercial Code by which the PLEDGEE, as the secured party, is deemed to take possession of said instrument for perfection.

IN WITNESS WHEREOF, the undersigned have executed this Agreement on or about _____ to be effective from and after _____ .

.

PLEDGOR: _____
                            A. Junior, O.D.

PLEDGEE: _____
                            A. Senior, O.D.

ESCROWEE: _____
                            A.N. Attorney, Inc.

STOCK PURCHASE AGREEMENT
DRS. SENIOR AND JUNIOR, INC.

THIS AGREEMENT, made and entered into by and between Drs. Senior and Junior, Inc., as a (State) corporation, organized under the (State) Professional Corporation Act, hereinafter called "OPTOMETRY CORPORATION", and A. Senior, O.D. and A. Junior, O.D., hereinafter called "SHAREHOLDERS";

W I T N E S S E T H :

In consideration of the mutual covenants herein contained, the OPTOMETRY CORPORATION and SHAREHOLDERS agree as follows:

1. **Restrictions on Transfer.** The pledge, encumbrance, transfer, sale, transfer by operation of law, or any other disposition of the stock of the OPTOMETRY CORPORATION, is hereby limited and restricted to the manner and methods hereinafter set forth, and by the terms of the (State) Professional Corporation Act. SHAREHOLDERS agree that there shall be endorsed on all certificates evidencing such stock, not outstanding, and all such certificates as may be issued in the future, notice of the above stated restricton by the following statement:

"The pledge, encumbrance, transfer, sale, assignment, or any other disposition of the share(s) of stock evidenced by this certificate is restricted and controlled by the terms of a certain **Stock Purchase Agreement** dated _____ , which, with any subsequent amendment(s), if any, is on file with the issuer of these securities and by this reference is incorporated herein. Any assignment, transfer, etc., of the shares of stock evidenced by this certificate can become effective, only after first complying with the provisions of said **Stock Purchase Agreement,** as amended."

2. **Option to OPTOMETRY CORPORATION.** One of the shares of the stock of the OPTOMETRY CORPORATION, owned by the parties hereto, shall be sold, assigned, transferred, given away, pledged, or in any manner disposed of, or in any manner transferred on the books of the OPTOMETRY CORPORATION from the name of the party now owning such stock, including, but not limited to, transfers by operation of law, without first notifying in writing the OPTOMETRY CORPORATION, stating the number of shares of stock proposed to be sold, assigned, transferred, given away,pledged, or otherwise disposed of, provided, that in the event of a proposed sale, assignment, pledge, gift or other disposition, the said notice shall state the name of the proposed purchaser, assignee, pledgee, donee, transferree, and, for a period of sixty (60) days following the receipt of such notice, the OPTOMETRY CORPORATION shall have an option to purchase such shares, or any of them, at the then book value of such shares. The amount of such purchase price shall be paid in three (3) equal annual installments, with the first installment to be paid within ninety (90) days following the exercise of its option by the OPTOMETRY CORPORATION. No interest shall be owed unless payment of an installment becomes delinquent, then interest at the rate of ten percent (10%) per annum shall be owed until the delinquent installment and interest are fully paid. The OPTOMETRY CORPORATION may pay any part or all of the purchase price for stock so acquired ahead of what otherwise would be the normal due date for payment. The sale, assignment, transfer, gift or other disposition by any manner whatever to any person who is not duly licensed to practice optometry by the State Board of Optometry of the State of _____ is strictly prohibited, and no provision of this Agreement shall be construed and interpreted as permitting the ownership of any stock of OPTOMETRY CORPORATION by any person not so licensed.

3. **Purchase on Death.** Upon the death of any SHAREHOLDER, the OPTOMETRY CORPORATION does hereby agree to purchase and SHAREHOLDERS, for themselves, their executors and administrators, do hereby agree to sell all of the stock of the OPTOMETRY CORPORATION then owned by the deceased SHAREHOLDER at a price equal to the book value of such shares. In the event that such purchase price shall exceed the amount of net proceeds of any life insurance owned by the OPTOMETRY CORPORATION upon the life of the deceased SHAREHOLDER which is then in effect and not encumbered by loans or prior

commitments, the net amount of the insurance proceeds received by the OPTOMETRY CORPORATION shall be paid to the estate of the deceased SHAREHOLDER within ten (10) days after its receipt, and the balance of such purchase price shall be paid by the OPTOMETRY CORPORATION to such estate, or the distributees of the deceased SHAREHOLDER in three (3) equal annual installments without interest, with payment to be made in the manner as provided in paragraph 2 hereof. The payment, however, shall be computed only on the excess, if any, of the book value of such stock at the date of death over the amount of insurance proceeds paid. If the amount of insurance proceeds paid exceeds the book value of the stock, the OPTOMETRY CORPORATION shall have no further obligation for any payment and shall be entitled to have the stock of the deceased SHAREHOLDER assigned and delivered back to it.

4. **Purchase — Permanent Disability.** If a party to this Agreement becomes permanently disabled, so that in the opinion of competent medical authority satisfactory to all other parties hereto, it is very improbable that the party so permanently disabled will ever be able to practice again, the OPTOMETRY CORPORATION does hereby agree to purchase and SHAREHOLDERS, for themselves, their executors, guardians, conservators, administrators and heirs, do hereby agree to sell all of the stock of the OPTOMETRY CORPORATION then owned by such permanently disabled SHAREHOLDER at a price equal to the book value of such shares. The other parties to this Agreement shall determine whether such a party is permanently disabled and the decision thereof shall be final and binding and not otherwise subject to review. The time, method and manner for payment for such stock shall be the same as provided for in paragraph 2 hereof.

5. **Purchase — Voluntary Withdrawal.** If a party to this Agreement voluntarily withdraws from employment with the OPTOMETRY CORPORATION then the OPTOMETRY CORPORATION does hereby agree to purchase and SHAREHOLDERS, for themselves, their executors, administrators and heirs, do hereby agree to sell all of the stock of the OPTOMETRY CORPORATION then owned by such withdrawing SHAREHOLDER at a price equal to one-half (1/2) of the book value of such shares. The time, method and manner for payment for such stock shall be the same as provided in paragraph 2 hereof.

6. **Option to Purchase — Involuntary Military Service.** If a party to this Agreement is involuntarily called to active duty with an armed service branch of the United States or of a State, or if a party hereto enlists in such a branch of the armed forces to avoid being drafted and there is a clear and definite danger of being drafted, then the SHAREHOLDERS hereof, give, grant and transfer to the OPTOMETRY CORPORATION, for themselves, their executors, administrators and heirs, continuing option under which the OPTOMETRY CORPORATION at any time during the involuntary military service, may repurchase the stock of such a SHAREHOLDER and if the OPTOMETRY CORPORATION exercises its continuing option then the SHAREHOLDER, his heirs and executors agree to cause all the stock of the OPTOMETRY CORPORATION then owned by such SHAREHOLDER to be assigned and delivered back to the OPTOMETRY CORPORATION. The price to be paid for such stock shall be the book value as determined on the last calendar day of the month preceding the exercise by the OPTOMETRY CORPORATION of its option to purchase said stock. The time, method and manner for payment for such stock shall be the same as provided for in paragraph 2 hereof.

7. **Book Value.** The term "book value" wherever used herein shall be defined to mean that portion of the excess of the tangible assets of the OPTOMETRY CORPORATION over the liabilities according to its records and books of account represented by such shares in proportion to the total number of shares outstanding with no allowances to be made for going concern value, or any similar intangible assets except goodwill, provided however, that for the purposes of this Agreement, cash on hand, cash deposited in any bank or banking institutions, and shares of capital stock in any other corporation, which are issued in the name of the OPTOMETRY CORPORATION, accounts receivable owned by OPTOMETRY CORPORATION shall be regarded as tangible assets for the purpose of arriving at book value

and provided further, that any and all real property, including buildings and improvements thereon, shall be valued at their then fair market value without regard to their valuation appearing upon the books of the OPTOMETRY CORPORATION. Real Estate leases and equipment leases in which the OPTOMETRY CORPORATION is named Lessee shall not be treated as either a tangible asset or as a liability in computing "book value". The total value of the goodwill of the CORPORATION shall not exceed the sum of _____ . Unless another method is unanimously agreed to in valuing accounts receivable, all accounts over one hundred twenty (120) days old shall be excluded and the value of the remaining accounts shall be fixed at a sum not to exceed ninety percent (90%) of the face thereof. The book value paid by the OPTOMETRY CORPORATION is the book value on the last day of the calendar month immediately preceding the month in which the need to value the stock of OPTOMETRY CORPORATION occurs. No greater valuation is given to such accounts because recognition of these values have been made in the separate Employment Agreement. In case there is any disagreement as to the price at which this OPTOMETRY CORPORATION shall purchase such shares, the matter shall be resolved by arbitration of three arbitrators appointed in accordance with the rules of the American Arbitration Association.

8. **Certificate of Agreed Value.** The foregoing to the contrary notwithstanding, the SHAREHOLDERS may at any time fix the book value of the stock of the OPTOMETRY CORPORATION by a certificate setting forth an agreed value, signed by all of the SHAREHOLDERS and filed with the OPTOMETRY CORPORATION. If at any time,when it becomes necessary to determine the book value of the stock of the OPTOMETRY CORPORATION for the purposes of this Agreement, a Certificate of Agreed Value is filed with the OPTOMETRY CORPORATION which is dated less than eighteen (18) months prior to the date the book value is to be determined, the agreed value set forth in such Certificate shall be conclusive as the book value and shall be accepted as the book value as of the date on which the book value is to be determined. In such event, no appraisal or accountant's determination of the book value shall be required or made, provided, that in no event shall a Certificate of Agreed Value be effective unless signed by all of the SHAREHOLDERS within eighteen (18) months prior to the date as of which the book value is to be determined. The SHAREHOLDERS may at any time execute a new Certificate of Agreed Value in the manner hereinbefore provided. Upon filing the same with the OPTOMETRY CORPORATION, it shall replace all prior Certificates of Agreed Value and in no event shall any but the last Certificate of Agreed Value be effective, if at all, for the purpose herein specified.

9. **Instruments of Transfer.** If, under the terms of this Stock Purchase Agreement, the stock of any SHAREHOLDER is purchased or retired in accordance with the provisions of this Agreement, such selling SHAREHOLDER or the legal representative thereof shall execute and deliver all necessary Stock Certificates and other documents that may be reasonably required for accomplishing a complete transfer of such stock for the purpose of the purchase or retirement transaction.

10. **Option to Purchase Life Insurance Policy.** If this Agreement is terminated as to any SHAREHOLDER during his lifetime, such SHAREHOLDER shall have the right, within thirty (30) days thereafter, to purchase any and all policies of life insurance issued to the OPTOMETRY CORPORATION upon his life, upon paying to the OPTOMETRY CORPORATION an amount equal to the cash surrender value thereof, as of the date of purchase of such SHAREHOLDER. Such purchase shall be subject to such collateral assignments or pledge as may be then in existence against such policies.

11. **Notice.** Whenever, under this Stock Purchase Agreement notice is required to be given, it shall be given in writing by registered mail and shall be deemed to have been given on the date such notice is posted, with postage prepaid, addressed to the last address of the addressee, according to the records of the OPTOMETRY CORPORATION.

12. **Binding on Assigns.** This Agreement shall be binding upon the parties hereto, their heirs, successors, assigns, executors, administrators and is also binding upon any person to

whom any of the stock of any of the SHAREHOLDERS is transferred in violation of, or contrary to any of the provisions of this Agreement, and the executor or administrator of any such person.

IN WITNESS WHEREOF, the parties hereto have caused this Agreement to be executed to be fully binding upon the individuals and upon such CORPORATION and to be effective from and after 12:01 a.m., _____ .

Dated this _____ day of _____ , 19 _____ .

SHAREHOLDER: _____
                                      A. Senior, O.D.

                                      _____
                                      A. Junior, O.D.

OPTOMETRY CORPORATION: _____
                                      Drs. Senior and Junior, Inc.

                                      By: _____
                                          A. Senior, O.D., President

(SEAL)

ATTEST:

_____
A. Junior, O.D., Secretary

SUMMARY PLAN DESCRIPTION:
EMPLOYEE PROFIT SHARING PLAN

1. **Eligibility for Participation and Benefits.** All employees are eligible to participate in the plan on the entry date coinciding with or next following employment by the employer. Persons covered by collective bargaining agreements and those who are non-resident aliens who receive no earned income from sources within the United States are ineligible to participate.

The vesting schedule for this Plan which would be applicable in determining that part of a participant's account balance which belongs to him in the event he terminates service with the Employer, voluntarily or involuntarily, for any reason other than death, retirement or disability is:

Total "Years of Service"	Applicable Percentage
0-1	0%
1	50%
2	60%
3	70%
4	80%
5	90%
6	100%

A "Year of Service" is defined in the Plan as being a Plan Year in which a participant receives credit for 1000 "hours of service". "Hours of Service" are defined in detail in the Plan but generously represent hours for which compensation is received by the participant.

Normal retirement age is defined as being the 65th birthdate of the participant.

The benefit available on retirement is that which can be provided with the funds in the individual participant's account. An individual's account is composed of his share of the company contribution, earnings on his account and that part of other participants accounts who leave before they are fully vested.

Company contributions and forfeitures are allocated on the following basis:

1) First, all participants whose salary exeeds $ _____ receive an allocation to his account equal to _____ % of basic compensation (regular wages, not including overtime and bonuses) over $ _____ . If there are not sufficient funds to make said contribution in full to all participants the allocations to each participant are reduced proportionally.

2) Then all participants, regardless of salary, receive an allocation of any remaining funds in the proporation that a participant's compensation bears to the total of all participant's compensation.

Earnings are allocated to individual participants in the same ratio that an individual's account balance bears to the total account balances of all participants.

If a participant dies while he is employed and participating in the plan, his account will fully vest. His designated beneficiary will receive all funds in his account regardless of the number of years of service he has to his credit. Likewise, a participant who becomes disabled while employed and participating in the Plan shall receive credit for his entire account balance regardless of the number of years of service he has completed.

"Disability" is a certification by a medical examiner that:

(1) A participant has become permanently disabled by bodily injury or disease so as to be completely prevented thereby from engaging in any useful occupation or employment for remuneration or profit, and

(2) That such condition of complete disability has continued for a period of twelve consecutive months, and will thereafter continue continuously during the remainder of the participant's normal lifetime.

Death, disability and retirement benefits shall be payable as soon after the event as determination of the following can be made: the amount in a participant's individual account, how payment is to be made, and to whom payment is to be made. When an employee enters the plan he will complete a written Beneficiary Designation Form which will determine to whom his benefits are to be paid in the event of his death. This designation can be changed at any time.

If a participant's employment is interrupted, he has what is referred to as a "break in service". A break in service is a Plan Year in which a participant receives credit for less than 500 hours of service. If a participant has a break in service, the vesting of his benefits will be determined according to the above vesting schedule. Generally, benefits because of termination will be paid within 60 days after the end of the Plan Year in which a participant's break in service occurs. If a participant receives credit for more than 500 hours of service but less than 1000 hours of service or has an approved leave of absence he will continue to participate in the Plan but will not receive vesting credit for those years.

Unless a participant submits a written request to the Plan Administrator stating the benefit and date on which payment is to commence, payment of his benefits must start not later than 60 days after the end of the Plan Year in which occurs the latest of:

a) Age 65;
b) 10 years participation in the plan;
c) termination of participant's service with Employer.

Benefits under the Plan are paid in one of the following ways:

(1) Lump sum;
(2) Placed in bank savings account and paid in equal installments, at least annually, extending over not more than 10 years, however, the period of payment cannot exceed the actual life expectancy of the participant.
(3) By the purchase of an insurance or annuity contract.
    I. **Life Annuity.** Substantially equal monthly installments (with variable installments permitted under a variable annuity) payable directly to the participant during his lifetime only.
    II. **Ten Years Certain.** Substantially equal monthly installments (with variable installments permitted under a variable annuity) payable directly to the participant during his lifetime only, with a minimum of one hundred twenty (120) payments guaranteed.
    III. **Cash Refund Annuity.** Substantially equal monthly installments (with variable installments permitted under a variable annuity) payable directly to the participant during his lifetime only, with a lump sum payment at death to his designated beneficiary if the aggregate payments thereto received are less than the commuted value of his annuity immediately before the first annuity payment.

If a participant is married at the close of the Plan year in which he becomes eligible to receive benefits, he can have a qualified joint and survivor annuity. A "qualified joint and survivor annuity" shall mean an annuity for the life of the participant with a survivor annuity, annuity for the life of his spouse which is not less than one-half, or greater than the amount of the annuity payable during the joint lives of the participant and his spouse, and which is the acturial equivalent of a single life annuity for the life of a participant. A participant is entitled to receive a written explanation of the terms and conditions of the joint and survivor annuity, and if he requests, the effect in dollar amounts per annuity payment of such election. After receiving the written explanation, the participant will have a reasonable period of time before the starting date of the annuity to elect a different option of payment if he desires. The election must be in writing and mailed to the Plan Administrator.

2. **Loss of Benefits.** As long as one is a full-time employee who is eligible to participate in the Plan or a retired employee or beneficiary who is eligible to receive benefits under the Plan, one may not be disqualified, declared ineligible, or be denied or lose benefits. A participant may lose some of his benefits if he leaves the Company before his account is fully vested. A participant may also lose benefits if he has allocated to his account more than is allowed by law.

A participant cannot have allocated in any one year to his benefit under all profit sharing and pension plans of the Employer more than 25% of his basic compensation or $ _____ , whichever is less.

The Employer retains the right to terminate the Plan at anytime. The Employer also retains the right to determine the amount of contribution to be made to the Plan each year.

3. **Insurance.** Benefits under the Plan are not insured by the Pension Benefit Guaranty Corporaton (PBGC). The law does not require nor provide PBGC with the duty to insure the benefits of this profit sharing plan.

4. **Contributions.** Employer contributions to the Plan are determined by the Board of Directors of the Company. The amounts vary from year to year. No contribution can be made unless the Company has a profit at the year end or unless the Company has accumulated earnings over the past year's operation.

Employees are not required to make contributions to the plan. Employees can contribute a total of up to 10% of their compensation from the Company to all the profit sharing and pension plans of the Company per year. Contributions by the employees are fully vested at all times.

The funds contributed to the plan are held and administered by the Trustee under a Trust Indenture. This Instrument details the power and authority, duties and responsibilites of the Trustee.

5. **Claims.** A claim for benefit is to be submitted in writing to the Plan Administrator whenever an event causing benefits to become payable occurs. The claim should state the event causing payment to be due, the method of payment preferred if more than one method is available. If the Plan Administrator approves the claim, it will be sent to the Trustee for payment.

If the Plan Administrator does not approve the claim, the claimant will be notified within 60 days. Within 60 days of receipt of a denial, the claimant may request review of the decision by the full Committee of Supervisors. In connection with such review, the claimant or his representative, upon reasonable request, may review any pertinent documents. The Committee of Supervisors will then issue its decision.

6. **ERISA Rights.** A Participant is entitled to the following statement of ERISA rights by Federal law and regulations:

As a participant in this Employee Profit Sharing Retirement Plan you are entitled to certain rights and protections under the Employee Retirement Income Security Act of 1974 (ERISA). ERISA provides that all plan participants shall be entitled to:

Examine, without charge, at the plan administrator's office all plan documents, including insurance contracts, and copies of all documents filed by the plan with the U.S. Department of Labor, such as detailed annual reports and plan descriptions.

Obtain copies of all plan documents and other plan information upon written request to the plan administrator. The administrator may make a reasonable charge for the copies.

Receive a summary of the plan's annual financial report. The plan administrator is required by law to furnish each participant with a copy of this summary annual report.

Obtain a statement telling you whether you have right to receive a pension at normal retirement age (age 65) and if so, what your benefits would be at normal retirement age if you stop working under the plan now. If you do not have a right to have pension, the statement will tell you how many more years you have to work to get a pension. This statement must be requested in writing and is not required to be given more than once a year. The plan must provide the statement free of charge.

In addition to creating the rights for plan participants, ERISA imposes duties upon the people who are responsible for the operation of the employee benefit plan. The people who operate your plan, called "fiduciaries" of the plan, have a duty to do so prudently and in the interest of you and other plan participants and beneficiaries. No one, including your employer, or any other person may fire you or otherwise discriminate against you in any way to prevent you from obtaining a pension benefit or exercising your rights under ERISA. If your claim for a pension benefit is denied in whole or in part, you must receive a written explanation of the reason for the denial. You have the right to have the plan reviewed and reconsider your claim. Under ERISA, there are steps you can take to enforce the above rights. For instance, if you request materials from the plan and do not receive them within 30 days, you may file suit in a federal court. In such a case, the court may require the plan administrator to provide the materials and pay you up to $100 a day until you receive the materials, unless the materials were not sent because of reasons beyond the control of the administrator. If you have a claim for benefits which is denied or ignored, in whole or in part, you may file suit in the state or federal court. If it should happen that plan fiduciaries misuse the plan's money, or if you are discriminated against for asserting your rights, you may seek assistance from the U.S. Department of Labor, or you may file suit in a federal court. The court will decide who should pay court costs and legal fees. If you are successful the court may order the person you have sued to pay these costs and fees. If you loose, the court may order you to pay these costs and fees, for example, if it finds your claim is frivolous. If you have any questions about your plan, you should contact the Plan Administrator. If you have any questions about this statement or about your rights under ERISA, you should contact the nearest Area Office of the U.S. Department of Labor-Management Services Administration, Department of Labor.

Note: This Summary Plan Description is provided in accordance with requirements of the Employee Retirement Income Security Act of 1974 and the rules and regulations issued therein. It is not intended to be a full statement of all rights and duties under said Plan. If a participant should desire further information about his rights under this Plan, he should contact the Plan Administrator. A complete copy of the Plan and Trust are on file in the office of the Plan Administrator and available for a participant's review during regular business hours. In case of any conflict between this Summary and the actual provisions of the Plan and Trust, the provisions of the Plan and Trust shall prevail. This Summary is based on the Plan and Trust provisions as of _____ , and does not represent any amendments or changes in provisions that may be made to the Plan and Trust from and after that date.

LEASE AGREEMENT

This Agreement made and entered into this the _____ day of _____ ,
19_____ , by and between General Partner, Midwest Professional Building, Ltd., a limited
partnership, whose principal office is located at _____ ,
_____ , hereinafter referred to as "Landlord",

— and — _____ ,
_____ ,
of _____
hereinafter referred to as "Tenant", witnesseth:

PROPERTY DESCRIPTION

1. For and in consideration of rents to be paid, and the covenants and agreements to be
performed by Tenant, Landlord does hereby lease until Tenant and Tenant hereby takes from
Landlord the following described premises located in building owned by the Landlord, at
_____ , _____ , situated within the County
of _____ , State of _____ ; and being more
particularly described as follows:

The Exhibit "A" attached hereto and made a part hereof

Together with all rights, and privileges belonging to or in any way pertaining to the said
premises. The demised premises are shown outlined in red on the attached Exhibit "A",
identified by the signatures of the parties and made a part hereof. It being understood that the
demised premises have approximately _____ square feet. The address of the
demised premises is located in a building located at _____ .

TERM OF LEASE

2. The term of this lease shall be for a period of _____ years and _____
(_____) months beginning on _____ or when the
building in which the premises rented is completed. If the commencement date of this lease
shall be a day other than the first day of a month, then the period between the commencement
date and the first day of the month next following shall be added to the term of the lease.

RENTS

3. Tenant will pay rent at the annual rental rate of _____
Dollars, payable in equal monthly installments of _____
(_____) Dollars in advance on the first day of each and every calendar month until
the expiration of said term. The rent in respect of any period of less than a calendar month shall
be prorated.

PLACE FOR PAYMENT OF RENTS

4. All rents shall be payable without prior notice or demand at the place hereinafter
specified for the giving of notice to Landlord.

DEPOSITS

5. Simultaneously with the execution and delivery of this lease, Tenant has paid to the
Landlord the sum of _____ (_____) Dollars
representing the first and last month's rent in advance and as security for full and faithful
performance by Tenant of each and every covenant, condition or agreement. Landlord may
and without diminishing, waiving, or affecting any other Landlord's rights and remedies
provided in this lease, use, apply or retain the whole or any part of said deposit for the payment
of any such default or for any other sum which Landlord may expend or be required to expend
by reason of Tenant's default, including any damages or deficiencies in the reletting of the
premises.

ASSIGNMENT & SUBLETTING

6. Tenant shall not, without the prior written consent of Landlord, transfer or assign this
lease or sublet or license the use of all or any portion of the demised premises. In the event of
any transfer, assignment, subletting or licensing without said written consent, Landlord may

terminate this lease and re-take possession of the demised premises. Provided, further, that Tenant shall remain primarily liable for the payment of the rent herein reserved and for the performance of each and all of the terms, covenants and conditions hereof Tenant's part to be performed.

ALTERATIONS BY TENANT

7. Tenant shall make no alterations, decorations, installations, additions or improvements in or to the demised premises without Landlord's prior written consent, and then only by contractors approved by Landlord. All such work, alterations, decorations, installations, additions or improvements shall be done at Tenant's sole expense and at such times and in such manner as Landlord may, from time to time, designate. All alterations, decorations, installations, additions or improvements upon the demised premises, made by either party, shall, unless Landlord elects otherwise, become the property of Landlord, and shall remain upon, and be surrendered with said premises, as a part hereof, at the end of the lease term or renewal terms, as the case may be.

UTILITIES

8. Tenant shall pay for all gas and electricity consumed by it in the demised premises from and after the commencement date of this lease. If Landlord shall furnish to, and shall be paid or reimbursed by Tenant for any of the aforesaid utilities, Tenant shall pay for the utilities consumed by it at the same rate Landlord is charged for such utilities by the primary supplier or utility company. Sewer charges and sewer taxes, regardless of the manner billed or assessed, shall be paid by Landlord. Landlord warrants that all utilities, to the extent necessary to service Tenant's business, shall be available to Tenant at the commencement of this lease.

LANDLORD'S RIGHT OF ENTRY

9. Tenant agrees that Landlord, Landlord's agent and other representatives, shall have the right, without abatement of rent, to enter into and upon the leased premises, or any part thereof, during regular business hours for the purpose of examining the same, or for making such repairs or alterations to the leased premises as may be necessary for the safety and preservation thereof, provided, however, that such examinations, repairs or alterations (unless of an emergency nature) shall be so made as to cause a minimum of interference with the operations of Tenant's business conducted in the leased premises.

COMMON FACILITIES

10. Landlord shall maintain all parking areas, paving, lawn, flower and shrub areas, sidewalks and necessary access roads adjacent to the buildings in which leased premises is located.

USE OF THE PREMISES

11. During the term of this lease, and any renewals and extensions thereof, the demised premises may be used and occupied only for the operation of Visual Care and Optical Goods and no other, without written consent of Landlord. Tenant agrees to operate the demised premises during the entire term of this lease and Tenant shall, at all times, conduct its operation on the demised premises so as to comply with all laws, orders and regulations of the Federal, State, County and Municipal authorities to the best of its information and knowledge; Tenant shall intentionally not do or permit to be done any act or thing upon said demised premises which shall invalidate or be in conflict with fire insurance policies covering the building of which the demised premises form a part,and shall not intentionally do or permit to be done any act or thing upon said demised premises which shall or might subject Landlord to any liability or responsibility for injury to any person or persons or to property by reason of any business or operation being carried on upon said demised premises or for any other reason.

REPAIRS

12. Landlord shall keep and repair all of the exterior of the leased premises and building except as herein provided. Tenant shall keep all of the interior of the leased premises in repair and all fixtures and equipment in good working order, including but not limited to exposed plumbing, electrical fixtures, (heating and air conditioning equipment), floors, ceilings, walls and re-decorating, and except for initial installation shall furnish all electric lightbulbs and tubes

so that the leased premises will revert to Landlord in the same general condition in which it was at the time of the letting, unavoidable casualty and reasonable wear and tear excepted. Tenant will replace, repair, and maintain all plate glass windows and doors. Tenant agrees to use the premises in a tenant-like manner and exercise reasonable care to prevent damage to the leased premises. If Tenant fails to make any repairs, restorations or replacements required of Tenant by this paragraph, same may be made by Landlord at Tenant's expense after giving tenant 10 days written notice and shall be paid by Tenant within five (5) days after rendition of a bill or a statement therefor.

Neither Landlord nor Tenant is responsible or liable to the other for any loss or damage which may be occasioned by or through the acts or omissions of persons occupying adjoining premises or any part of the premises adjacent to or connected with the demised premises.

TAXES

13. Landlord shall pay all real estate taxes and assessments levied, assessed or imposed upon the leased premises and upon all improvements erected thereon and all installments of principal and interest required under any mortgage or deed of trust and all rent reserved under all underlying leases affecting the leased premises as and when the same shall become due and payable. Tenant shall reimburse Landlord each year as additional rental, on a pro rata basis all increases in real estate ad valorem taxes on the building wherein leased premises is located, which exceed the amount of real estate and valorem taxes assessed for the year 19_____ as a base period. All such increased ad valorem taxes shall be paid by Tenant within ten (10) days after rendition of a bill or statement therefor by Landlord. Tenant will pay all personal property taxes. The pro rata share shall be determined as the percentage of leased space of the premise in relation to the total net leasable square feet of the building.

INSURANCE

14. Landlord shall carry no insurance on the property of Tenant, and Landlord shall incur no liability to Tenant, his employees, or invitees for damages caused by or resulting from fire, explosion, windstorm, tornado, earthquakes, leakage of water, gases, steam, rain, snow, falling plaster, glass breakage, theft, burglary, robbery, vandalism, riot or any other casualty or other risks incident to the extended coverage applicable under standard fire insurance contracts, and from the acts or omissions of other tenants, their employees or invitees or trespassers.

In addition to the rentals herein before specified, Tenant agrees to pay as additional rental on a pro rata basis in the same manner as in paragraph 3 above, any increase on premiums charged on policy or policies of insurance which exceed the amount of premiums charged on policy or policies of insurance paid for the year 19_____ as a base period. Tenant will pay such increased insurance premiums within ten (10) days after rendition of a bill or statement therefor by Landlord.

HOLD HARMLESS

15. Tenant agrees to indemnify and save Landlord harmless from all damages, claims and demands of any person or persons by reason of the operation and conduct of the business of Tenant on the leased premises not the result of Landlord's negligence of breach of this lease or for any condition existing on the leased premises under control of Tenant and in any suit or action for damages arising from the negligence of Tenant in this respect, in which action Landlord is included or made a defendant and Tenant agrees to assume all the burden, cost, and expense of the defense or settlement of suit or causes of action, including attorney fees in the defense or settlement of such action or claim.

During the term of this lease including any extension thereof, Landlord agrees to indemnify and save harmless Tenant from and against any and all other claims, demands, and causes of action of any nature whatsoever and any expense incident to the defense of any by Tenant therefrom for injury to or death of persons, or loss of, or damage to property other than that described in the preceding Paragraph. Parties agree that in any action to enforce any of the terms, covenants, and conditions of this lease, the prevailing party shall be entitled to an award for his reasonable attorney's fees and the costs of this action. Notwithstanding anything to the contrary herein contained, Landlord especially waives any right of recovery against Tenant that it may have by virtue of any loss or damage to the leased premises caused by fire, windstorm, or other risks incident to the extended coverage applicable under standard fire insurance contracts, except any loss or damage which is caused by willful negligence on the part of Tenant or its agents, servants, or employees.

SIGNS AND EXTERIOR LIGHTING

16. All signs and advertising displayed in and about the demised premises shall be such only as to advertise the business carried on by Tenant, and Landlord shall control the character and size thereof. No signs or door lettering shall be erected or displayed until approved in writing by Landlord.

HOLDING OVER

17. Should Tenant, or any of its successors in interest, hold over the demised premises, or any part thereof, after the expiration of the term of this lease, unless otherwise agreed in writing, such holding over shall constitute and be construed as Tenancy from month to month only, at a monthly rental equal to the rent paid for the last month of the term of this lease.

DEFAULT BY TENANT

18. The following events shall be deemed to be events of default by Tenant under this lease:

(a) Tenant shall fail to pay any installment of the rent of the date that same is due and such failure shall continue for a period of ten (10) days.

(b) Tenant shall fail to comply with any term, condition or covenant of this lease, other than the payment of rent, and shall not cure such failure within thirty (30) days after written notice thereof to Tenant, or if such failure cannot reasonably be cured within the said thirty (30) days and Tenant shall not have commenced to cure such failure within said thirty (30) days and shall not thereafter with reasonable diligence and good faith proceed to cure such failure.

(c) Tenant shall become insolvent, or shall make a transfer in fraud of creditors, or shall make an assignment for the benefit of creditors.

(d) Tenant shall file a petition under any section or chapter of the National Bankruptcy Act, as amended, or under any similar law or statute of the United States thereof; or Tenant shall be adjudged bankrupt or insolvent in proceedings filed against Tenant hereunder.

(e) A receiver or Trustee shall be appointed for substantially all of the assets of Tenants.

(f) Upon the occurrence of any such events or defaults, Landlord shall have the option to pursue any one or more of the following remedies without any notice or demand whatsoever:

(1) Terminate this lease, in which event, Tenant shall immediately surrender the premises to Landlord, and if Tenant fails so to do, Landlord may, without prejudice to any other remedy which it may have posession or arrearages in rent, enter upon and take possession of the demised premises and expel or remove Tenant and any other person who may be occupying said premises or any part thereof, by force if necessary, without being liable for prosecution or any claim or damages therefor; and Tenant agrees to pay to Landlord, on demand, the amount of all loss and damage, which Landlord may suffer by reason of such termination, whether through inability to relet the premises on satisfactory terms or otherwise.

(2) Enter upon and take posession of the demised premises and expel or remove Tenant and any other person who may be occupying said premises or any part thereof, by force, if necessary without being liable for prosecution or any claim for damages therefor, and relet the premises and receive the rent therefor; and Tenant agrees to pay to Landlord on demand any deficiency that may arise by reason of such reletting.

(3) Enter upon the demised premises by force if necessary without being liable for prosecution or any claim for damages therefor, and do whatever Tenant is obligated to do under the terms of this lease, and Tenant agrees to reimburse Landlord on demand for expenses which Landlord may incur in thus effecting compliance with Tenant further agrees that Landlord shall not be liable for any damages resulting to the Tenant from such action, whether caused by the negligence of Landlord or otherwise.

Pursuance of any of the foregoing remedies shall not preclude pursuit of any of the other remedies herein provided or any other remedies provided by law, nor shall pursuit or any remedy herein provided constitute a forfeiture or waiver of any rent due to Landlord hereunder or of any damages accruing to Landlord by reason of the violation of any of the terms, conditions and covenants herein contained.

LANDLORD'S LIEN

19. In addition to the statutory Landlord's lien, Landlord shall have, at all times, a valid contractural lien for all rentals and other sums of money becoming due hereunder from Tenant, upon all goods, wares, equipment, fixtures, furniture and other personal property of Tenant situated in or upon the demised premises, and such property shall not be removed therefrom without the consent of Landlord until all arrearages in rent as well as any and all other sums of money then due to Landlord hereunder shall first have been paid and discharged. Upon the occurrence of an event of default by Tenant, Landlord may, in addition to any other remedies provided herein or by law, enter upon the demised premises and take possession of any and all goods, wares, equipment, fixtures, furniture and other personal property of Tenant situated on the premises without liability for trespass or conversion and sell the same with or without notice at public or private sale, with or without having such property at the sale, at which Landlord or its assigns may purchase, and apply the proceeds therof, less any and all expenses connected with the taking of possession and sale of the property, as a credit against any sums due by Tenant to Landlord. Any surplus shall be paid to Tenant; and Tenant agrees to pay any deficiency forthwith.

ATTORNEY'S FEE

20. If, on account of any breach or default by Landlord or Tenant of their obligations to any of the parties hereto, under the terms, conditions and covenants of this lease, it shall become necessary for any of the parties hereto to employ an attorney to enforce or defend any of its rights or remedies hereunder, and should such party prevail, it shall be entitled to any reasonable attorneys fees incurred in such connection.

DESTRUCTION BY CASUALTY

21. If the building in which the premises are situated is destroyed by casualty or damaged to such extent that it cannot be repaired within sixty (60) days from the happening of such injury, this lease shall terminate and rent shall be adjusted as of the date of such destruction or damage. If the premises are damaged from casualty and can be repaired within sixty (60) days from the happening of such injury; Landlord shall, with reasonable diligence, at Landlord's expense, repair same. If during the period of repair or any part thereof the premises cannot be used, rent shall abate for such part of the period. Tenant further convenants and agrees that the term and duration of this lease shall be extended from its termination date herein provided for a period of time equal to that required to complete such repair and during which rental shall be abated. If the premises can be partially used during said period there shall be an equitable rebate of a portion of the rent. Repairs may be made during business hours and there shall be no abatement of rent by reason of inconvenience. Damage to the premises resulting from the negligence of Tenant or his employees or invitees shall be repaired at the expense of Tenant. Landlord and Tenant hereby expressly waive each in favor of the other, and all rights of recovery that either of them might have against the other for any and all liability and expense for loss, damage or destruction of property resulting from perils ordinarily covered by standard policies of fire and extended coverage insurance and originating from any cause whatsoever, including negligent acts or omissons of the parties, their agents or employees.

WAIVER OF DEFAULT

22. No waiver by the parties hereto of any default or breach of any term, condition or covenant of this lease shall be deemed to be a waiver of any subsequent default or breach of the same or any other term, condition, or covenant contained herein.

REMOVAL OF TENANT

23. Tenant shall have the right to remove from the demised premises all of its signs, and equipment, and any and all other trade, fixtures, which it has installed in and upon the demised

premises, all of said property being hereby expressly reserved and restrained by Tenant; provided, however, that Tenant is not in default of any of the terms and conditions of this lease agreement and that Tenant shall repair any damage caused by removal of its property.

FORCE MAJEURE

24. Neither Landlord nor Tenant shall be required to perform any term, condition, or convenant in this lease so long as such performance is delayed or prevented by force majeure, which shall mean acts of God, strikes, lockouts, material or labor restrictions by any governmental authority, civil riot, floods, and any other cause not reasonable within the control of Landlord and which by the exercise of due diligence, Landlord is unable, wholly or in part, to prevent or overcome.

EXHIBITS

25. All exhibits, attachments, and instruments and agenda referred to herein shall be considered a part hereof for all purposes with the same force and effect as if copied at full length herein.

USE OF LANGUAGE

26. Words of any gender used in this lease shall be held and construed to include any other gender, and words in the singular shall be held to include the plural, unless the context otherwise requires.

CAPTIONS

27. The captions or headings of paragraphs in this lease are inserted for convenience only, and shall not be considered in construing the provisions hereof if any question of intent should arise.

NOTICES

28. Whenever, under this lease, provisions are made for notice of any kind, it shall be deemed sufficient notice and sufficient service thereof if:

(a) Such notice to Landlord is in writing, addressed to Landlord's executive offices located at _____ , _____ , _____ , or at such other address as Landlord may notify Tenant in writing, and deposited in the United States mail by registered or certified mail, return receipt requested, with postage prepaid, and

(b) Such notice to Tenant is in writing addressed to last known post office address of Tenant and deposited in the United States mail by registered or certified mail, return receipt requested, with postage prepaid.

RIGHT OF ASSIGNMENT

29. Landlord reserves the right to assign and subordinate this lease at all times to the lien of any mortgage or mortgages now or hereafter placed upon Landlord's interest in the demised premises; provided, however, that no default by Landlord, under any mortgage or mortgages, shall affect Tenant's rights under this lease, so long as Tenant substantially performs the obligations imposed upon it hereunder.

EMPLOYEE PARKING

30. Tenant shall require its employees to park their automobiles in parking areas designated by Landlord in order that parking for patrons will be convenient, and available at all times. Landlord agrees to provide adequate parking space for Tenant, his employees and invitees within reasonable proximity to the leased premises at all times.

ENTIRE AGREEMENT

31. This lease shall constitute the entire agreement of the parties hereto; all prior agreements between the parties, whether written or oral, or merged herein and shall be of no force and effect. This lease cannot be changed, modified or discharged orally but only by an agreement in writing, signed by the party against whom enforcement of the change, modification or discharge is sought.

CUMULATIVE RIGHTS

32. The various rights, powers, elections and remedies of the Landlord and the Tenant contained in this lease shall be construed as cumulative, and no one of them as exclusive of the

other, or exclusive of any rights or priorities, allowed by law, and no rights shall be exhausted by being exercised on one or more occasions.

ASSIGNS

33. The covenants, conditions and agreements made and entered into by the parties hereto shall be binding upon and inured to the benefit of their respective heirs, representatives, successors and assigns.

IN WITNESS WHEREOF, the parties hereto have executed this lease agreement this the day and year first above written.

_____
Landlord

ATTEST:
                      _____

                      By _____

                                 ITS _____
                                 "TENANT"

_____

_____
"Tenant"

STATE OF _____

COUNTY OF _____

BEFORE ME, the undersigned authority in and for said County, on this day personally appeared _____ , known to me to be the person whose name is subscribed to the foregoing instrument and acknowledged to me that he executed the same for the purposes and consideration therein expressed.

GIVEN UNDER MY HAND AND SEAL OF OFFICE, this _____ day

of _____ , 19 _____ .

_____
Notary Public

My Commission Expires:

_____

*****

STATE OF _____

COUNTY OF _____

BEFORE ME, the undersigned authority, on this day personally appeared _____ known to me to be the person _____ whose name _____ _____ subscribed to the foregoing instrument, and acknowledged to me that _____ he _____ executed the same for the purposes and consideration therein expressed.

GIVEN UNDER MY HAND AND SEAL OF OFFICE, this _____ day

of _____ , 19 _____ .

_____
NOTARY PUBLIC

My Commission Expires:

_____

*****

STATE OF _____

COUNTY OF _____

BEFORE ME, the undersigned authority, in and for said County, and State, on this day personally appeared _____ , known to me to be the person and officer whose name is subscribed to the foregoing instrument and acknowledged to me that the same was the act of the said _____ , a corporation, and that he executed the same as the act of such corporation for the purposes and consideration therein expressed, and in the capacity therein stated.

GIVEN UNDER MY HAND AND SEAL OF OFFICE, this _____ day

of _____ , 19 _____ .

_____
NOTARY PUBLIC

My Commission Expires:

_____

SS: SS: SS:

Initial

Appendix **C** | **Investigating Locations**

HARRIS NUSSENBLATT, O.D., M.P.H.

The answers to the questions raised in chapter 3 regarding the choice of a practice location, will come from a variety of sources and will take a significant amount of time to collect. It will be necessary to talk with various community leaders, practitioners, and individuals in the area as well as collecting information about the area. Sources of information available that can assist in the process are listed at the end of this chapter but the best sources of information will be those produced at the local level in that they will frequently be the most up to date and relevant, though other types of information (such as census information) can be valuable.

Students who are undecided as to where to set up practice or who have narrowed their choice only so far as state or region can obtain help from the Department of Health and Human Services (HHS) designation of vision care shortage areas. The Federal Government, in 1978, listed about 850 counties across the U.S. that were deemed to need vision care practitioners. Though the formula used to determine these areas has been criticized, someone who is interested in locating potential practice areas should review the list and investigate these communities in detail.

Students who have narrowed potential practice locations down to 3-4 should subscribe to the town newspaper. This is an ideal source of information concerning the area and reading it on a regular basis allows one to become familiar with an area even if some distance away. Phone directories for the area should be requested from the phone company (they are available at no charge) and should be looked at carefully (primarily the Yellow Pages). As an example, one can get an idea of the competitiveness of the ophthalmic marketplace by looking at the way practitioners advertise in the Yellow Pages (and possibly newspapers) and the same follows for other health professionals such as physicians and dentists.

The area Chamber of Commerce, banks, city planning agencies, and local library often have economic data on the city with such information as the industrial base, unemployment, percent of the population on public assistance (and Medicaid), past and future residential and commercial building activities, and number of new electrical, sewer, water, and telephone connections. Many states also have state planning agencies that look at all areas of community growth and have information available for public use.

In 1974, Congress created local health planning agencies which were responsible for planning health resources in given areas. These Health System's Agencies (HSAs) collected demographic, economic, and health related information as part of their activities and this information can be obtained from these agencies. Though some of these agencies have closed down, their responsibilities have been taken over by state health planning agencies such as the state health department. If an area does not have an HSA currently operating, then a practitioner could contact the state health department for this type of information.

The types and number of ophthalmic practitioners (optometrists, ophthalmologists, and opticians) are important in the decision making process, but it is often a gray area. Most of the previous literature on the subject recommend a certain number of practitioners on the basis of formulas such as the practitioner to population ratio or other formulas based on demand for services or the needs of the population. These ratios are often based on assumptions that may or may not be true for a community and should be viewed with caution. As an example, the most often quoted practitioner to population ratios of 1 optometrist to 7000 population and 1 optometrist to 10,000 population require only two pieces of information; the number of practitioners (optometrists) and the population. This type of ratio makes many assumptions such as the size of the community being the major determinant of manpower requirements; that all factors influencing the supply of manpower such as productivity, technology change, and fees do not change; and that factors affecting demand are also unchanged such as demographic shifts, socioeconomic conditions, and third party care. So while it is a relatively simple way to specify manpower, it has serious disadvantages including ignoring future changes in delivery mechanisms and other components that affect both the supply and demand for services.

Another common way to calculate manpower needs in a community is by evaluating the number of services delivered to an area. This method assumes that the community has a fixed number of people, requiring a specific amount of services and each practitioner, in turn, provides a certain amount of services. The focus is on the provision of services and the community's practitioners' productivity. The problem with this type of formula is that the data needed to utilize this formula are difficult to locate and often times based only on the judgment of other practitioners. It also implies that there is sufficient knowledge and information available to set appropriate norms for community services. The Department of HHS Vision Care Shortage Area designations are based on this type of calculation.

In spite of these problems with formulas for determining the ideal mix of practitioners, one must try to get an idea of the number and distribution of practitioners in the community. The best source is usually the area Yellow Pages which will generally have the listing of all practitioners, except new practitioners who have moved into the community since their publication. Though the directory is available from the phone company, an excellent source of both the white and Yellow Pages is a product called Phone Fiche, a directory on microfiche which contains the phone books of virtually all communities in the U.S. and Canada. Phone Fiche is available at most large libraries and is updated yearly. The Blue Book of Optometrists and Red book of Ophthalmology are also sources of manpower but since these are published every two years, they tend to be more out of date than other pieces of information. These books do, however, contain some biographical information on practitioners which can be of value in analyzing age characteristics of the practitioners. The state licensing board of each health professional will normally provide a listing of all practitioners in the state which can then be analyzed by city or area. There is normally a small charge for the list but this information is usually public information and can be readily obtained (Medical Boards lists normally do not contain physicians listed by specialty so a listing of just ophthalmologists may not be available from the Board, though a listing of physicians could be be obtained).

Practice location selection depends on a wide variety of information obtained through a long period of investigative work on the part of the new practitioner. Information from a number of sources must be collected and analyzed so that the practitioner can make an informed judgment as to a community's potential for supporting another doctor. This process must rely not only on hard data such as community population, growth, and income levels but must also rely heavily on judgmental evaluations of the local practitioners, patient acceptance of a new practitioner, and projected demand for optometric services in the community.

COMMUNITY DATA SOURCES
Census Information

1. Statistical Abstract of the U.S., 1981

This volume contains a summary of statistics on the social, political, and economic organization of the United States. It includes a selection of statistics used by public officials, business analysts, educators, and researchers. 1031 pages

2. State and Metropolitan Area Data Book–1982

This volume contains the information listed below in three formats: 1) Regions and divisions of the U.S. 2) Standard Metropolitan Statistical Areas (SMSA) and component counties and 3) SMSAs by population size. Information is provided in the following areas for regions, divisions, and states:

Areas and population	Business enterprise
Births and deaths	Construction, housing
Marital status, marriage	Divorces
Households and families	Banking
Health and hospitals	Life insurance
Education	Elections, voters
Employment and labor force	Energy

Income	Highways, transportation
Personal wealth	Communications
Federal government	Mineral industries
State government	Farms and farming
Local government	Land ownership, parks
Government employment	Forestry and fisheries
Social insurance and welfare	Manufacturers
Vocational programs	Wholesale trade
Veterans	Retail trade
Crime	Selected services

Information is provided for SMSAs in the following areas:

Area and population

Births and deaths

Marriages, divorces, living arrangements

Physicians and hospitals

Education

Employment and labor force

Income

Government finances and employment

Social insurance and welfare

Crime

Housing

Banking, elections

Manufacturers

Wholesale and retail trade

Selected services

3. County and City Data Book-1977*

    This volume contains statistical data for each county in the United States, 277 SMSAs and for each of the 910 cities of 25,000 or more inhabitants in 1975. The information is based on the 1972 censuses of business, industry, and governments, the 1974 census of agriculture, and the 1970 census of population and housing. Information is provided in the following areas:

Population and area	Housing
Vital statistics	Local government

Labor force	Government employment
Employment	Crime and police
School enrollment	Manufacturers or manufacturing
Health	Income
Public assistance	Selected services
Education	Farm and agriculture
Banking	

* The 1982 edition is due to be released in the Fall, 1983.

4. Directory of Federal Statistics for Local Areas–1976

This is a comprehensive guide to sources of Federal statistics for metropolitan areas. This volume contains specific sources for items of information in agriculture, banking, insurance, business, construction, governments, housing, income, labor, manufacturers, industry, population, transportation, and other subjects. 372 pages. Issued in 1978.

5. Directory of Federal Statistics for Local Areas, Urban Update–1977–78

This is a supplement to the Directory listed above and includes reports published before January 1, 1979 and focuses on urban areas. It was issued in 1980 and gives the source of tables describing the social, economical, and technical data about local areas that is available from the Federal government.

6. Bureau of the Census Catalog–1981

This catalog includes a description of all reports by title and subject issued by the Bureau for 1980–81. (GPO 003–024–05001–03)

7. Census of Service Industries–1977

This book contains information on service industries including number of businesses, receipts, payroll, and employee numbers for the U.S. as a whole (1972 and 1977), for the states (1977), and for SMSAs and Standard Consolidated Statistical Areas (SCSAs) (1977). Issued in April, 1980. (SC77–A–52)

8. Census of Manufacturers–1977

This report is available for each state (51 separate reports) and contains historical employment statistics (1963–1977) for the state and SMSA. Counties and selected cities statistics are included for manufacturing establishments between 1972 and 1977 as are employment statistics by county for 1972 and 1977. (MC–77–A–44)

9. Census of Retail Trade–1977

This book is issued by state and contains statistics by SMSA, major retail centers, and central business districts for 1972–1977. It also contains maps of each central business district with appropriate street boundaries. (RC77–C–44)

10. City Employment in 1980

This booklet contains summary information for all cities concerning city employment from 1970–1980 broken down into such categories as education, police, fire, etc. It includes 1980 population figures as well as break downs by city (50,000 or more population). Issued in July, 1981. (GE80–NO. 2)

11. Current Survey Statistics

Information is available in a number of areas on a monthly, quarterly, or annual basis by state, SMSA, county, or city and is the best source for current information. The areas covered and the appropriate publication series number are given below:

Population P-20, P-23, P-24, P-25, P-26, P-27, P-28, P-60

Housing H-150, H-170, H-111, H-130

Construction C-20, C-21, C-22, C-25, C-27, C-30, C-40, C-41, C-45, C-50

Trades and Services BR, CB, BD, BS, BW, BI, BG-41

Governments GF, GR, GE

12. Standard Metropolitan Statistical Areas and Standard Consolidated Statistical Areas: 1980

This report includes information for all 323 SMSAs and 17 SCSAs and their components of the 1980 Census including counts of persons in the major race groups, persons in households, and the SMSAs and SCSAs ranked by population. (PHC80–S1–5)

13. Summary Characteristics for Governmental Units and SMSAs

This report has both complete count and sample data for the 1980 census for states, SMSAs, counties, county subdivisions, and incorporated places. Complete count information is available on age, race, sex, Spanish origin, household type, housing units, persons in units, housing value, and contract rent. Sample information covers unemployment, poverty status, percent with work disability, per capita and median income, percent with air conditioning, and year structure built. (PHC80–3)

Health Statistics

Area Resource File

A computer based county specific health information system which is updated every six months and utilizes health related data for all U.S. counties. The following information is available on either U.S., state, HSA, or county basis:

Health manpower (including optometrists)
Health facilities
Health training schools
Population characteristics
Economic data
Hospital utilization levels
Hospital and Medicare expenditures
Environment

Individual state, HSA, or county reports available from the National Technical Information Service, U.S. Department of Commerce, 5285 Port Royal Rd., Springfield, Virginia 22161. 703-487-4650.

Manpower Information

1. Blue Book of Optometrists

This book, issued in even numbered years, contains the listing of optometrists by city and state, names and addresses of optical supply houses, addresses of state optometric associations, and abbreviated copies of state optometric laws. Published by Professional Press, Inc.

2. Red Book of Ophthalmology

This book is issued in odd numbered years and contains the listing of physicians practicing ophthalmology by city and state. Published by Professional Press, Inc.

3. Vision Care Shortage Areas–Department of HHS

Lists all counties in the U.S. that meet HHS criteria for designation as a vision care shortage area. The method of calculation takes into account the number of optometrists and ophthalmologists and the productivity of each type of practitioner. County listings of shortage areas are in the Federal Register Volume 45, Number 167, August 26, 1980, Page 57002. Criteria for designation of shortage areas is in the Federal Register 42CFR, Part 5, January 10, 1978.

4. Directory of Medical Specialities, 1981–1982

This directory includes the individual biographical listings by city of all medical specialists who are board certified. Published for the American Board of Medical Specialists by Marquis Publishing, Chicago, Il.

5. American Medical Directory, 1979 and Update, 1981

This directory is published by the American Medical Association and includes individual listings of all physicians by state, county, and city.

6. Physician Characteristics and Distribution in the U.S., 1981

This book is published by the American Medical Association and includes summaries on the geographic distribution of physicians including age, sex, and board certification by regions, states, and counties.

7. Phone Directory

White and Yellow Pages of the area's phone directory. Phone Fiche is a system of microfiches containing both directories for virtually all communities in the U.S. and Canada.

8. Health Systems Agency

Local health planning agency with information on area demographics, economic data, and health related information. If a Health Systems Agency is not operating in a specific area, then the same information can be obtained from the State Health Planning Agency, normally the state health department.

Other Sources

1. State Almanacs

State almanacs contain summary information by counties and/or cities for the entire state including data on agriculture, business, population, geography, weather, banking, per capita income, manufacturing, insurance, and public facilities (libraries, schools, etc.). Most of the information is compiled from the U.S. Government such as the Census and state agencies. Usually issued yearly.

2. Chamber of Commerce

3. Area newspapers/microfilm

Appendix **D** | **Practice Location Worksheet**

Practice philosophies and practice location evaluation. Before starting a practice these issues should be addressed.

A. Practice Philosophies

    1. Attitude towards patients

    2. Types of services to be offered

    3. Quality of standards for materials and services

    4. Areas of special interest in practice

    5. Personnel hiring and management

    6. Community involvement

    7. Interaction with other health care professionals

B. Practice Location Evaluation

    1. County

        a. Population:

           20 Yrs _____ 10 Yrs _____ 5 Yrs _____ Present _____

        b. Median Age: Males _____ Females _____

    2. City

        a. Population:

           20 Yrs _____ 10 Yrs _____ 5 Yrs _____ Present _____

        b. Median Age: Males _____ Females _____

        c. Population of surrounding areas: 10 mi radius _____

           15 mi radius _____ 20 mi radius _____

        d. Projected growth of city: _____

        e. Average Income: _____

	Previous 5 Yrs	Previous 3 Yrs	Previous 1 Yr	Present
Individual	_____	_____	_____	_____
Family	_____	_____	_____	_____

f. Unemployment: _____

	Yrs Ago Four	Yrs Ago Three	Yrs Ago Two	Last Year	Present
Yearly Average	____ %	____ %	____ %	____ %	____ %

g. Current Number of Health Care Professionals:

		Total
1.	Medical Doctors:	_____
2.	Dentists:	_____
3.	Optometrists:	_____
4.	Osteopaths:	_____
5.	Podiatrists:	_____
6.	Chiropractors:	_____
7.	Opticians:	_____
8.	Ophthalmologists:	_____

h. Hospitals — Number of beds, emergency services: _____

i. School System:

		Number of Schools	Total Enrollment
1.	Elementary:	_____	_____
2.	Secondary:	_____	_____
3.	High School:	_____	_____
4.	College:	_____	_____

j. Nursing Homes — Number of beds: _____

k. Financial Institutions:

		Number	Total Assets
1.	Banks:	_____	_____
2.	Savings & Loans:	_____	_____

l. Housing: Number of dwellings, % owner occupied: _____

m. Churches: Number and denomination: _____

n. Retail Business Sales: 4 Yr Past $ _____

3 Yr Past $ _____ 2 Yr Past $ _____

1 Yr Past $ _____ Present _____

o. Retail business: # _____

   Number employed _____

p. Wholesale businesses: # _____

   Number employed _____

q. Major Employers in Area:

	Product	No. Employees
1. Company #1	_____	_____
2. Company #2	_____	_____
etc.		

3. Practice Location within City:

   a. Determine professional spaces available

   b. Evaluation of location

       1. Neighbors — professional climate and reputations

       2. Aesthetics of building and landscaping

       3. Size and outlay of space available

       4. Traffic flow past location

       5. Parking availability

       6. Present upkeep

       7. Reputation of the owner and manager

       8. Plumbing, electrical, heating and air conditioning

       9. Cost of renovation

       10. Age of building, maintenance costs

C. Design Office Space
   (review the "101 Facts That Every Doctor Should Know".)

Appendix E | Loan Request Worksheet

When starting a new practice, relocating a practice, or building a new office, a business plan is needed to acquire a loan and to plan for the future.

The following outline will include a sample resume', financial statement, loan request, income projection, operating expenses, and basic equipment needed to start a practice.

Resume'

1. Name Address, Age and Family Information
2. Introduction Paragraph
3. Professional Work Experience
4. Collegiate Work Experience
5. Education
6. Attitude, Values and Opinions
7. Honors and Awards
8. Professional Affiliations
9. Extra-curricular Activities
10. Hobbies and Interests
11. Credit References
12. Personal References
13. Conclusion Paragraph

Individual Financial Statement

Assets		Liabilities	
Cash	$ 500.00	Note for School Loan	$ 1,500.00
Automobile	8,000.00	Note to Bank — Car	4,000.00
Home	30,000.00	Note to Mortgage Co. — House	28,000.00
Total Assets	$38,500.00	Total Liabilities	$33,500.00
		Net Worth	5,000.00
		Total	$38,500.00

Loan Request

Name: _____ , O.D.

Purpose: To establish an optometric practice in (City) _____ ,

      (State) _____ .

Estimated Financing Needed:

1. Six months Operating Expenses	$10,000.00
2. Equipment/Furniture	21,000.00
3. Frames/Contact Lens Inventory	6,000.00
4. Building Renovation	3,500.00
Total Loan Request	$40,500.00

Loan Terms Desired: First six months — no payments.

                    Second six months — make interest payments.

                    Second year — start monthly payments on

                              principal and interest.

Minimum Income Projection For First Year

Quarter	Patients/Wk	Gross Income Avg Per Patient	Monthly Gross	Quarterly Gross
First	2	$150.00	$1,200.00	$ 3,600.00
Second	5	150.00	3,000.00	9,000.00
Third	7	150.00	4,200.00	12,600.00
Fourth	9	150.00	5,400.00	16,200.00
			Total	$41,400.00

Operating Expenses

		Per Month	Per Year
1.	Office Rent	$1,000.00	$12,000.00
2.	Salaries	800.00	9,600.00
3.	Lab Fees (34%)	1,173.00	14,076.00
4.	Utilities	250.00	3,000.00
5.	Supplies	100.00	1,200.00
6.	Interest	450.00	5,400.00
7.	Insurance	50.00	600.00
8.	Taxes (Business)	100.00	1,200.00
9.	Miscellaneous	200.00	2,400.00
	Total		$49,476.00

Estimated cost of Furniture and Equipment

1. Reception Room
   - a. Chairs, (7) — $1,400.00
   - b. Lamp Tables, (2) — 400.00
   - c. Coat Rack — 50.00
   - d. Magazine Display — 50.00
   - e. Wall Decor — 150.00
   - f. Drapes — 200.00

   $2,250.00

2. Business Office
   - a. Typewriter — 200.00
   - b. Calculator — 150.00
   - c. Office Chair — 200.00
   - d. File Cabinet — 150.00
   - e. Built-in File System — 400.00
   - f. Stationery and Paperstock — 250.00
   - g. Telephone System (2 lines) — Lease — 250.00
   - h. Office Supplies — 100.00
   - i. Bookkeeping System (Pegboard) — 150.00

   $1,850.00

3.   Laboratory and Dispensing

   a.   Dispensing Table   300.00

a.	Dispensing Table	300.00
b.	Chairs, (2)	300.00
c.	Mirrors	200.00
d.	Frame Warmer	100.00
e.	Tools	150.00
f.	Lensometer	1,100.00
g.	Radiuscope	1,200.00
h.	Job Trays (20)	100.00
i.	CL Magnifier and Reticle	50.00
j.	Supplies (Screws, hinges, bulbs)	200.00
		$3,700.00

4.   Styling Area

a.	Frames (200 @ $27 each)	$5,400.00
b.	Frame Displays, (3)	450.00
c.	Chairs, (2)	400.00
d.	Mirrors, (2)	250.00
e.	Wall Decor	100.00
		$6,600.00

5.   Contact Lens Dispensing

a.	Solutions	500.00
b.	Contact Lens Stock (Most CL's on Consignment)	1,000.00
c.	Dispensing and Instruction Table	250.00
d.	Chairs, (2)	300.00
		$2,050.00

6.   Private Office

a.	Bookcase	250.00
b.	Chair	200.00
c.	Desk	550.00
		$1,000.00

7.   Examination Room

a.	Chair and Stand (Used)	$ 5,000.00
b.	Phoroptor (Used)	2,500.00
c.	Slit Lamp (New)	4,500.00
d.	Applanation Tonometer (New)	800.00

e.	Projector (Used) and Slide	500.00
f.	Polarized Screen	100.00
g.	Keratometer (Used)	750.00
h.	Trial Lenses and Trial Frame (Used)	750.00
i.	Indirect Ophthalmoscope and Lens	600.00
j.	Adjustable Stool with Back	200.00
k.	Chairs, (2)	250.00
l.	Retinoscope, Opthalmoscope	300.00
m.	Vectograph Slide	150.00
n.	Color Plates	50.00
o.	Stereo Fly	50.00
p.	Pharmaceuticals	50.00
q.	Bulbs	150.00
r.	Tangent Screen and Targets	100.00
s.	Miscellaneous	400.00
		$17,200.00
	TOTAL	$34,650.00

First Year Income Projection

A.	Loan	$40,500.00
B.	Practice Gross	41,400.00
C.	Spouse Income	12,000.00
		$93,900.00

First Year Expense Projection

A.	Operating Expenses	$49,476.00
B.	Equipment and Supplies	34,650.00
		$84,126.00
	Net Income with Spouse's Salary	$ 9,774.00

The above figures are for demonstration purposes only to acquaint the beginning practitioner with the method of applying for a loan, projecting expenses and income. One should be sure a significant part of the budget is in a contingency category to cover those multitues of expense items not considered: such as first and last month's rent, utility deposits, etc. When starting a practice all details must be evaluated in order to avoid future surprises.

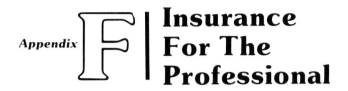

Appendix **Insurance For The Professional**

WESLEY K. WYATT

Every person in professional practice today, whether just starting or several years into a career, realizes the need for insurance planning. If you are new in your practice, you will get all kinds of advice from many salespeople or insurance specialists eager to do business with you. This is as it should be as you are just as eager to get business from them. If you have been in practice for a number of years, you have the continual opportunity to keep your coverages current with your needs and the times. Like your practice, the practice of insurance planning for the professional changes with the times and your needs and must be kept up to date. The big question is, **what** kinds of insurance do I need and how much? There is a point at which you can be over-insured, just as you can be under-insured. As long as you don't need it or have a claim, all insurance is good! The whole point of insurance planning is to have as perfect of a blend of all coverages needed in your practice, while at the same time not over-insuring or paying too much for the wrong kind of insurance.

Let's talk about life insurance first, then we can discuss other types of coverages such as disability income insurance, overhead interruption insurance, liability coverage, etc. During the last three decades, particularly the past three years, there has been a new revolution in the insurance business! The life insurance business in particular. If you are not aware of the new products available and plan your program accordingly, you could be throwing many thousands of dollars down the drain.

The new life insurance revolution has created a diversity of new life insurance plans. The giant life insurance industry has finally started listening to what the people are telling them. People are looking for places to put their life insurance dollars where they can do some good in today's, and probably tomorrow's, climate of high inflation, high taxes and high interest rates. The competition for the consumer's dollars, along with high interest rates, improved mortality rates and the computer age, has created a diversity of life insurance plans of which most people are not aware. You as a professional should be aware so that you might choose the plan that suits you the best.

It is ironic that after we have built a large estate with enough income to support us without working, we will still need life insurance and must plan our life insurance program accordingly. We must keep in mind that death does not just cost working people their livelihood, the expenses of death can also cost wealthy people a sizable portion of their estate. We have all seen it, death taxes whittling down estates that were once adequate to live on. Probate costs, administrative fees and various other estate settlement costs can force families to liquidate assets that were earmarked for other purposes. When this happens, the estate no longer provides what the deceased intended, a suitable standard of living. Adequate life insurance can provide the funds to pay the estate settlement costs at death, thus leaving the estate intact. The estate is preserved and so is the family's standard of living, if life insurance is properly provided. Life insurance not only completes an estate, but it also preserves an estate. The event that creates the need, which is death, also creates the money with which to satisfy the need.

TERM INSURANCE

This is the type of life insurance that offers protection only. It is like car insurance, if you have a wreck, or die, it pays off. If you don't, you have paid for pure protection. You may or may not realize something for your premium payment, other than peace of mind. You should think of term insurance as renting your home compared to buying it. The lease comes up for renewal at the end of a rental period, much the way the life insurance protection comes up for renewal at the end of the term. No matter how long you stay in the rented home, and no matter how many payments you make on it for someone else, you don't build up any equity or financial interest in it. The same is true of term insurance. To answer the question as to whether you should buy term or permanent, you might ask yourself whether you rent or own your home and your office building. We all know the benefits of property ownership versus renting. The building is profitable to someone!

The advantage of term insurance is that the premiums are generally lower than for the premiums of any other kind of life insurance, especially at the younger ages. The rates are calculated simply by taking the risk factors of someone your age dying within the coverage period and you are charged accordingly. The risk is less at the younger ages and increases as we get older. The premium increases proportionately. Annual renewable term is the best type to buy, but regardless of the type of term you buy, you pay a higher premium every time you renew the policy.

We have to look at term insurance as to whether or not it will meet your objectives. Many people decide that they are going to buy term and invest the difference between term and whole life premiums. On paper, that is the most profitable route to go. In reality, most will not do that! Experience has showed me that in most cases, the only money clients have over a period of years is the low yielding cash value in their policies, yet they have made many investments over the years!

Statistically, approximately 1 percent of the term policies written, end up as death claims! In a study of one group of term policies, it was revealed that 45 percent were terminated or converted to other forms of protection the first year. During the first three years, 72 percent were terminated or converted. These figures tell us that the majority of term insurance buyers don't keep their temporary protection in force as long as it's needed. When you are young, need a lot of coverage and don't have much extra cash, low cost term works well. Or, if you only need life insurance for a short period of time, such as security for a loan, term insurance works well. Situations like these and other situations fit very well into the lower premiums of term insurance. If we are speaking of lifetime protection, the increasing premium, lack of equity, and the potential lack of availability at later ages when the risk is the greatest, term insurance is often a less than ideal solution.

PERMANENT LIFE INSURANCE

Just what does permanent life insurance offer? Mainly, it offers lifetime protection with premiums leveled over the entire period that the protection is in force. This is an averaging process. The high premiums you would expect to pay at later ages are reduced and the premiums you would expect to pay at younger ages are raised. Premiums that are prepaid earn interest over time which create a reserve from which the higher protection costs at the later ages can be paid. This makes life insurance protection both available and affordable over an entire lifetime.

Other advantages in addition to the level lifetime premium is that prepaid sums offer guaranteed, tax deferred, steadily increasing cash values that are payable whether you live or die. This makes for a triple benefit — protection, peace of mind and "living benefits" from all of the premium payments made over the years. With permanent insurance, we own our home as opposed to renting, as was discussed with term insurance. Your home is yours as long as you make the payments! No one can come in and tell you that your lease won't be renewed, or that it might be renewed if you pay higher rent. With renting comes a handful of rent receipts; with ownership, each mortgage payment brings you closer to the full possession of a deed to your home!

No plan is perfect, and certainly not traditional permanent life insurance. All financial instruments have their limitations and that is what permanent life insurance is, a financial instrument. From an investment standpoint, the interest rates earned by your cash values might look fairly low compared to what some investments are earning, especially in today's investment climate. Even this is changing, mainly because of competition and a greater return on investment portfolios of companies along with a better mortality experience.

UNIVERSAL LIFE

With all of the advertising and with all of the agents and financial planners talking about Universal Life, you probably have heard of it more than any of the other new plans. Very simply, universal life offers death protection plus cash value accumulations, just like a traditional permanent product. The difference is that it adds a number of features not found in the traditional permanent products, like the cash values being credited with interest that reflects current rates on Treasury bills, or other government securities, or money market funds. With money continually rolled over into these instruments, the cash value earnings usually reflect current economic conditions. Since interest is a part of a life insurance policy, the earnings accumulate without being currently taxed to the policyholder. The company usually pays only a modest tax on its total investment earnings. We will probably see an increasing number of new permanent life policies offering an opportunity to invest one's cash values in investments that pay current interest rates. The public will demand it now that they have been educated to current rates and competition will supply the products.

With Universal Life, you also have the flexibility of premium payments. As long as you maintain a minimum of cash value to handle the cost of the protection portion, the timing and amount of premium payments is largely up to the policyholder.

Another feature about the new policies, such as Universal Life or Current Value Life, is that adjustments can be made in the amount of the death benefit, which cannot be made in some ordinary life policies. You can either maintain a level death benefit, which includes both the cash values and death benefit, or, you can keep the insurance amount constant in addition to the steadily growing cash values. This results in an increasing total benefit that has a better chance of keeping pace with inflation. You can switch back and forth between these two options, depending on your own long range plans.

Universal Life cash values are more accessible than in traditional policies. There are limits, of course, but within these limits, you can make withdrawals from your cash values without an interest charge. Or you have the option of borrowing them, just as you do in a traditional policy. You have to be sure that you leave enough money in the policy to pay the cost of the protection.

CURRENT VALUE LIFE

Much more could be written on Universal Life products as the new products of the future. While the IRS still has its head lingering in the shadows of whether or not to tax the cash value buildup, a new product called Current Value Life does not have this tax problem. It works with the same flexibility as Universal Life, mainly because of the same concept, that of offering low premiums, high current return and flexibility. Let's discuss the two types. Current Value Life meets the requirements that must always exist in any product. It must be good for the consumer, for the company and for the agent. If a product cannot be marketed then the public cannot benefit. Compensation is vital to the effectiveness of any product if the consumer is to benefit. Current Value Life does allow the agent to survive and be compensated well enough to provide the services needed by the consumer. Universal life does not.

The Current Value Life product is immune to some of the concerns now circulating in the marketplace about the Universal Life concept. Specifically, the Internal Revenue Service may rule unfavorably on the tax aspects of Universal Life.

The concerns about Universal Life arise because of its basic design, which is fundamentally different from a traditional cash value life insurance policy. Technically, Universal Life is a combination of an annually renewable term policy and an investment fund. While both are provided through a single contract form, they operate essentially independently. The contract holder pays money into the investment fund, at such times and in such amounts as he chooses. The investment fund earns interest and is available to the contract holder for full or partial withdrawal at any time. The fund is then used to pay premiums for the term insurance. If the insured dies, the beneficiary receives both the term insurance and the fund balance. In short, "buy term and invest the difference" wrapped into a single contract form.

The questions about Universal Life all center on the status of the investment fund. First, does including the "side fund" in the same contract as the term insurance convert the fund into life insurance proceeds on the death of the insured. (The IRS issued a favorable private ruling to an individual. This ruling does not apply to other purchasers, even from the same insurer. We understand that the IRS has subsequently declined to give similar rulings to other purchasers.)

The second main issue is whether the interest earned on the fund should be treated as an increase in life insurance reserves, as interest paid (or credited) to the policyholder, or as a life insurance dividend. This issue affects the potential taxes of both the policyholder and the insurance company. In the case of some Universal Life policies, there may also be a question as to whether the link between the investment income credited to the fund and the investment performance of specific investments or an investment pool may make the fund a security subject to SEC regulation.

The design of Current Yield Life policy is much different. They have taken the traditional cash value life insurance policy and made some important, but technically modest, modifications. First, they separated the contract into one year segments. Second, they promised to use fair current assumptions to calculate each year's premium in advance. Third, they offered the policyholder the opportunity to modify his plan (future death benefits, premiums and cash values) on each annual renewal date. But, unlike Universal Life, the essential unity of the cash value life insurance policy is maintained. Like Universal Life, Current Value Life provides the advantages of low cost financial needs. But, Current Value Life provides these advantages within the traditonal life insurance framework.

Current Value Life does not include a separate "fund" from which "term insurance premiums" are "paid" monthly. Therefore, it is not possible for them to seek an opinion as to whether the "fund" is a life insurance cash value, or, upon death, a life insurance death benefit.

Current Value Life provides low cost through its current basis premiums, rather than through excess interest credits on a fund. All three basic elements: current premium, death benefit and cash value, are fully guaranteed in advance, year by year. Therefore, it is not possible for them to seek an opinion as to the treatment of excess interest credits under tax and insurance laws.

Current Value Life annual statement reserves are calculated using traditional life contingency formulas and the statutory 1958 CSO mortality table at $4\frac{1}{2}\%$ interest. Therefore, it is not possible for us to seek an opinion as to whether a fund accumulated at interest only qualifies as a life insurance reserve.

Current Value Life provides fair current value without being tied to the investment performance of specific marketed securities or of pools of securities.

Therefore, it is not possible for them to seek an opinion as to whether such ties would make the policy subject to federal and state securities laws.

These comments will help you to better understand why Current Value Life needs to be distinguished from the Universal Life family of products.

The highlights of the CVL products include:

1) Current interest rates, flexible return to buyer. Current Value Life features a competitive current interest rate. And since life insurance cash values build free of income tax, a good interest rate can be quite attractive. The interest rate in the policy is flexible. If interest rates on investments increase, the CVL interest rate can increase. If interest rates fall, the CVL rate can fall. At the same time, Current Value Life preserves the security of traditional life insurance policies. They have a guaranteed basis minimum interest rate of $4\frac{1}{2}\%$.

2) Flexibility of death benefit scheduling. The policyowner has the right to increase or decrease the policy death benefit on every policy anniversary. The buyer can change benefits as his or her needs change, or can establish a schedule of benefit changes in advance. One important plus is that if scheduled increases are established in advance, they may be underwritten in advance.

3) Flexibility of premium payment plans. While there is a minimum premium for CVL, which is their current rate basis whole life rate, there is no maximum. Extra premium payments create extra values inside the policy, since they will never charge more than their current basis factors. Extra values can pay up the policy early (on either a current basis or a guaranteed basis), or create an endowment or retirement income plan. The policyowner can select any number of years to pay premiums, and they can provide a level premium payment plan to suit his needs. Large "pour-in" premiums are also possible. Pour-ins will build policy values and will create extra policy death benefits as well.

4) Current Value Life is exceptionally good for the special risk. Current interest and mortality rates are used to calculate extra premiums for the special risk. This makes the CVL policy a tremendous value for the special risk.

VARIABLE LIFE

Now that you have had a look at Universal Life and Current Value Life, let's take a look at still another form of life insurance call Variable Life, what it is, and how and why you might use it.

Variable Life is more like a traditional permanent life insurance policy. That is, it has fixed premiums and a minimum guaranteed death benefit. The difference is that the cash values are not fixed or guaranteed, either in respect to minimums or maximums. Instead, the cash values are invested in a portfolio of common and preferred stocks, bonds, money market funds, or a combination of those three that the policy owner chooses.

If we choose the stock portfolio, and the performance is high, then both the cash values and the death benefit increase with a Variable Life insurance policy increasing proportionately. Of course, if the fund performance falls off, the benefit may drop also, but never below a guaranteed fixed amount. Probably a new Variable Life with some of the privileges of Universal Life will eventually be created by the actuaries. Variable Life has been around for some time and lost part of its attractiveness in the seventies when fund performance was down. With the market on the rise, there is now more interest in it.

The Variable Life will do a great job of protection and investment, which will account for a rise in its popularity. Term insurance, while on the rise in the past, will probably decrease mainly because of the more aggressive investment stances in Universal Life, Current Value Life and the new Variable Life plans. The insurance industry is finding new ways of meeting the needs of policy owners, with the end result benefiting the client.

No one knows what interest rates are going to be in the future, nor what the equally slippery quantity, inflation, will be. Whatever happens, the insurance industry, once based on fixed assumptions and constitutions, is adapting to the times. In the end, it's the policyholders who dictate to the company. The insurance industry will, and has, created choices to suit various needs and goals. The biggest change in all of these new plans is that you can readily change your program to keep abreast of changes in the economy or in your personal situation. With so many options available, it would be wise to take a good look at where you are, what you own, the premiums you are paying, and the benefits you are getting so as to be sure you are current with the products themselves, as well as your current needs. Remember, nothing is forever. Change is inevitable in everything, including your life insurance program and it must be reviewed periodically.

DISABILITY INCOME INSURANCE

Disability income insurance is vitally important to anyone depending on their income from working. If you strip away your ability to work and earn income, then you strip away the ability of most individuals to provide the basic building blocks of any financial plan. This is especially true of a professional person. An unexpected injury or illness could mean low or no income, and a drain of savings that could be devastating. If you don't believe this, think about your last medical bill!

It doesn't take long to recognize that a successful financial planner includes a means of protecting the plan from a loss of income. One such tool that financial planners and insurance agents use is Life and Disability Income Insurance. This type of insurance protects against the loss of human capability due to death or disability and helps prevent a drain on the accumulated assets. When you consider this type of insurance, two basic rules should be followed. First, you always insure against catastrophic loss no matter how remote the possibility of long term disability or illness might be. Second, you do not insure against smaller losses if the cost can easily be absorbed by current income. Coverage for smaller, more frequent losses is costly and, in most cases, unnecessary.

Health and Accident Insurance genuinely refers to those coverages providing the insured with benefits as a result of sickness or injury. Recently, preventive care costs and health maintenance provisions have been added. Health and Accident Insurance takes two major forms. First, in Disability Income Insurance and second, in Medical Expense Insurance, which we will talk about later. This coverage includes hospital and surgical benefits, major medical insurance, and, in some cases, dental coverage.

If we look at social security administration figures published in 1978, financial losses resulting from disability were expected to affect about 16 million Americans in 1982. The trends we have seen recently indicate that one out of every 7 working individuals in their mid-thirties will be disabled for a period of 90 days or more before they retire at age 65. The Life Insurance Marketing Research Association tells us that almost 70% of their lost income will never be replaced. When income stops, long term disability amounts to economic death.

Disability Income Insurance can be defined as health insurance that provides income replacement payments when the insured is unable to work, owing to sickness or injury. Some disability contracts cover both risks, some provide only for disability resulting from accidental injury.

For the professional person who has group health insurance, you may only have some form of disability insurance. You should check this out carefully. In any event, you should question its adequacy relative to your cost of living expenses. Whether you have group coverage or are self-employed and own an individual Disability Income policy, you can evaluate the adequacy of your coverage by estimating your monthly expenses and comparing the total figure to the total disability provided. If your cost of living expenses exceed your disability income provisions, you will want and need to supplement your coverage. The total disability benefit available is based on three things, first, the amount of weekly or monthly payment, second, the length of the intital elimination or waiting period and third, the maximum period for which benefits are payable.

Let's take a look at the basic benefit amount. This is the basic benefit provided by a Disability Income Insurance policy. The scheduled payment is also referred to as weekly or monthly indemnity. The proper amount of indemnity is determined by the insured's income.

In choosing disability benefits, you should consider the elimination or waiting period, which works like a deductible on any other type of insurance. Your disability benefits begin when the elimination period ends. This waiting period can range from zero days to two years, however, most Disability Income Insurance policies are based on elimination periods of 30, 60, 90 or 180 days. The reason for this waiting period is to discourage short-term disability claims which the insured can usually budget for, thus reducing the cost both to the company and the insured. Take a look at how long you can survive before income comes in and that will tell you the waiting period you should choose.

We now have to take a look at the maximum benefit period, which is the indemnity limit, or the longest period of time for which benefits are payable for any one disability. Generally, these benefit periods range from one year to age 65, and are of the same duration for both accident and sickness under one contract. You will want to check to see if your policy is an old or new policy, as that will determine many of the benefits and elimination periods. The newer contracts provide longer benefit periods and assume that income for the deductible time will be covered by the personal assets of the insured. This is why an emergency fund is most important in the professional's planning, usually about three months of income. Again, remember the longer the elimination period, the lower the premiums.

You, of course, must qualify for the disability benefits. When you get your Disability Income policy, look at the definition of "total disability." To collect any of the benefits you must satisify the policy definition of total disability. The more liberal the definition, the better off you are.

Disability Income policies used to state that a person was not considered totally disabled until he or she was unable to perform any kind of work. That made it pretty difficult for anyone to collect benefits. Today, the policy definitions are more liberal, such as on the inability to perform job functions in the insured's regular occupation. Even if the insured continues to work, the loss of speech, hearing, sight or the loss of use of two limbs is recognized as total disability by many insuring companies. Partial disability benefits are provided to the insured in some, not all, Disability Income Insurance policies. When an insured is unable to perform one or more of the important duties of his or her occupation, then partial disability benefits are provided, following a total disability benefit period. Most contracts pay approximately 50% of the total disability benefits for six months or one year. Some contracts also have a residual disability benefit that pays benefits if recovery is not complete and partial disability remains. These policies emphasize a loss of earned income rather than an inability to perform the duties of a particular occupation and are paid to the insured in the same proportion as a reduction in earned income. These residual benefits may also be subject to qualification periods and earned income figures.

There are many additional Disability Income policy provisions that you will want to be aware of. They are waiver of premium, recurrent disability and transplant surgery benefits, cost of living rider, and Social Security benefits replacement rider.

You will certainly want to take a good look at the renewability and rates. There are three basic types of renewal provisions that you will want to review. First, Cancellable. This means the contract renewal is at the option of the insurer. Second, Guaranteed Renewable. Here the company guarantees contract renewal, but reserves the right to change premiums. And third, Non-Cancellable. This is where the insured has the right to renew the contract and the company cannot change the premiums or refuse renewal. This is the type of policy to look for. You will also want to look at the exclusions and limitations as well as how pre-existing conditions are treated.

MEDICAL EXPENSE INSURANCE

This type of coverage is designed to cover hospitalization costs and general nursing care, medical fees for physicians, surgeons, private nurse care, costs of necessary medical and health care services, supplies, extended care facilities, medicines, dental care, plus prosthetic appliances. There are three major types of medical insurance programs. First, the Hospital-Surgical policy. Second, the Major Medical policy, and third, the Comprehensive Medical Expense policy.

The Hospital-Surgical policy may also be called a basic coverage policy. There are typically seven benefit provisions related to hospitalization and surgical care. 1) Hospital room and board, 2) Miscellaneous hospital expenses, 3) Maternity benefits, 4) Surgery, 5) Physician's nonsurgical services provided during the hospital stay, 6) Extended care facility room and board, and 7) Out-patient diagnostic X-ray and laboratory expenses. Most Hospital-Surgical coverages have no deductible with hospital coverage usually beginning your first day of hospital stay. Surgical coverage goes into effect with the first fee, however, some policies may have a small deductible. If it does you may choose a higher deductible to cover some ortion of the hospital and surgical expenses yourself and save on the premimum. Remember, we are back to the larger deductible, the lower the premium. In many cases, this is the best route to go. All benefits paid out for each service or fee under a basic Hospital-Surgical coverage are limited by schedule, allocation, or specified maximum benefit amounts outlined in the medical expense policy.

A review of each of the seven benefit provisions, is necessary. On hospital room and board, pay attention to your policy definition of "period of hospital confinement." Confinement may be defined by cause, time separation or both. On Miscellaneous Hospital Expenses, pay attention to any maximum limits on miscellaneous expenses. Some policies offer a flat dollar limit, some follow a schedule of service fees. Anything over the allowable benefit is paid by the policyholder. In maternity benefits, check the specific amout of maternity benefits offered under your Hospital-Surgical coverage, if any. Depending on your geographic area and maternity care desired, you may want to increase your coverage. Under surgical benefits, you should be aware of the scheduled amounts for common surgical procedures. Since policies vary, choose the one with the most liberal schedule. You will particularly want to pay attention to the maximum surgical benefits. This is the largest amount allowed for any listed operation. For physicians' in-hospital expenses, note as to how the physician's in-hospital benefit is handled in your policy. In most policies, in-hospital expenses and surgical expenses incurred by the same physician will not be payable under both provisions of the policy. The insured must choose the larger benefit and pay the lesser amount out of pocket. On extended care, you will want to pay attention to the policy's definition of "extended care facility." Most definitions require the facility to have six or more beds, to be supervised by a physician or registered nurse, and to care for and treat primarily those individuals convalescing from sickness or injury. On the out-patient diagnostic and laboratory expenses, to encourage people to use less-expensive medical facilities and to practice preventive medicine, many policies include coverage for laboratory and X-ray expenses provided by clinics and other facilities. This benefit is usually a modest flat dollar amount.

MAJOR MEDICAL INSURANCE

This type of insurance was developed in response to catastrophic medical expenses, and the inadequacies of basic hospital-surgical coverage. This type of coverage may be provided as an optional provision to a basic hospital–surgical contract or as a separate contract. The emphasis on major medical is on large medical bills, major medical expense provisions that are based on large deductibles and co–insurance, or shared risk, between the insured and the insurance company. There are five key factors that determine the amount and distribution of Major Medical benefits. They are: 1) Eligible medical expense, 2) Deductible amount and accumulation period, 3) Benefit period, 4) Co–insurance percentage and, 5) Maximum benefit. Breaking these down further, the eligible medical coverage says that major medical plans cover all reasonable charges including hospitalization, medical and nursing care, and any additional supplies and treatments as prescribed by a physician. Although hospital confinement is not necessary, the physician's prescribed care is. For the deductible amount and accumulation period, the deductible is the amount of expenses paid for by the insured before any benefit is paid. This could range from $500 to $5,000 and must be satisfied with per illness or per calendar year. After the deductible amount is satisfied and the first eligible medical expense incurred, then the benefit period begins. The benefit periods will vary in length from one to five years, unless the insured remains in the hospital when the benefit period is due to expire, then it is extended until the hospitalization period is over. Once the deductible is satisfied, a new benefit period may begin. Under co–insurance percentage, major medical expenses are shared by the insured and the insurance company. The typical cost split is 80:20%, with the insurance company assuming the greater part of the cost. The maximum benefit is simply the maximum amount the insurance company will pay per illness or per life of the policy.

SHOPPING HINTS ON HEALTH AND ACCIDENT INSURANCE

1) Compare policies. They do vary in coverage. Just make sure you are getting what you want.

2) Don't over–insure. You simply will wind up paying premiums for duplication in coverage. Know what policy covers what expenses.

3) Check for pre–existing conditions or exclusions. You don't want to eliminate coverage you need.

4) Know your maximum benefits. These are described in terms of dollar amounts and time frame. Know how long you will be paid benefits and how much.

5) Check for guaranteed renewability and non–cancellable coverage. Avoid the headache of cancelled coverage. You want to be in control of policy renewal.

6) Check for premium adjustment privileges. Can the insurance company raise your rates? If so, how often and under what circumstances?

7) Take advantage of the 10–day free look. If you decide not to purchase a coverage, just return it and get a refund.

SUMMARY

Health and Disability Income Insurance play vital roles in the success of your personal financial plan. For the professional person, there is no substitute for having the right kind and the right amount at the right time. When you consider Disability Income policies, do insure catastrophic loss although the possibility may seem remote. Do consider longer elimination periods to lower your premiums. Don't accept just any definition of "total disability". Be sure the definition is liberal, otherwise you may not be eligible for benefits.

When considering Medical Insurance, do choose a higher deductible or shared risk to help reduce premiums. Do look at the premium differentials between schedule benefits for hospital–surgical costs and 80:20 or 75:25 shared risk contracts. It may be worth sharing the risk. Do be aware of conversion option under your group medical contracts. You may need to supplement coverage when you leave the job or retire. Don't assume you are covered for everything! Many people think maternity benefits are automatically part of the contract. This is not so. And last, become an informed consumer. It will be in your favor. The important thing is, have the knowledge to feel confident about making the proper decisions and providing yourself and your family with adequate coverage. Remember, a wise guy or gal makes a wise buy!

PROFESSIONAL OFFICE PACKAGE

Many of your major carriers offer a Professional Office Package for professionals in practice. Take a look at these packages rather than try to piecemeal your coverage out separately, whether it be with one or with several companies. With one Professional Office Package, you will usually wind up with more benefits and less premium. Most of your Professional Office Packages combine property and liability coverages that you as a professional should have. Let's go over a few of these coverages.

OFFICE PROPERTY: Provides all–risk coverage for buildings and business personal property, with no coinsurance! All loss settlements are made on a replacement cost basis, new for old without a deduction for depreciation. Business personal property includes furniture in your offices, waiting rooms and examination areas; laboratory equipment, optical equipment, etc. Usual office supplies and machinery such as copying machines, dictaphones and microfilm are covered. The improvements you make to the building if you're a tenant are automatically included.

OFFICE LIABILITY: The company's comprehensive office liability automatically provides coverage for bodily injury and property damage with limits that range from $300,000 to $1,000,000. Also included in this section are medical payments up to $1,000 per person, employees as additional insureds, products liability for give–away items, all–risk tenants legal liability, host liquor liability, blanket contractual and owners protective liability.

PROFESSIONAL LIABILITY: This coverage is critical to protect you and your practice from liability losses. Claims–made coverage is available as determined by the professional liability lines offered in your state.

MALPRACTICE INSURANCE: Malpractice insurance should not be an option for the professional. Be sure your professional office package has sufficient coverage on this area.

BONUS COVERAGES INCLUDED IN THE PACKAGE OF PROFESSIONAL PROTECTION

LOSS OF EARNINGS AND EXTRA EXPENSE: The company will pay for the income you lose as a result of a loss covered by the policy. They'll also pay for reasonable extra expenses to keep your practice in operation after a covered loss. Such payments are for the actual loss you sustain, without a dollar limitation for a period of up to one year.

MONEY AND SECURITIES: Covers your money, checks and securities against loss of up to $10,000 while they are inside your office and $2,000 while off your premises.

OFF-PREMISES AND TRANSIT PROTECTION: Covers your business personal property when off-premises or in transit up to a $5,000 limit.

VALUABLE PAPERS AND RECORDS: Covers the cost of research and other expenses needed to replace valuable papers and records and data processing materials up to a $5,000 limit.

NEWLY ACQUIRED LOCATIONS: Covers business personal property at new locations during the first 30 days for up to $25,000.

BUILDING INFLATION PROTECTION: Automatically increases the insurance value on your building every three months to help keep your coverage in line with inflation.

KEY OPTIONS AVAILABLE WITH THE PROFESSIONAL OFFICE PACKAGE

BLANKET POSITION EMPLOYEE DISHONESTY: Limits of $10,000 or $25,000 per employee. Optional welfare and pension plan endorsement is available.

OUTDOOR SIGN/OUTSIDE GLASS: All-risk coverage for your outdoor signs and all-risk coverage for outside glass breakage are available.

ERISA LIABILITY COVERAGE: Covers the fiduciary responsibilities imposed under the Employee Retirement Income Security Act of 1974 (ERISA).

LIABILITY PROTECTION FOR AUTOS YOU DON'T OWN: Covers non-owned and hired autos and can include partnership liability. Combined single limits of $300,000, $500,000 or $1,000,000 are available.

Many other options can be selected to supplement your professional insurance protection. Your financial planner or your local independent agent can help you select the coverage you need. The insurance plans for the professional man or woman are almost limitless, so you must choose wisely. There is also business interruption insurance that would pay you while your business was being rebuilt, after a fire or storm damage. What you have to do is take the money you have, figure out where you would be hurt the most if a loss occurred, and insure accordingly. An experienced financial planner can be a valuable help to you.

411 South Washington
Stillwater, Oklahoma 74076
(405) 372-3177

Glossary Of Insurance Terms And Vision Insurance Information

Appendix G

Administrative Costs — The overhead expenses incurred in the operation of a plan which are distinct from the costs of professional services.

Beneficiary — A person who is entitled to service under a plan.

Benefits — The reimbursement or payment for services to a beneficiary according to the insurance policy or service plan. This also refers to the list of services or procedures covered by the policy. Same as coverage.

Carrier — Insurance company, health underwriter, or other organization that guarantees that covered services will be paid.

Certificate of Insurance — A statement issued to a group member describing in general terms the policy provisions.

Claim — A demand by an insured person for benefits provided by the policy.

Closed Panel — Benefits are available only when provided by a limited group of providers, that is, only by panel providers. Panel providers must agree to see any beneficiary.

Co-Insurance — A plan requirement in which the beneficiary shares a portion of the cost of the services.

Deductible — A specified amount the beneficiary must pay before being eligible for coverage. Typical amounts vary between $100 and $500 per year. This is in contrast to "first dollar coverage" in which there is no deductible.

Dependent Coverage — Benefits are also available to spouses, children, or other dependents of the insured member's family.

Eligibility — Conditions which must be satisfied before an individual becomes eligible to receive benefits.

Exclusions — Specific conditions or diseases which the policy will not pay for services.

Fee For Service — A fee is charged the patient for each task or service performed.

Freedom Of Choice — Beneficiaries are entitled to select the practitioner of their choice from whom services can be obtained.

Group Member — A person who is a direct member of a group who has subscribed for services.

Group Policy — The policy between the insurer and the group which is providing the benefits to its members.

Indemnity Policy — The beneficiary receives a specific amount for a specific service rather than having the service paid in full. The beneficiary receives a fixed dollar amount according to a schedule to meet the cost of services.

Insurance Company — An organization chartered under state laws to engage in the business of furnishing insurance protection to the public.

Insured — The person whom the insurer agrees to provide coverage.

Insuror — The organization that provides either payment for covered expenses or who provides the service.

Major Medical Coverage — Coverage for catastrophic illness or injury which normally goes into effect after expenses have exceeded a stated amount.

Non Participating Practitioner — A practitioner with whom the carrier does not have an agreement to provide services to plan members.

Open Panel — A panel that is open to all licensed practitioners so that any practitioner can elect whether or not he/she wishes to participate in the plan and in which beneficiaries can select from all licensed practitioners.

Panel Member — A practitioner who has agreed to provide services on a full service basis to beneficiaries according to a contract.

Participating Practitioner — Any licensed practitioner with whom the plan has an agreement to provide care to beneficiaries.

Policy — The document which details the insurance coverage.

Policy Holder — Under a group plan, the employer or union to whom the group plan is issued. In an individual plan, the person to whom the contract is issued.

Premium — The amount charged for coverage under a plan for a specific period.

Prepayment — A plan in which services are provided in exchange for a fixed regular (usually monthly) payment.

Self Insurance — The group covers its own members for services by setting aside funds to meet expected claims. Funds are used to provide benefits directly without going through an insurance carrier.

Service Plan — A plan which provides services to the insured or makes some provision for services and pays the practitioner for services rendered.

Third Party Payment — Payment for services by someone other than the person receiving the services.

Utilization — The percentage of persons under the plan who utilize services during a given time period.

Vision Service Corporation — A professionally sponsored nonprofit corporation legally constituted to contract with groups of consumers to administer vision care plans on a prepaid basis.

Statement Of Policy On
Vision Care Benefit Programs

The American Optometric Association believes that vision care benefit programs can provide a sound mechanism for making vision care more readily available to the American people. The Association encourages the development of various types of comprehensive vision care benefit programs.

In order to assure availability of the highest level of care under vision care programs, the AOA recommends the following concepts:

1. The optimal vision care program would include the full scope of examination, diagnosis, and treatment of conditions of the visual system on an "as needed" basis.

2. Provisions shall be made to assure the highest quality of both services and materials.

3. The patient shall have the freedom of choice concerning provider of services.

4. All legally qualified optometrists shall be eligible providers.

5. The optimal vision care program would provide for covered benefits without requiring the beneficiary to pay a deductible and/or co-insurance.

6. The cost of vision care should take into consideration accurate and current statistical data, and be subject to adjustment at reasonable intervals. Reimbursement should not act as a deterrent to high quality vision care.

7. Reimbursement policies for covered benefits shall differentiate between professional service fees and the acquisition cost of materials.

8. Administrative requirements shall not usurp the professional judgment of the practitioner in the right to render optimal vision care.

9. Programs should provide equal payment or reimbursement to participating and non-participating providers as a means of enabling the beneficiaries to obtain quality care from the providers of their choice.

10. Peer review shall be the mechanism for maintaining standards.

11. When a program provides reimbursement at the provider's actual charge up to a maximum stated amount, the program should not discriminate between different provider groups when payment is made for covered benefits as defined by the program. In claims administration, carriers should not develop differential screens based on provider classification.

Guidelines For
Vision Care Benefit Programs

The American Optometric Associaton encourages the development of various types of comprehensive vision care benefit programs. This paper discusses guidelines for such programs. Programs which do not meet all of these guidelines may nevertheless serve the public interest.

Each individual provider may determine whether or not he/she wishes to participate in any particular program. Individuals may wish to consult with their attorney or accountant with respect to some specific features of a particular program.

Information will be made available concerning the name of the group, term of contract, the identities and responsibilities of the carrier and administrator and the types of beneficiaries under major multi-state contracts.

I. PLAN DESCRIPTION

A. Benefits — A comprehensive vision care program involving the full scope of examination, diagnosis and treatment of conditions of the vision system is recommended. (See e.g. **Optometric Care in Third Party Programs, Current Optometric Procedural Terminology** (COPT) and **Current Optometric Information and Terminology** (COIT) for reference in this area.)

B. Options — When a program allows for options, the patient shall have the right to obtain said options at the provider's usual and customary charge.

C. Exclusions — Exclusions must be listed and should be reviewed for possible inclusion as either Benefits or Options.

D. Benefit Frequency — The optimal vision care program would cover examination of the vision system and any necessary treatment on an "as needed" basis. The minimal criteria, however, should allow for full scope examination, diagnosis, and treatment of conditions of the vision system on an annual basis.

E. Prior Authorization — Prior authorization may be desirable in certain non-routine conditions which may require extraordinary treatment.

II. COPAYMENT/DEDUCTIBLES

The optimal vision care program would provide for "paid in full" covered benefits, since copayments/deductibles may deter the timely receipt of needed services. When deductibles or copayments are necessary they should be applicable for treatment and/or materials only, since it is the patient's best interest that priority be given in diagnostic services. For ease of administration, and since a patient has a right to know his exact cost prior to the ordering of materials, it is recommended that copayments and deductibles be a stated dollar amount as opposed to a percentage.

III. PANEL PARTICIPATION

A. Freedom of choice of the provider of examination, diagnosis and treatment is exposed.

B. Equal payment for participating and non-participating providers is recommended.

C. Capping and Steering which would affect freedom of choice of the patient is discouraged.

IV. LABORATORIES

Providers should have freedom of choice of laboratories as a means of assuring quality. Quality standards are discussed in the AOA's Guidelines for Peer Review.

V. ELIGIBILITY/GUARANTEED PAYMENTS

Programs should utilize appropriate forms which, when presented to providers, will establish eligibility and guarantee payment for covered benefits.

VI. REIMBURSEMENT

A. The cost of vision care should take into consideration accurate and statistical data, and be subject to adjustment at reasonable intervals. Reimbursement should not act as a deterrent to high quality vision care.

B. Payment to providers should be current, prompt and at least semi-monthly.

C. When a program provides reimbursement at the provider's actual charge up to a maximum stated amount, the program should not discriminate between different provider groups when payment is made for covered benefits as defined by the program. In claims administration, carriers should not develop differential screens based on provider classification.

D. The provider should be reimbursed for materials on a laboratory acquisition cost basis plus a fee for attendant professional services based on usual, customary, reasonable or similar basis.

VII. USE OF OPTOMETRIC CONSULTANTS

It is recommended that carriers and administrators utilize the American Optometric Association Guidelines for Optometric Consultants.

VIII. STANDARD CLAIM FORM

It is recommended that a universal claim form be developed.

IX. LIAISON TO UNDERWRITER/ADMINISTRATOR

It is recommended that open lines of communication between providers, underwriters and administrators be established and maintained.

X. DISSEMINATION OF BENEFITS INFORMATION TO BENEFICIARIES

The American Optometric Association encourages the development, and offers its assistance in the preparation of appropriate information concerning vision plan benefits for dissemination to plan beneficiaries.

XI. PEER REVIEW MECHANISMS

The development and utilization of appropriate peer review mechanisms are endorsed.

FISCAL INTERMEDIARIES
MEDICARE

Alabama

Medicare
Blue Cross-Blue Shield of Alabama
P.O. Box C-40
Birmingham, Alabama 35205

Alaska

Medicare
Aetna Life & Casualty
Crown Plaza
1500 S.W. First Avenue
Portland, Oregon 97201

Arizona

Medicare
Aetna Life & Casualty
Medicare Claim Administration
3010 West Fairmount Avenue
Phoenix, Arizona 85017

Arkansas

Medicare
Arkansas Blue Cross and Blue Shield
P.O. Box 1418
Little Rock, Arkansas 72203

California

Counties of: Los Angeles,
Orange, San Diego, Ventura,
Imperial, San Luis Obispo,
Santa Barbara
Medicare
Transamerica Occidental Life
Insurance Co.
Box 54905
Terminal Annex
Los Angeles, California 90054

Rest of State:
Medicare
Blue Shield of California
P.O. Box 7968, Rincon Annex
San Francisco, California 94120

Colorado

Medicare
Blue Shield of Colorado
700 Broadway
Denver, Colorado 80273

Connecticut

Medicare
Connecticut General Life
Insurance Co.
100 Barnes Road, North
Wallingford, Connecticut 06492

Delaware

Medicare
Pennsylvania Blue Shield
P.O. Box 65
Camp Hill, Pennslyvania 17011

District of Columbia

Medicare
Pennsylvania Blue Shield
P.O. Box 100
Camp Hill, Pennsylvania 17011

Florida

Counties of: Dade, Monroe
Medicare
Group Health, Inc.
P.O. Box 341370
Miami, Florida 33134

Rest of State:
Medicare
Blue Shield of Florida, Inc.
P.O. Box 2525
Jacksonville, Florida 32231

Georgia

The Prudential Insurance Co. of
America
Medicare Part B
P.O. Box 95466
Executive Park Station
Atlanta, Georgia 30347

Hawaii

Medicare
Aetna Life & Casualty
P.O. Box 3947
Honolulu, Hawaii 96812

Idaho

Medicare
The Equitable Life Assurance Society
P.O. Box 8048
Boise, Idaho 83707

Illinois

E.D.S. Federal Corp.
Medicare Claims
P.O. Box 66906
Chicago, Illinois 60666

Indiana

Medicare Part B
120 West Market Street
Indianapolis, Indiana 46204

Iowa

Medicare
Iowa Medical Service
636 Grand
Des Moines, Iowa 50307

Kansas

*Counties of: Johnson,
Wyandotte*
Medicare
Blue Shield of Kansas City
P.O. Box 169
Kansas City, Missouri 64141

Rest of State:
Medicare
Blue Shield of Kansas
P.O. Box 239
Topeka, Kansas 66601

Kentucky

Medicare
Metropolitan Life Insurance Co.
1218 Harrodsburg Road
Lexington, Kentucky 40504

Louisiana

Medicare
Pan-American Life Insurance Co.
P.O. Box 60450
New Orleans, Louisiana 70160

Maine

Medicare
Blue Shield of Massachusetts
Maine
P.O. Box 1010
Biddeford, Maine 04005

Maryland

*Counties of: Montgomery,
Prince Georges*
Medicare
Pennsylvania Blue Shield
P.O. Box 100
Camp Hill, Pennsylvania 17011

Rest of State:
Maryland Blue Shield, Inc.
700 East Joppa Road
Towson, Maryland 21204

Massachusetts

Medicare
Blue Shield of Massachusetts, Inc.
55 Accord Park Drive
Rockland, Massachusetts 02371

Michigan

Medicare
Blue Shield of Michigan
P.O. Box 2201
Detroit, Michigan 48231

Minnesota

*Counties of: Anoka, Dakota,
Filmore, Goodhue, Hennepin,
Houston, Olmstead, Rumsey,
Wabasha, Washington, Winona*
Medicare
The Travelers Insurance Company
8120 Penn Avenue, South
Bloomington, Minnesota 55431

Rest of State:
Medicare
Blue Shield of Minnesota
P.O. Box 43357
St. Paul, Minnesota 55164

Mississippi

Medicare
The Travelers Insurance Co.
P.O. Box 22545
Jackson, Mississippi 39205

Missouri

*Counties of: Andrew, Atchison,
Bates, Benton, Buchanan,
Caldwell, Carroll, Cass, Clay,
Clinton, Daviess, DeKalb,
Gentry, Grundy, Harrison,
Henry, Holt, Jackson, Johnson,
Lafayette, Livingston, Mercer,
Nodaway, Pettis, Platte, Ray,
St. Clair,Saline, Vernon, Worth*
Medicare
Blue Shield of Kansas City
P.O. Box 169
Kansas City, Missouri 64141

Rest of State:
General American Life
Insurance Co.
P.O. Box 505
St. Louis, Missouri 63166

Montana

Medicare
Montana Physicians' Service
P.O. Box 4340
Helena, Montana 59601

Nebraska

Medicare
Mutual of Omaha Insurance Co.
P.O. Box 456, Downtown Station
Omaha, Nebraska 68101

Nevada

Medicare
Aetna Life & Casualty
P.O. Box 11260
Phoenix, Arizona 85017

New Hampshire

Medicare
New Hampshire Vermont
Physician Service
Two Pillsbury Street
Concord, New Hampshire 03306

New Jersey

Medicare
The Prudential Insurance Co. of
America
P.O. Box 3000
Linwood, New Jersey 08221

New Mexico

Medicare
The Equitable Life Assurance
Society
P.O. Box 3070, Station D
Albuquerque, New Mexico
87110

New York

*Counties of: Bronx, Columbia,
Delaware, Dutchess, Greene,
Kings, Nassau, New York,
Orange, Putnam, Richmond,
Rockland, Suffolk, Sullivan,
Ulster, Westchester*

Medicare
Blue Cross-Blue Shield of
Greater New York
P.O. Box 458
Murray Hill Station
New York, New York 10016

County of: Queens
Medicare
Group Health, Inc.
P.O. Box A966,
Times Square Station
New York, New York 10036

Rest of State:
Medicare
Blue Shield of Western New York
P.O. Box 600
Binghamton, New York 13902

North Carolina

The Prudential Insurance Co. of
America
Medicare B Division
P.O. Box 2126
High Point, North Carolina
27261

North Dakota

Medicare
Blue Shield of North Dakota
4510 13th Avenue, S.W.
Fargo, North Dakota 58121

Ohio

Medicare
Nationwide Mutual Insurance Co.
P.O. Box 57
Columbus, Ohio 43216

Oklahoma

Medicare
Aetna Life & Casualty
Jamestown Office Park
3031 N.W. 64th Street
Oklahoma City, Oklahoma 73116

Oregon

Medicare
Aetna Life & Casualty
Crown Plaza
1500 S.W. First Avenue
Portland, Oregon 97201

Pennsylvania

Medicare
Pennsylvania Blue Shield
Box 65 Blue Shield Bldg.
Camp Hill, Pennsylvania 17011

Rhode Island

Medicare
Blue Shield of Rhode Island
444 Westminster Mall
Providence, Rhode Island 02901

South Carolina

Medicare
Blue Shield of South Carolina
Columbia, South Carolina 29260

South Dakota

Medicare
Blue Shield of North Dakota
4510 13th Avenue S.W.
Fargo, North Dakota 58121

Tennessee

Medicare
The Equitable Life Assurance
Society
P.O. Box 1465
Nashville, Tennessee 37202

Texas

Medicare
Group Medical and Surgical Service
P.O. Box 222147
Dallas, Texas 75222

Utah

Medicare
Blue Cross and Blue Shield of Utah
P.O. Box 30270
2455 Parley's Way
Salt Lake City, Utah 84125

Vermont

Medicare
New Hampshire Vermont
Physician Service
Two Pillsbury Street
Concord, New Hampshire 03306

Virginia

Counties of: Arlington, Fairfax
Cities of: Alexandria, Falls,
Church, Fairfax
Medicare
Pennsylvania
P.O. Box 100
Camp Hill, Pennsylvania 17011

Rest of State:
Medicare
The Travelers Insurance Co.
P.O. Box 26463
Richmond, Virginia 23261

Washington

Medicare
Washington Physicians' Service
Mail to your local
Medical Service Bureau
If you do not know which bureau
handles your claim, mail to:
Medicare
Washington Physicians' Service
4th and Battery Bldg., 6th floor
2401 4th Avenue
Seattle, Washington 98121

West Virginia

Medicare
Nationwide Mutual Insurance Co.
P.O. Box 57
Columbus, Ohio 43216

Wisconsin

Medicare
Wisconsin Physicians' Service
Box 1787
Madison, Wisconsin 53701

Wyoming

Medicare
The Equitable Life Assurance
Society
P.O. Box 628
Cheyenne, Wyoming 82001

American Samoa

Medicare
Aetna Life & Casualty
P.O. Box 3947
Honolulu, Hawaii 96812

Guam

Medicare
Aetna Life & Casualty
P.O. Box 3947
Honolulu, Hawaii 96812

Puerto Rico

Medicare
Seguros De Servicio De Salud
De Puerto Rico
G.P.O. Box 3628
San Juan, Puerto Rico 00936

Virgin Islands

Medicare
Seguros De Servicio De Salud
De Puerto Rico
G.P.O. Box 3628
San Juan, Puerto Rico 00936

Appendix H | Office Building And Floor Plans Of The Authors' Offices

The two offices that are the professional homes of the authors of this book are relatively new having been built within the last five years. Studying these floor plans will show a completely different approach, yet good patient flow in both. They are both located in a high traffic area of suburbia, each with more than adequate parking. One office is a three story structure in a multi-health care setting while the other houses a single health care facility (optometrist).

Both offices use wall coverings to convey a warm and friendly atmosphere utilizing paint, wall paper and wood paneling in combination. Both offices supply interesting photographs taken by the doctors as part of the decorating scheme. One office harmonizes oil paintings and sculptures done by the wives. Both offices have carpet for visual effects and additional sound proofing.

The two offices are contrasted in furnishings and decorating style with one being ultra-modern while the other highlights numerous antiques.

Alike, yet so different, they show two different settings that complement the personalities of the men who practice there.

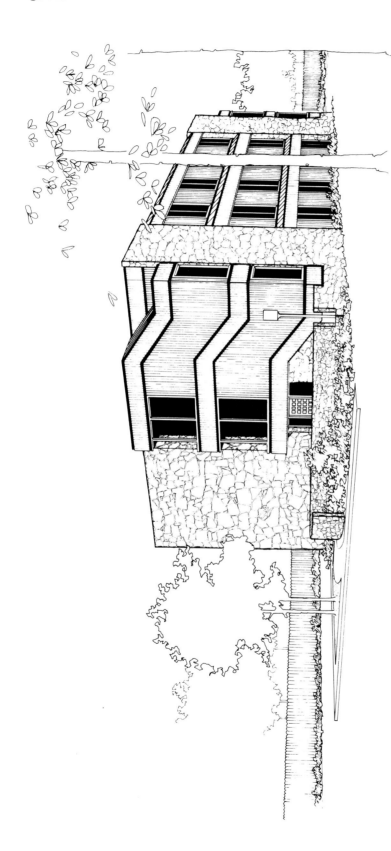

BOB L. BALDWIN, O.D., F.A.A.O.
AND
BOBBY CHRISTENSEN, O.D., F.A.A.O.
MIDWEST CITY, OKLAHOMA

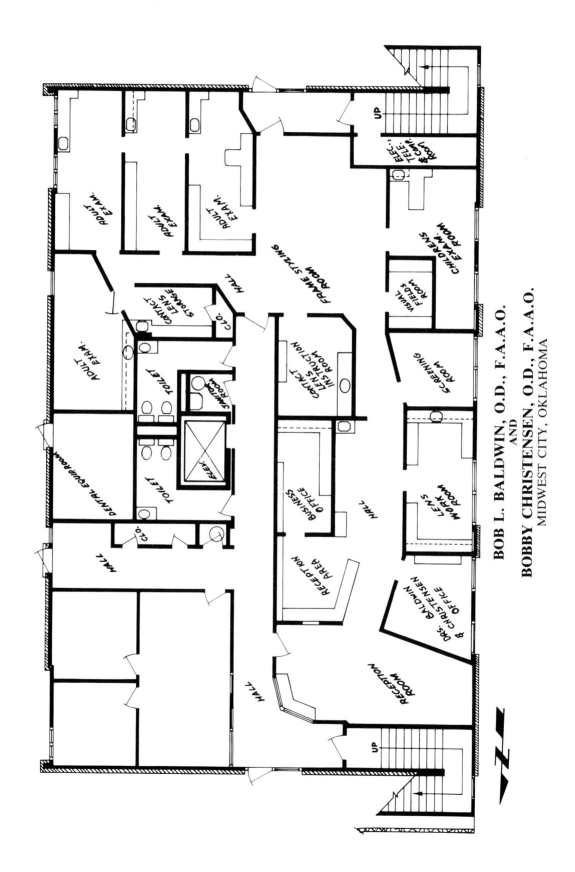

BOB L. BALDWIN, O.D., F.A.A.O.
AND
BOBBY CHRISTENSEN, O.D., F.A.A.O.
MIDWEST CITY, OKLAHOMA

**JACK W. MELTON, O.D., F.A.A.O.
AND ASSOCIATES**
PRACTICE LIMITED TO CONTACT LENSES
OKLAHOMA CITY, OKLAHOMA

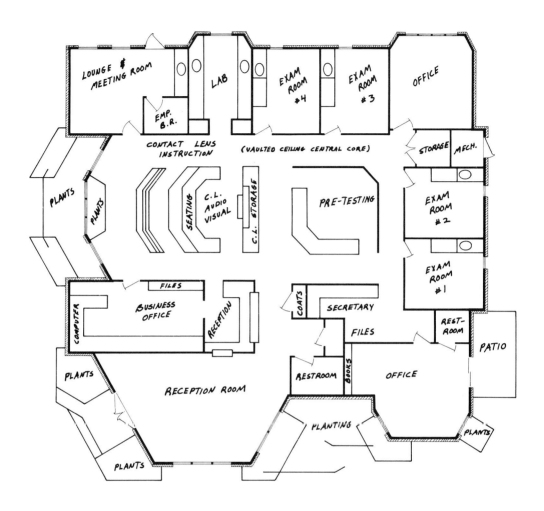

JACK W. MELTON, O.D., F.A.A.O.
AND ASSOCIATES
PRACTICE LIMITED TO CONTACT LENSES
OKLAHOMA CITY, OKLAHOMA